# The Making of an Economist, Redux

# THE MAKING
# OF AN ECONOMIST, REDUX

**David Colander**

PRINCETON UNIVERSITY PRESS

PRINCETON AND OXFORD

Copyright © 2007 by Princeton University Press
Published by Princeton University Press, 41 William Street,
Princeton, New Jersey 08540
In the United Kingdom: Princeton University Press,
6 Oxford Street, Woodstock, Oxfordshire OX20 1TW

*All Rights Reserved*

Second printing, and first paperback printing, 2009
Paperback ISBN: 978-0-691-13851-0

The Library of Congress has cataloged the cloth edition of this book as follows

Colander, David C.
The making of an economist, redux / David Colander.
p.   cm.
Includes bibliographical references and index.

ISBN-13: 978-0-691-12585-5 (hbk.)
ISBN-10: 0-691-12585-6 (hbk.)

1. Economics—Study and teaching (Graduate)—United States.
2. Economists—United States. 3. Graduate students—United States. I. Title.

HB74.8.C65 2007
330.071'173—dc22          2006051039

British Library Cataloging-in-Publication Data is available

This book has been composed in Helvetica medium and Minion

Printed on acid-free paper. ∞

press.princeton.edu

Printed in the United States of America

3   5   7   9   10   8   6   4   2

# CONTENTS

CONTENTS

# PREFACE

OVER THE PAST TEN YEARS, I've been continually asked, "Colander, when are you going to do a followup of your 'Making of an Economist' study?" I'd answer, "Don't know; I'm working on other things." Actually, I wasn't eager to do the followup study. Part of the fun of the initial study was doing it with Arjo Klamer, who was a strange bird as an economist, but who brought some neat perspectives to the project, and who was the one heavily into conversations. Unfortunately, soon after our initial study he was given a chair in cultural and economic studies over in the Netherlands, where he had become one of those policy wonks and talking heads you see on TV. In his new role, he was really quite removed from the economics profession here in the United States, and not interested in doing a followup.

Then another couple of friends pulled me into a project considering recent changes in the profession. That project was started in 2002, and published in 2005 (Colander, Holt, and Rosser 2005). On the basis of that project I came to believe that the profession was indeed changing, which led me to wonder whether, and how, those changes were being reflected in graduate training. That wondering, in turn, led me back to the topic and to two related projects. In one I followed up respondents in the previous study to see if and how their views had changed. The results are reported in chapter 4. The second project was a redo of the earlier study. The initial results were published in the *Journal of Economic Perspectives* (Colander 2005), and the extended results of that study make up the bulk of this book.

The book has the same general structure as the last book—an introductory chapter discussing the nature of the economics profession, a group of chapters presenting the results of the surveys, a group of chapters reporting the conversations with graduate students, and a concluding group of chapters reflecting on the survey and on graduate economic education in general.

Like the last book, this book is written for three audiences: students thinking of becoming economists, economists, and the lay public. The most obvious readers are the students. I am told that the last book became almost required reading for U.S. students thinking of becoming economists and that the greater information for students led to better matches between those who chose to go to graduate school and those whom the graduate schools were looking for. I think those results are fortunate. The book, however, also discouraged many students from entering economics, and thereby contributed to the filtering of the type of students who enter economics, and decreased the diversity within the economics profession. I think that is unfortunate.

One group that the last book did not significantly affect was the group of economists who are at the top programs and who decide on the structure of the core in economics. The core was quite unaffected by the previous book. In my view, the core exists as it currently does, not because that's the core that the majority of economists want, but rather because of inertia and lack of desire for the political fight that it would take to change it. I had hoped that the book, and the Commission on Graduate Education in Economics (COGEE) Report that followed, would lead to departments taking control of the core and collectively deciding what should be in the core, rather than leaving it to the invisible hand of inertia. That didn't happen, and I'm hoping that this book will generate some department activism about the core.

The third audience for this book is the lay reader. For those lay readers, I offer a word of caution about interpretation. Don't assume from this discussion that economics graduate training is in some sense unique in having problems. All institutions have their foibles and internal debates, and academic institutions have more than most. So see this as what it is—a peek into the training that economists receive—and not a sign that economics training is in any more trouble than any other type of training. The economics profession is succeeding: its graduates are in high demand, and its graduates are happy with the training that they are getting.

## Acknowledgments

I have been very lucky to teach at a liberal arts school where there is flexibility about the type of research one does; I thank Middlebury for creating the environment where one can do this type of research. I also would like to thank the Christian A. Johnson Foundation, which funds my chair here at Middlebury. It has provided me with a number of research assistants who have helped at various stages of this project, including Neli Georgieva, Yanling Cao, John Oliver, and Iqbal Sheikh; I very much appreciate their help.

Survey research requires much more cooperation than other types of research, and I am indebted to friends at a variety of graduate schools who helped me in arranging to do the surveys and interviews, including Marty Weitzman at Harvard, Xavier Gabaix at MIT, Brendan O'Flaherty at Columbia, Robert Shiller at Yale, Robert Hall at Stanford, Allen Sanderson and Derek Neal at Chicago, and Ben Bernanke at Princeton. I thank them all.

The people who know most about graduate economic departments are the administrative assistants who handle the nitty gritty of the administration of the departments. They are wonderful people, and I sincerely want to thank them for helping me distribute the questionnaire and set up the interviews. These include Julie Less at Chicago, Pat Brown at Yale, Sharon Wynne at Columbia, Shelley Weiner at Harvard, Susie Madsen at Stanford, Gary King at MIT, and Kathleen DeGennaro at Princeton. I cannot thank them enough.

This book is part of my continuing study of the economics profession, and sections of it are based on various articles that have been previously published. Chapter 1 includes selections from the original *Making of an Economist* book (Klamer and Colander 1990) as well as selections from an article entitled "The Sounds of Silence," which was published in the *Journal of Agricultural Economics* (Colander 1998). Chapter 2 is a modification of "The Making of an Economist Redux," which was published in the *Journal of Economic Perspectives* (Colander 2005). Chapter 4 is a modification of an article entitled "The Aging of an Economist," which was published in the *Journal of the History of Economic Thought* (Colander 2003). I thank these journals for permission to reprint the selections.

As I have carried out this study, I have benefited from comments by many people, some of whom I have forgotten. Helpful comments on drafts of the article and book that I remember came from Jacques Dreze, Lee Hansen, James Hines, Jessica Holmes, Joanna Lahey, David Laibson, Steve Levitt, Deirdre McCloskey, Casey Rothschild, Andrei Shleifer, John Siegfried, Wendy Stock, Tim Taylor, Michael Waldman, and two anonymous reviewers. I would also like to thank Robert Solow and Arjo Klamer, who wrote reflections on the survey and interviews (chapters 11 and 12). Those perspectives add much to the study.

At Princeton University Press, Tim Sullivan and Peter Dougherty were very helpful with suggestions about the project and in seeing the book through the production process. I'd also like to thank Helen Reiff, who edited the manuscript and prepared the index, Jill Harris, who oversaw the production process, and Linda Truilo, who did a great job copyediting the manuscript.

Most of all I want to thank the students who took the time to fill out the questionnaire and to come in for the interviews. This is their book and their story. I hope that the presentation does them justice.

# The Making of an Economist, Redux

---

# Introduction: Understanding Economics and Economists

ECONOMISTS HAVE BECOME ubiquitous. You turn on the TV news and you hear from them—economists say inflation is slowing; economists question the tax cut proposal; economists predict that a recession is likely. You pick up your newspaper or newsmagazine, and you read about economists.

As with many things ubiquitous, there is an ambiguity about what precisely an economist is, and what it is that he (most economists are male) is supposed to know. Thus, nowhere will one find a specified body of knowledge that an economist must know to call himself or herself an economist. In fact, unlike in law or medicine, where there are licenses that one must have to be called a lawyer or doctor, anyone can simply put the suffix "economist" after his name and call himself an economist.

One way of specifying who is an economist might be to consider who studies economics as an undergraduate. Each year approximately 25,000 undergraduate students (about 2 percent of all college seniors) major in economics.[1] The large majority of these majors have no intention of becoming economists; they are planning to go into business, with banking, finance, and general management the most popular fields. So, undergraduate economics majors do not, for the most part, consider themselves economists. Most are majoring in economics because business is not an acceptable liberal arts major, and the undergraduate economics major is a surrogate for a business major. Another way of limiting the number of economists might be to restrict it to members of an economic association. That wouldn't work either, however, since anyone can join these associations—there are no restrictions. Pay your dues and you are a member.[2]

So it seems that anyone can be an economist. The lack of formal requirements about who can call himself or herself an economist, however, masks another reality by which individuals who are economists judge whether or not someone is a "true" economist. For example, were an undergraduate student to ask an economist how to become an economist, he would tell her to go to graduate school. She might demur, asking, "Wouldn't it make more sense to go to Wall Street and learn how markets work?" Getting firsthand experience may sound like a good idea to her, but most economists would briskly dismiss the suggestion. "Well, maybe I should get a job in a real business—say, turning out automobiles." The answer will be "no" again: "That's not how you learn economics." She might try one more time. "Well, how about if I read all the top economists of the past—John Stuart Mill, David Ricardo, Adam Smith?" Most economists would say, "It wouldn't hurt, but it probably won't help." Instead, he would most likely tell her, "To become an economist who is considered an economist by other economists, you have to go to graduate school in economics." So the reality is that, to economists, an economist is someone who has a graduate degree (doctorates strongly preferred) in economics.[3] This means that what defines an economist is what he or she learns in graduate school.

## A Profile of Economics Graduate Students

To get an idea of who becomes an economist, let's consider a profile that Wendy Stock and John Siegfried compiled.

As you can see, each year somewhat more than 900 Ph.D.'s are awarded, a rate slightly higher than in the past. Assuming the rate of production has averaged 800 over the past forty years, and that the average economist works for approximately forty years, and that few economists trained outside the United States come to work in the United States, and that 20 percent of the students who get Ph.D.'s do not stay in the United States, then there are about 25,000 Ph.D. economists currently in the United States. The composition of this group is constantly changing, and each year a bit over 2 percent of the economists are replaced with younger cohorts, which means that over a decade the nature of economists is likely to change considerably, with new graduate students replacing retiring economists.

This table gives you a pretty good sense of who the graduate students are who are replacing the old economists. The first thing to note is that the percentage of U.S. citizens in graduate economics programs is declining; economics, like many of the sciences, is becoming a field dominated by non-U.S. citizens, the majority of whom stay in the United States to work. Notice also that while the percentage of women is increasing, the economics profession remains a primarily male profession. Another point to note is that most students finance their education with fellowships, along with research and/or teaching assistantships, although about 30 percent finance it themselves.

Graduate economics students attend one of the over one hundred Ph.D. programs in economics within the United States. The group as a whole, however, isn't the subject of this book. Instead, the book's main focus is the graduate students at elite graduate schools. These elite schools are disproportionately influential, and the students at these schools are destined to become the future elite of economics. This follows, since schools seldom hire from other schools ranked significantly lower than themselves, which means that this group will populate the top schools in the future and decide how economics is done.

Schools' rankings are generally well understood by economists, and conversations with newly minted economists often begin with, "Where did you get your Ph.D.?" Upon hearing where, the questioner will make a judgment about the quality of one's training and whether or not one should be considered a serious economist. (It's a bit like two dogs marking out their territory.) If you are planning to go on in serious economic research, you had better be able to answer that question with "I went to (fill in the name of one of the twenty of the top-ten-ranked economics graduate programs)." Otherwise you don't pass the initial sniff test.

Notice that I said "twenty of the top ten." The reason is that there are many different ranking systems. Developing rankings, and discussing the advantages and disadvantages of various rankings, is an industry in itself. There can be survey rankings (done in a variety of different ways), publication-based rankings (with publications weighted in a variety of different ways), and citation-based rankings (with citations weighted in a variety of different ways). Each of these

Table 1-1: A Profile of Doctoral Training in Economics in the United States: 1977, 1986/1987, 1996, and 2001

| Measure | 1976–1977 | 1985–1986 or 1986–1987 | 1995–1996 | 2000–2001 |
|---|---|---|---|---|
| Number of doctorates awarded in economics and econometrics | 838 | 861[a] | 1,008 | 930 |
| Percentage U.S. citizens | 67.3 | 55.7[a] | 42.9 | 38.0 |
| Percentage female | 8.7 | 19.3[a] | 22.4 | 28.0 |
| Percentage with B.A./B.S. degree in economics | 63.6 | 59.7[a] | 57.8 | 56.6 |
| Number of full-time first-year graduate students (including master's) | 2,886 | 2,584[a] | 2,466 | 2,562 |
| Number of full- and part-time graduate students (including master's) | 12,063 | 12,830[a] | 12,080 | 11,340 |
| Number of full-time graduate students in economics (including master's) at doctoral institutions | 9,938 | 10,473[b] | 10,991 | 10,755 |
| Median years to Ph.D. | 5.7 | 6.3[a] | 6.8 | 7.0 |
| Type of support for full-time graduate students at doctoral institutions (percentage distribution)[c] | | | | |
| Fellowship and traineeship | 18.4 | 15.3[a] | 18.8 | 19.4 |
| Research assistant | 14.5 | 11.9[a] | 11.3 | 13.3 |
| Teaching assistant | 25.6 | 30.9[a] | 28.9 | 31.5 |
| Other | 41.5 | 41.9[a] | 41.0 | 35.8 |
| Source of support (percentage distribution) | | | | |
| Federal | 7.4 | 3.1[a] | 4.1 | 4.6 |
| Institutional | 44.9 | 52.4[a] | 52.9 | 59.6 |
| Other | 11.5 | 9.4[a] | 7.8 | 6.8 |
| Self | 36.2 | 35.1[a] | 35.2 | 28.9 |

Table 1-1 (*cont.*)

| Measure | 1976–1977 | 1985–1986 or 1986–1987 | 1995–1996 | 2000–2001 |
|---|---|---|---|---|
| Postdoctoral plans of new Ph.D.'s (percentage distribution)[c] | | | | |
| Employment | 90.5 | 85.4[b] | 82.9 | 82.9 |
| Postdoctoral study | 3.9 | 6.0[b] | 9.3 | 8.4 |
| Postdoctoral status unknown | 5.6 | 8.6[b] | 7.8 | 8.7 |
| Percentage accepting employment outside United States | 16.2 | 19.6[b] | 30.3 | 26.2 |

*Sources*: W. Lee Hansen (1991 tables 1 and 2) and the NSF WebCASPAR database system.

[a]1985–1986.
[b]1986–1987.
[c]Distributions do not always sum to 100 percent because some categories are not reported.
Reprinted from Wendy Stock and John Siegfried, "The Labor Market for New Ph.D. Economists," *American Economic Review* 94, no. 2 (May 2004): 272.

rankings can be measured on a per-faculty or a total-number criterion (using various alternative measures of what is determined a faculty member). With so many ways of creating a ranking, there are many different possible rankings. Most possible rankings are explored and published, since college administrations often determine the level of support they will give a program on the basis of these rankings.[4]

Where there is general agreement about rankings is about the schools at the top, and six of the seven schools that I included in this study—Harvard, Stanford, Chicago, MIT, Princeton, and Yale—are consistently ranked in the top ten. (They are ranked as the top six in a recent survey, and the seventh school in this study—Columbia—is ranked twelfth; Thursby 2000.) These elite schools compete vigorously for top students. They invite accepted candidates to campus, wine and dine them, have them meet with faculty members, and work hard to sell their school to them. Except at Chicago, which follows a somewhat different model, the large majority of students at these schools get fellowships that provide them with as much as $30,000 to $35,000 a year in addition to tuition and fees, often guaranteed for three years. The large majority of the students who start the programs at these elite schools finish the programs.

Once they graduate, these students tend to dominate the profession: they are the majority of members on American Economic Association (AEA) boards, and they are the economists called upon when a reporter is seeking economists' view on an issue. Of course, not all of these graduates manage to remain in the elite, but it is from this group that the majority of the elite come. How large is this elite? There are probably around 100 to 150 of the definitely elite, 700 to 800 of the elite, and another 1,500 economists might be seen as peripheral elite. All have Ph.D.'s, and most have academic appointments, although some move back and both between academia and government.

*The Graduate Economics Program*

It generally takes a bit over five years of graduate study for students to get a Ph.D.[5] In the first year or two of most Ph.D. programs, students take courses in micro, macro, and econometrics, with some electives mixed in. At elite schools each of the core courses is usually taught by two, or sometimes three, graduate professors, each concentrating on his or her area of specialty. These three courses—micro, macro, and econometrics—are known as the core, and they are what define the common training of economists. At the end of these courses, an exam, generally made up by the professors teaching the course, is given, and successful completion of those exams means successful completion of the core. At some schools the core exam is separate from the final exam for the course, but that separation is decreasing. Also, in the past, the department, not the professors, made up the core exam, but that too has changed. Thus, the professors teaching the core have enormous power in determining what an economist is in the sense that they determine what common core is taught.

After completing the core, graduate economics students move on to field courses, and they usually have to pick two areas of specialty. Often, at the end of the field courses, there are field exams, which end the formal required course work. After passing the field exams, students become known as ABD's (All But Dissertations). Thereafter students work on their dissertations, which generally can take anywhere from one to three years. During this time students typically work part-time as teaching or research assistants, attend seminars, and work on publishing papers. Often, students will write three essays as their dissertation, to make the translation into journal articles easier. (Journal articles, not books, are most important to academic economists in advancing in their careers.)

In their final year of study ABDs go on the job market. For the majority of graduate students there is a definite pecking order of desirability among jobs: (1) high-ranked graduate programs; (2) middle-range graduate programs; (3) international agency or top government (especially central bank) programs; (4) top undergraduate programs; (5) lower-range graduate programs; (6) lower-ranked undergraduate programs; and (7) private business—although, depending on a graduate's specific field, there will be some shifting among the lower-numbered choices in the order of preference. This pecking order reflects views inculcated during the student's graduate school training. Graduate programs at the elite schools are designed to prepare students to do academic research in economics at other graduate programs, and departments generally rank themselves on how well they do in placing their students into academic jobs.

7

## What Academic Economists Do

Academic economists teach, do extensive committee work at the college or university that employs them, and carry on "research," which generally takes the form of writing articles. Books tend to count for little in economics department rankings. To provide outlets for all the articles, there has been a steady increase in the number of economics journals, many of which have also become available online: while there were about 200 journals in 1980, today the online database EconLit provides access to more than 600 journals. Moreover, the focus on articles is different from that in other social science disciplines, such as history and political science, where researchers generally write books rather than articles. Writing articles is, however, common in physics and the other natural sciences. Most elite economists judge other economists by their journal article output. In calculations of department rankings, books are seldom even counted.

Paul Samuelson, a Nobel Prize–winning economist and perhaps the dominant figure in economics from the late 1930s through the 1960s, captured an important aspect of the profession when he said that it is not for the applause of the public that economists work, but for the praise of their peers. Most economists at the elite level are primarily concerned with what other elite economists think of them, as opposed to whether they are looked on positively by the broader public. Elite economists are more likely to stay within academic institutions and use their skills to advance the knowledge of their peers. A few are hired as consultants, textbook writers, or court witnesses, but devoting too much time to such activities is looked down upon by the profession. Economists who dedicate their careers to such outside services for pay are treated with suspicion.

## The Original *Making of an Economist*

In the mid-1980s, Arjo Klamer and I did a study of these elite graduate economic programs that was much discussed in the profession and widely reported in the popular press. That study did not paint a flattering picture of graduate economics education. It was a picture of a profession lost in pure theory and technicalities, with little focus on ideas. There was a sense that economics dealt with mind games, not real economics problems. For example, in our earlier introduction, Arjo Klamer and I cited numerous views that were critical of economists, and quoted Robert Kuttner, who wrote, "Departments of economics are graduating a generation of idiot savants, brilliant at esoteric mathematics yet innocent of actual economic life."

Whether that assessment was right or not (many mainstream economists argued that it was quite wrong and, in any case, was far too simplistic), it was an assessment shared by numerous people at the time. It was the buzz, especially among critics of the profession, that economics had gone off the deep end on theory. The feeling was that the teaching of graduate economics had lost something that made economics special—that it focused too much on abstract theory, that it focused too much on modeling for the sake of modeling, and that there was too little empirical grounding for the theoretical work that was done. This situation existed in micro because many of the graduate micro courses were still digesting Arrow/Debreu general equilibrium theory, and in macro because the New Classical revolt against Keynesian economics seemed to be pulling macro along the same pure analytic corridor.

As with much successful research, a lot of the success of our original study was due to "right place/right time." We were not alone in our beliefs: the beliefs were shared by a large number of economists, many of whom were not critics of economics but were mainstream economists. The movements for change had already occurred. A new journal, the *Journal of Economic Perspectives*, was being created by the AEA, whose purpose was to provide an outlet and discussion forum for less esoteric research, and there was much discussion among economists over coffee or drinks about the changing way in which economics was done.

Our actual collection of data started in 1983, which led to a paper entitled "The Making of an Economist," written in 1985 and published in 1987 in the newly formed *Journal of Economic Perspectives*.[6] The paper caught on and was much discussed long before it was published. The results in it gave people some numbers to focus on and to put the issues in perspective. Our results, however, were hardly scientific. The survey was far from inclusive—we covered only a small group of elite schools—and there were many aspects of graduate economics education that it did not touch. In other words, it was a decent conversation piece, but it was not a stepping stone for something actually to be done.

Our initial paper also left out much discussion of implications. We did so on purpose—to let the numbers speak for themselves and not let our critical views of the profession color the way in which the numbers might be interpreted. Our book, by contrast, was much more extensive: it included not only the initial study but also the conversations that we had had with the students. At the end of that book both Klamer and I reflected on the implications. Our reflections were quite different. Klamer concentrated on the lack of policy relevance; I concentrated on incentives for workmanship.

## The COGEE Report

Since there were a number of economists who felt that something should be done, a consensus developed that a more substantive study might actually bring about change. It was for this reason that the Commission on Graduate Education in Economics (COGEE) was set up by Robert Eisner, then president of the AEA. The charge to the commission was to "take stock of what is being done (in graduate education), what results we are getting. . . . In all of this . . . the concern is, of course, very largely with the direction of research and focus of resources." In short, the commission was to look more deeply at graduate education than Klamer and I had done, and to do it right.

While there was a general agreement that what Arjo and I had reported was, in general, correct, our work was certainly not systematic. (We had financed our limited surveys ourselves, with help from small grants from our schools.) COGEE was a much larger fact-finding effort, with substantial NSF funding. It was felt that a commission made up of leading economists, basing their assessment on a more systematically structured study than ours, would provide more insight into what was really going on, and, if it was felt that change was necessary, could better articulate those changes that were necessary. It was also felt that, if changes were necessary, the commission would carry more weight in bringing them about. Thus, COGEE was appointed with representatives of the top graduate schools, and one government economist.[7] Lee Hansen oversaw the statistical work that underlay the commission's project, and he directed publication of a number of supporting studies for the report.

In its makeup, the commission was broadly sympathetic to reform, although there was a diversity of views represented, as necessarily had to be the case if the commission was to be seen as representative of the mainstream economics position. To reduce political infighting it was decided that the report would not be an official report of the AEA, but instead a report that reflected the views of the members and nothing more. Still, given the distinguished stature of the commission members, it was felt that the report would make a difference.

Before I saw the commission's report, I predicted, in print (Colander and Brenner 1992) that the report would find that all was generally well with the profession, but that there were some areas for concern. I was partially right. Toward its beginning, the report announced that "the current state of the profession is healthy." I was pleasantly surprised, however, by the degree to which the commission considered the concerns of critics of the profession, and by the relatively strong (for a commission) recommendations that it made.

The commission's recommendations, published in September 1991 (Krueger et al. 1991), were the following:

1. Reasonable requirements in mathematics, statistics, and economics be established.
2. Remedial courses be offered to those who have deficiencies in economics, mathematics, or statistics.
3. Core courses be taught in a way that can balance breadth and depth, with sufficient attention to applications and real-world linkages to encourage students themselves to start applying the concepts.
4. The core should be regarded as a departmental "public good" and its content be the concern of the entire department.
5. Field courses should attempt to include more empirical applications.
6. Greater attention should be given to writing and communication skills.
7. Efforts should be made to ease the transition from course work to dissertation.
8. More differentiation should exist among departments.

## Response of the Profession to the COGEE Report

The COGEE Report was greeted with formal silence by the profession.[8] I am told that Anne Krueger, the head of the commission, said that if a pin had dropped at the same time as the report came out, the pin landing would have sounded like thunder. That may be a bit of an exaggeration, but there was no groundswell of change caused by the report. In 1999, I surveyed the members of the COGEE Commission about the changes brought about by the COGEE Report. The conclusions were the following:

1. No school changed its mathematical requirements in response to the commission's report, nor did any school lower its mathematical requirements. If anything, mathematical requirements have been raised. (The majority of the commission members felt that at whichever institution he or she represented the level of mathematical sophistication needed by incoming graduate students had increased.)

Moreover, the underlying culture continued to deemphasize reading the literature and studying economic issues outside a formal technical model approach. History of thought and history of economics requirements declined further. Moreover, graduate school culture lets students know that they should deemphasize these courses and focus on the "hardcore" courses. For example, at one top-ten school that had a core economic history requirement, I was told that either the requirement was overlooked or students were told to minimize their studying in the course to free up time for their other core courses.

2. Most schools already offered remedial courses in mathematics, so there was little change here. Most of these courses are given in August preceding the first semester. As Alan Blinder remarked, "We have always had 'remedial' math. (In fact, it is pretty advanced.) We still do." The content of these remedial courses has changed to a larger focus on game theory and dynamics to reflect the changes in the math used in the core courses—but not because of the report.

No school had a remedial program in economics before the COGEE Report, and none implemented one. This is the case even though many new graduate students have taken few, if any, economics courses. (Some have taken none.) It is still possible to do exceptionally well in the first two years in economics graduate programs without having taken undergraduate economics. For those students without an undergraduate degree in economics, this means that their economics training consists of the economics content of the core courses, and what they have learned on their own. When I asked one COGEE member about this,

I was told that most of the graduate students serve as TAs in a principles course, and they learn economics there.

3. At most schools, the emphasis on technique over intuitive application in the core course has remained roughly the same or even increased.[9] When I discussed the issue with graduate students in the late 1990s, some graduate students told me that they were encouraged to think of applying the models they learn. They are told to work on a paper in their first year, but they found doing that difficult because they have not had any in-class training in how to do so.

While the general focus on technique has remained constant, the techniques being learned are changing. Much more game theory is being taught and being made central to the core of the micro courses. This movement toward game theory makes the core more closely applicable to real-world events, since it allows a broader range of assumptions. This change, however, has not been in reaction to the COGEE Report; it has been part of the continuing evolution of microeconomic thinking.

4. The teaching of the core did change, but not to a "public good" as recommended by the commission. Instead it changed to a "subdivided private good." By this I mean that instead of one individual teaching the core course, as was common in the past, core courses are now taught by combinations of two or three professors. Essentially, the core courses now consist of a collection of mini-courses, each focusing on a separate area or modeling technique. These mini-courses are separable in that each professor sets the exam for his or her portion of the course. In one sense, this approach presents the students with more diversity, but in another, it removes any chance that a student might get an overall vision of the subject matter of the course. It increases the focus on the training of techniques. The development of these mini-courses has, in many ways, eliminated the micro/macro distinction, and one school, Stanford, has integrated the two while simultaneously developing departmental guidelines as to what will be taught in the subsections of the core.

To my knowledge, there are no integrative core courses, which provide an overview of economics, given at any top school. History of thought requirements and electives have been eliminated at most top schools, and older professors who took an integrative approach to teaching are generally assigned to non-core courses. Where such courses still exist, students are discouraged from focusing on them.

5. These is a sense that in field courses there was a slight movement toward more applications.

6. Some commission members said that at their schools more emphasis is being given to writing in workshops. Some schools have developed a second year requirement that each student present a field paper. Alan Blinder summed up the view of many when he wrote, "We keep experimenting with various types of workshops, papers, etc., but nothing works terribly well, and on the whole, it is much the same." So I would judge that attempts are being made to improve writing. These attempts, however, have been ongoing, and are not in response to the COGEE Report.

7. Based on general discussion with graduate professors, attempts are being made to improve the transition from course work to dissertation. One commission member stated that at his school there was more assignment of advisors if the graduate student failed to develop ideas on his or her own. At some schools, workshops and luncheon seminars are required in the third year; these workshops are meant to focus attention of the student on developing a thesis topic. A few years ago the Social Science Research Council started a program, including summer workshops and fellowships, to encourage more focus on intuitive foundations.

8. Among top schools there has been no recognizable movement toward differentiation. If anything, the process has gone the other way. When Arjo Klamer and I did our initial study, there was a significant difference among top schools, reflected in differences in what students believed. These differences often reflected the differing view, of some major professors who taught the core. With recent cross-hires among these top schools, and the division of the core courses into subcomponents, such differences in beliefs among schools are far less noticeable. This is because (1) there are fewer differences in the profession, and (2) even if there are differences, those differences will not be taught to the students because the core courses are divided among two or three professors focusing on the particular sub-area of that course within which they work.

# The Changing Face of Economics

So my conclusion is that Arjo's and my initial study, and the COGEE Report, had little direct effect on the profession. However, despite this, the profession has changed. Thus, if our study and the COGEE Report had an effect, it was an indirect effect that is not discernable from the broader evolution of the profession. The studies and the discussion around them become part of the profession's understanding of itself, which causes no specific changes but may change *proclivities* to change the system.

I say this because looking at the profession today, I am convinced that it is quite different than it was in the mid-1980s, when Arjo and I first sat over drinks and lamented the state of the profession. The commitment to theorems and proofs has declined, and there is a much stronger empirical branch of economics. Natural experiments and instrumental variables are now central to an economist's training. Behavioral economics has advanced enormously, and the macro that is done is fundamentally different from the macro that was done in the 1980s; advanced time-series statistics, such as cointegrated structural VARs and calibration, are commonplace, where they were hardly known before. What were taken as requirements of research in the 1980s are no longer requirements in the 2000s; the holy trinity of greed, equilibrium, and rationality has been replaced by a looser trilogy of purposeful behavior, sustainability, and enlightened self-interest. I could extend the list enormously, but there is no need to do that here. My point is simply that economics has changed and will continue to change, making it impossible to call the existing profession neoclassical any longer.

In *The Changing Face of Economics* (Colander, Holt, and Rosser 2004), I argued that these changes have occurred almost imperceptibly; economics changes not by revolution but by slow evolution. This reflects the continual exit of economists through retirement and the continual entrance of economists to replace them. In the fifteen years since the original "Making of an Economist" study, there has been about a 30 percent turnover, and it is this turnover that is changing the nature of economics. Our earlier study had little direct effect on the profession, but it, and the discussion that surrounded it, may have indirectly affected the profession by its effects on the participants of the earlier study, because these participants became the profession. So, in my view, there is no better place to see the changes at the cutting-edge of the profession than through a study of graduate economics education at elite schools. The views of the students at these schools will become the views of the profession in the coming decades, if only by one funeral at a time.

# PART I
## The Survey Results

I'VE ALWAYS FOLLOWED a relatively simple research strategy: let the question, not the tools or the availability of data, define the research. The advantage of that strategy is that it lets you ask interesting questions; the disadvantage is that it gives you only imprecise answers. That was not the normal economist's approach back in the 1970s, when I went to graduate school, or when I did the first study in the 1980s. Then, tools or available datasets, tended to define research programs.

Most of the profession still does not follow the simple research strategy that I follow, but now, with the enormous advancement in computational technology and in economists' knowledge of statistical techniques, students are less limited by tools and more willing to work creatively with datasets to make them fit the problem that they are interested in. Theory unconnected to reality has declined in importance, and empirical work—looking at real world problems—has increased in importance. The push for precision, however, remains a central part of economics and, in my view, it continues to limit economists' contribution to research. Precision is helpful in eking out the final 20 percent of knowledge that can be squeezed out of a dataset, and in getting published in journals, but, simple observation, case studies, knowing the institutions, reading the literature, and asking for knowledgeable people's opinions often gives you the first 80 percent of what you can know about a problem. To move into precise statistical analysis before you have used these other imprecise techniques is often an inefficient way to understand an issue.

Surveys are a form of asking knowledgeable people what they think, and thus they seem to be a natural way of finding out information. Economists, for the most part, have been highly suspicious of surveys. They point out the framing problems of surveys and that surveys are what people say they believe, whereas what one is generally interested in is what they actually believe and how they act. The two aren't necessarily the same. I agree that surveys have problems, but I also believe that other sources of data are also problematic, and that surveys are too little used by most economists as a source of data.

This part contains the results of two surveys that I did, and the comparisons of those surveys with my earlier survey. Because I do not want the results to convey more precisions than I believe they warrant, I present the quantitative data with no statistical precision tests—just the numbers. I also present the written comments of students to give the reader a deeper sense of the responses. These, combined with the conversations presented in Part II—where I asked students to tell me their interpretation of the results, and to tell me about graduate school—convey a good sense, in my view, of graduate economics education.

CHAPTER TWO

# The Making of an Economist, Redux

INDIVIDUALS ARE NOT born as economists; they are molded through formal and informal training. This training shapes the way they approach problems, process information, and carry out research, which in turn influences the policies they favor and the role they play in society. The economics profession changes as cohorts with older-style training are replaced with cohorts with newer-style training. In many ways, the replicator dynamics of graduate school play a larger role in determining economists' methodology and approach than all the myriad papers written about methodology. Arjo Klamer and I came to that belief in the early 1980s, and it led us to publish our "Making of an Economist" (Colander and Klamer 1987), which in turn led to a much more thorough study by a Commission on Graduate Education in Economics appointed by the American Economic Association (Hansen et al. 1991). Over the years, I have received numerous suggestions to update our earlier study.[1] This chapter provides that update.

The chapter reports the findings of a survey and interviews with graduate students at seven top-ranking graduate economics programs: University of Chicago, Columbia University, Harvard University, Massachusetts Institute of Technology, Stanford University, Yale University, and Princeton University. It consists of two parts. The first part explores who current graduate students are and what they think about economics, the economy, and graduate school. In doing so, it offers a snapshot of current training that can be compared to our earlier snapshot, giving us a sense of how graduate students and graduate education have changed over the past twenty years. The second part is more reflective, offering my interpretation of the nature of the changes in graduate school and in economics more generally. To maintain comparability, I followed the same procedures as last time, distributing a questionnaire identical to the one used earlier, and following a similar interview procedure. I also include three appendices. Appendix A presents specific information about the survey and interview procedures; appendix B presents the questionnaire; and appendix C presents tables on which some of the discussion is based.

## Profile of Students

The profile of the typical graduate student in economics at highly selective institutions has not changed significantly since the original 1985 study. The average age is still twenty-six years. Students are predominantly male, although the percentage of women in the survey increased from 19 to 29 percent. This percentage is in line with the fact that 30 percent of economics Ph.D.'s were awarded to women in the profession in 2003 (Blau 2004, 4). A slight majority of the students did not go to graduate school directly after completing their undergraduate degrees, but instead had a variety of jobs, primarily as economic research assistants.

The majority of the respondents (62 percent) are foreign. That percentage differed significantly by school: for example, 14 percent of the Chicago respondents were U.S. citizens, while 78 percent of the Stanford and MIT respondents were U.S. citizens.[2] On the question about race and ethnicity, 21 percent chose not to answer; of those who did answer, 68 percent were white, 18 percent Asian, 10 percent Hispanic, and 4 percent other. About two-thirds of students (69 percent) said they were nonreligious, and about two-thirds (65 percent) said they were involved in a long-term relationship. Most came from upper-middle-class families, many from academic backgrounds.

The large majority (81 percent) had majored in economics as undergraduates, while 21 percent had majored in mathematics and 22 percent had other majors. (A number of students had double majors.) U.S. students and foreign students who had done their undergraduate work in the United States were much more likely to have majored in math, reflecting the higher math content in foreign undergraduate economics programs. In the interviews, it was generally believed by both U.S. and foreign students that foreign students had the stronger math background, at least as it related to economics.

At these top schools, financial issues were not stressful for most students; 90 percent had fellowships in their first year. Only 9 percent found financial issues very stressful. Some students even stated that they were able to save during their studies. What students identified as most stressful was finding a dissertation topic: 29 percent found this very stressful and another 33 percent found it stressful.[3] Relations with faculty were generally not stressful. Those relations did, however, become more stressful over time, with 4 percent of first-year students finding relationships with faculty very stressful but 16 percent of fifth-year students finding those relationships very stressful.

Almost half of the students (47 percent) were involved in writing a scholarly paper. Most students beyond their third year were working; 65 percent of students beyond their third year were working as teaching assistants and about 38 percent beyond the third year were working as research assistants. Some were doing both.

Economists are often thought of as conservative, but that was not the case in the previous study nor in this study. In this study, 47 percent of the students classified themselves as liberal, 24 percent as moderate, 16 percent as conservative, and 6 percent as radical. (Six percent stated that politics were unimportant to them.) These percentages are very similar to the last study, although the share of those identifying themselves as radicals declined (from 12 percent). The students perceived their views as slightly more liberal than those of their parents, 40 percent of whom they classified as liberal, 36 percent as moderate, 16 percent as conservative, and 3 percent as radical.

The large majority of students (80 percent) felt that their political views did not change in graduate schools, although that changed by year, with 10 percent of first-year students reporting a change in their views, but 32 percent of fourth- and higher-year students reporting a change in their views. In particular, 10 percent of first-year students considered themselves conservative; by the fourth and fifth year, this number had risen to 23 percent. There was also a large drop by year in students who considered themselves radical; that percentage fell from 13 percent of first-year students to only 1 percent of fourth-year-and-higher students.

## Interests of Students

The majority of the students were positive about their graduate school experience, although students in the first and second year often were concerned by the lack of relevance of what they were learning. A typical comment of upper-level students was, "The first two years were miserable. Now it is kind of fun and exciting, but I'm not sure the pain was worth it." First-year students were more likely to question the relevance of economics. One wrote, "I'm not convinced I'm doing anything that matters outside the ivory tower of academia." Despite these feelings, the level of concern was slightly less than it was in the previous study, and there seemed to be less cynicism than in the previous study. Only 7 percent said they would not have undertaken the program if they could do it over; 16 percent said they were unsure.

In terms of future jobs, the majority of students planned on an academic career; only 7 percent said they did not plan to pursue an academic career. The majority of the students (59 percent) expected to be at a major university in 15 years, 18 percent at a major research institution, 18 percent at an institution involved in policy-making, and 9 percent at a good liberal arts school.[4] The students' outlooks reflected some changes from the previous study, when only 41 percent expected to be at a major university, 32 percent expected to be at a policy-making institute, and 16 percent expected to be at a good liberal arts school. Since graduate training is definitely geared toward training students for academic careers in major universities, this shift in attitudes suggests a more effective selection process than before.

In the interviews, the push by the faculty toward eventually working at major research universities was clear. One student stated, "There is definitely a perception among the graduate students that you're better off not advertising that you're not interested in a research university." Another said, "I mentioned to one of my advisors last year that I might be interested in policy research, which I really am interested in, and she was definitely dismissive." Creating researchers for major universities is clearly the role that these schools see for themselves.

Although approximately the same percentage of students listed a desire to engage in policy formulation as very important (50 percent compared to 53 percent in the previous study), in this study the students did not see policy interests as incompatible with their academic careers. My interpretation of this result is that the policy role they see themselves playing is not that of a person directly involved in making policy within a political arena, but instead as a person providing expert advice and empirical support rather than direct policy implementation. One student put it this way: "Although a direct link to policy formation is not always present, economists serve a crucial role in providing clarification of issues both technically and in policy debates." About two-thirds of students (68 percent) did not consider political reasons to be important in their decision to do graduate work in economics; only 11 percent saw it as very important.

There were some changes in the interest of students in various fields since the earlier study. Economic development, labor, and public finance increased in importance while macro theory, political economy, money and banking, international trade, industrial organization, and history of thought decreased in importance. In most areas, interest did not vary significantly by year, but it decreased somewhat by year for both macro and for money and banking. The largest change by year occurred in the interest in the history of thought, where interest fell as students progressed, with 19 percent of first-year students interested in history of thought, 16 percent of second-year students, and then about 3 percent of third-year-and-higher students being interested in the history of thought. Women were more interested in labor and less interested in theory, macro, and history of economic thought.

In the interviews, macro received highly negative marks across schools. A typical comment was the following:

> The general perspective of the micro students is that the macro courses are pretty worthless, and we don't see why we have to do it, because we don't see what is taught as a plausible description of the economy. It's not that macroeconomic questions are inherently uninteresting; it is just that the models presented in the courses are not up to the job of explaining what is happening. There's just a lot of math, and we can't see the purpose of it.

The students also pointed out that foreign students were more likely to study macro than were U.S. students.

*Perceived Importance of Alternative Skills*

Perhaps the most discussed finding in our earlier study concerned what students felt put them on the fast track. In the earlier study, having a broad knowledge of the economics literature was seen as very important by only 10 percent of the students, and having a thorough knowledge of the economy was seen as very important by only 3 percent of the students. Table 2–1 reports the results from the earlier study compared with those from this study.

The view of the importance of literature remained much the same, but the number of students who believed that having a thorough knowledge of the economy was very important increased from 3 to 9 percent. Interest in empirical research also increased significantly in importance, with the percentage finding it very important increasing from 16 to 30 percent. The increased emphasis given to empirical work could also be seen in other parts of the survey. For example, a typical response to the question regarding their idea of a successful economist was "someone who affects policies by empirical studies." Problem solving, the most important skill by far last time, went down somewhat in importance, from 65 to 51 percent finding it very important. Excellence in mathematics also went down significantly, from 57 to 30 percent finding it very important.

In many ways, table 2–1 summarizes my perception of the changes that have occurred in the profession over the past 20 years. Math is still important, but less importance is given to math for the sake of math, and more importance is given to empirical work, which means that knowledge of the economy is more important. Economics is still a field that gives its literature little importance, but the field has become more consciously empirical, and students believe that their ability to do good empirical work separates them from other social scientists.

The changes are not earth shattering; 51 percent still see a thorough knowledge of the economy as unimportant, and 35 percent still see a broad knowledge of the literature as unimportant. To an outside observer who was not familiar with economics graduate training 20 years ago, economics today would likely still appear highly technical, theoretical, and unconcerned with reality. Compared to our last study, how-

Table 2–1: Perceptions of Success

| | Very important | | Moderately important | | Unimportant | | Don't know | |
|---|---|---|---|---|---|---|---|---|
| | Previous | New | Previous | New | Previous | New | Previous | New |
| Being smart in the sense that they are good at problem-solving | 65% | 51% | 32% | 38% | 3% | 7% | 1% | 2% |
| Being interested in, and good at, empirical research | 16% | 30% | 60% | 52% | 23% | 12% | 1% | 4% |
| Excellence in mathematics | 57% | 30% | 41% | 52% | 2% | 14% | 0% | 3% |
| Being very knowledgeable about one particular field | 37% | 35% | 42% | 42% | 19% | 15% | 2% | 7% |
| Ability to make connections with prominent professors | 26% | 33% | 50% | 40% | 16% | 19% | 9% | 7% |
| A broad knowledge of the economics literature | 10% | 11% | 41% | 44% | 43% | 35% | 5% | 8% |
| A thorough knowledge of the economy | 3% | 9% | 22% | 24% | 68% | 51% | 7% | 15% |

ever, the change away from theory for the sake of theory, and toward empirical and applications, is strongly apparent.

Additional insight into the students' views can be gained by considering the views by year. Interest in doing outside reading in mathematics, which overall was an attitude shared by 35 percent of the respondents, declined from 53 percent of first-year students finding it very important to only 22 percent of fifth-year students. Similarly, excellence in mathematics was seen by 46 percent of the first-year students as very important in putting someone on the fast track; the number finding it very important falls to 18 percent by the fifth year.

A slightly different picture emerges when we consider views on the stress caused by mathematics by year and by gender. The share of students finding math stressful was greatest in the first year, with 18 percent of the first-year students finding it very stressful. By the third year that had decreased to 5 percent, but then it increased among the fourth- and fifth-year students to about 10 percent. My interpretation of that finding is that while the core program is centered on math, the field courses are not, and in the third year students are choosing a dissertation so math is not their main concern. But then in the fourth and fifth years when they are actually writing the dissertation, some students again face the problem of solving the models, which brings the math stress back. In terms of gender, 23 percent of women but only 7 percent of the men found mathematics highly stressful. This stress in women, however, is not because the women cannot do the math; all the women I interviewed had a strong math background and demonstrated a strong knowledge of mathematics.[5]

The share of those who thought that "having a thorough knowledge of the economy" did not rise as students progressed through their education. Instead it fell, with about 15 percent of first- and second-year students seeing it as very important to put them on the fast track, but with less than 1 percent of the fourth- and fifth- year students seeing it as very important. Foreign students were much more likely to see a thorough knowledge of the economy as very important (13 percent) compared to U.S. students (2 percent). My interpretation of this data is that foreign students are more likely to return home and work in policy positions, where a practical knowledge of the economy is important, whereas U.S. students are more likely to be going into academia, where they will specialize in a particular area of study and will not be using general knowledge of the economy. The decline in importance by year suggests that when students are writing their dissertations, their interests narrow from a general interest to an interest in their particular field.

## Relevance of Graduate Training

One criticism that has often been made of graduate economic education is its supposed lack of relevance. In this spirit, we started our 1987 paper with a discussion of the following view: "Departments of economics are graduating a generation of idiot savants, brilliant at esoteric mathematics yet innocent of actual economic life." That view is still around, but it is less widespread, and more economics students see relevance in their studies. In response to the question, "Do you consider the role that economists currently have in society relevant?" 73 percent said yes; 7 percent said no, and 16 percent were uncertain.[6] This compares with 53 percent who thought that the role of economists in society was relevant in the previous study. The change can also be seen in the answer to another question about relevance. In the previous study, 34 percent of the students strongly agreed that neoclassical economics is relevant for economic problems; this time the number increased to 44 percent. The number strongly supporting the view that economists agree on fundamental issues also rose, from 4 to 9 percent. Similarly, the increase in the number of students seeing economics as the most scientific of the social sciences rose from 28 to 50 percent.

My interpretation of these changes is threefold. First, students coming into graduate school are now better informed about what it will involve, so that those who think that what economists currently do is relevant are the ones choosing graduate study in economics. Second, while graduate economics education is still highly mathematical, it is much more empirical; the math often ties in with the empirical work, and hence is more relevant for policy analysis. Finally, in many top programs, while the math is presented in the first two years, the core exams and the class exams do not require an in-depth knowledge of the mathematical theory but simply an ability to do a variation of fairly well-defined problems. Given the strong math background of many of the students, math is no longer seen as a major obstacle; it is simply a tool to be used when appropriate. As one graduate student stated, "You learn the five tricks of the math as it applies to economics and that's it for the math."

Whatever their views, the students were well on their way to being acclimated to being economists. For example, a defining attribute of an economist is often thought to be his or her use of the concept of optimizing behavior, and the students fit this mold. In answer to the question about whether they use the notion of individual optimization behavior, and given the options—very often, infrequently, or never—74 percent said they used it very often, 23 percent said they used it only infrequently, and 3 percent said they never used it.

## Differences among Schools

The earlier study found distinctive views in various schools. Table 2–2 (pp. 30–31) reports several opinions about economics, organized by school, in the previous study and in the current one.

The breakdown by schools shows less difference among schools in this study compared to the previous. In the previous study, Chicago stood out on the high end as seeing neoclassical economics as relevant, and Harvard stood out on the low end. This time the overall results of students strongly agreeing that neoclassical economics was relevant increased, but the number strongly agreeing at Chicago decreased, while the number strongly agreeing at Harvard increased. Today, in terms of their views of the relevance of neoclassical economics, Harvard and Chicago differ only slightly; they both see neoclassical economics as more relevant than do the other schools.[7]

Another question where a school stood out was in the question of whether economists agreed on fundamental issues. Columbia had no student who strongly agreed with this statement. When I asked Columbia students about this, they stated that the policy views of two major professors at Columbia were starkly opposed, which may account for the result.

Overall, table 2–2 shows that economics is currently regarded as more relevant and more scientific, with slightly more agreement on fundamental issues, than twenty years ago. There was a substantial increase in students who agreed that economics is the most scientific of the social sciences, with an increase in the percentage of those students rising from 28 to 50 percent. While Chicago was still an outlier here, again it was less so than in our previous study. The most substantial change was in Harvard, where 54 percent now strongly agreed that economics is the most scientific social science, whereas only 9 percent had believed that earlier.

I also asked students to compare their current views on various issues with the views that they believed they held before they came to graduate school. Table 2–3 (pp. 32–33) reports those results. (To save space I report only "strongly agree.")

Overall, most students found themselves believing that neoclassical economists had become more relevant; the percentage strongly agreeing increasing from 37 to 44 percent. Chicago, however, showed the largest increase, jumping from 44 to 63 percent, while MIT actually declined. In terms of agreeing on fundamental issues, Chicago, MIT, and Columbia show decreases in the view that economists agree on fundamental issues, and Yale and Stanford show increases.

There were also changes in views that learning neoclassical economics is learning a set of tools, with all schools but MIT increasing, and Harvard remaining the same. In regard to seeing economics as the most scientific of the social sciences, Harvard, Yale, and Stanford decreased, while Chicago, Princeton, Columbia, and MIT increased.

## Differences in Political Orientation among Schools

Schools differed in political orientation, as table 2–4 (p. 34) shows. I found it surprising that Chicago is not a major outlier; Stanford students saw themselves as more conservative than Chicago. Stanford students were also least likely to change their views, while Yale students saw their views changing the most. In the survey, I also asked those who did change their views in what direction their views changed. For most schools the change went both ways. One student captured what likely is happening when he stated, "I became more eclectic. Both conservatives and liberals have their favorite pipe dreams at odds with rea-

Table 2–2: Opinions of Economics as a Science: Comparison among Schools

| | Strongly agree | | Agree somewhat | | Disagree | | No clear opinion | |
|---|---|---|---|---|---|---|---|---|
| | Then | Now | Then | Now | Then | Now | Then | Now |
| **Neoclassical economics relevant** | | | | | | | | |
| Total | 34% | 44% | 54% | 45% | 11% | 5% | 1% | 5% |
| Chicago | 69% | 63% | 28% | 25% | 3% | 7% | 0% | 5% |
| Princeton | | 29% | | 65% | | 3% | | 3% |
| Harvard | 20% | 55% | 56% | 43% | 22% | 0% | 2% | 3% |
| Yale | 33% | 40% | 60% | 47% | 8% | 7% | 0% | 7% |
| MIT | 31% | 26% | 56% | 74% | 22% | 0% | 2% | 0% |
| Columbia | 24% | 33% | 68% | 44% | 8% | 4% | 0% | 19% |
| Stanford | 34% | 29% | 60% | 46% | 6% | 21% | 0% | 4% |
| **Economists agree on the fundamental issues** | | | | | | | | |
| Total | 4% | 9% | 40% | 43% | 52% | 44% | 4% | 4% |
| Chicago | 3% | 8% | 47% | 53% | 44% | 37% | 6% | 2% |
| Princeton | | 6% | | 44% | | 47% | | 3% |
| Harvard | 2% | 13% | 27% | 55% | 68% | 29% | 2% | 3% |
| Yale | 13% | 14% | 33% | 21% | 47% | 50% | 7% | 14% |
| MIT | 4% | 9% | 31% | 43% | 60% | 39% | 4% | 9% |
| Columbia | 4% | 0% | 48% | 33% | 44% | 59% | 4% | 7% |
| Stanford | 2% | 13% | 51% | 22% | 43% | 65% | 4% | 0% |

Table 2–2 (cont.)

|  | Strongly agree | | Agree somewhat | | Disagree | | No clear opinion | |
|---|---|---|---|---|---|---|---|---|
|  | Then | Now | Then | Now | Then | Now | Then | Now |
| We can draw a sharp line between positive and normative economics | | | | | | | | |
| Total | 9% | 12% | 23% | 34% | 62% | 40% | 6% | 14% |
| Chicago | 22% | 14% | 38% | 38% | 34% | 38% | 6% | 10% |
| Princeton | | 13% | | 19% | | 52% | | 16% |
| Harvard | 9% | 11% | 4% | 47% | 84% | 32% | 2% | 11% |
| Yale | 7% | 7% | 33% | 20% | 60% | 53% | 0% | 20% |
| MIT | 7% | 13% | 16% | 22% | 73% | 48% | 4% | 17% |
| Columbia | 0% | 15% | 32% | 27% | 52% | 42% | 16% | 15% |
| Stanford | 9% | 4% | 30% | 52% | 55% | 26% | 6% | 17% |
| Economics is the most scientific of the social sciences | | | | | | | | |
| Total | 28% | 50% | 39% | 27% | 19% | 16% | 14% | 6% |
| Chicago | 47% | 69% | 28% | 25% | 9% | 10% | 16% | 7% |
| Princeton | | 56% | | 13% | | 22% | | 9% |
| Harvard | 9% | 54% | 43% | 23% | 30% | 15% | 18% | 8% |
| Yale | 13% | 33% | 47% | 53% | 40% | 0% | 0% | 13% |
| MIT | 27% | 43% | 36% | 26% | 24% | 22% | 13% | 9% |
| Columbia | 36% | 50% | 24% | 23% | 28% | 27% | 12% | 0% |
| Stanford | 27% | 35% | 31% | 48% | 23% | 17% | 19% | 0% |

Table 2–3: Current vs. Earlier Perspectives on Economics

|  |  | Current view Strongly agree | View before entering grad school Strongly agree |
|---|---|---|---|
| Neoclassical economics is relevant for today. | | | |
| | Total | 44% | 37% |
| | Chicago | 63% | 44% |
| | Princeton | 29% | 30% |
| | Harvard | 55% | 48% |
| | Yale | 40% | 31% |
| | MIT | 26% | 30% |
| | Columbia | 33% | 29% |
| | Stanford | 29% | 27% |
| Economists agree on the fundamental issues. | | | |
| | Total | 9% | 11% |
| | Chicago | 8% | 16% |
| | Princeton | 6% | 9% |
| | Harvard | 13% | 14% |
| | Yale | 14% | 0% |
| | MIT | 8% | 13% |
| | Columbia | 0% | 7% |
| | Stanford | 13% | 4% |
| We can draw a sharp line between positive and normative economics. | | | |
| | Total | 12% | 15% |
| | Chicago | 14% | 15% |
| | Princeton | 13% | 19% |
| | Harvard | 11% | 10% |
| | Yale | 7% | 7% |
| | MIT | 13% | 22% |
| | Columbia | 15% | 19% |
| | Stanford | 4% | 12% |

Table 2–3 (*cont.*)

|  | Current view Strongly agree | View before entering grad school Strongly agree |
|---|---|---|
| **Learning neoclassical economics is learning a set of tools.** | | |
| Total | 36% | 26% |
| Chicago | 32% | 18% |
| Princeton | 34% | 21% |
| Harvard | 33% | 33% |
| Yale | 47% | 31% |
| MIT | 23% | 35% |
| Columbia | 48% | 29% |
| Stanford | 42% | 23% |
| **Economics is the most scientific of the social sciences.** | | |
| Total | 50% | 46% |
| Chicago | 69% | 47% |
| Princeton | 56% | 42% |
| Harvard | 54% | 64% |
| Yale | 33% | 38% |
| MIT | 43% | 39% |
| Columbia | 50% | 29% |
| Stanford | 35% | 48% |

sonable economics." There were two exceptions. At Chicago, nine students reported becoming more conservative, and only one more liberal, while at Princeton six students reported becoming more liberal and only one more conservative. Since Princeton and Chicago reported roughly the same percentage of conservative students, it seems that Princeton brings in conservative students and turns them into liberals, while Chicago brings in liberal students and turns them into conservatives. When asked about this tendency of students to move toward a conservative point of view, one student noted that one of the teachers in the first year stated, "I'm not here to teach you; I'm here to brainwash you." The student continued, "And that's been pretty much successful."

Table 2–4: Political Views of Different Schools

| | | Chicago | Princeton | Harvard | Yale | MIT | Columbia | Stanford | Total |
|---|---|---|---|---|---|---|---|---|---|
| Indicate your political orientation: | Conservative | 19% | 19% | 13% | 0% | 9% | 14% | 28% | 16% |
| | Moderate | 21% | 23% | 21% | 31% | 30% | 25% | 24% | 24% |
| | Liberal | 43% | 39% | 64% | 62% | 43% | 50% | 44% | 48% |
| | Radical | 3% | 13% | 3% | 8% | 13% | 4% | 0% | 6% |
| | Politics are unimportant to me | 14% | 6% | 0% | 0% | 4% | 7% | 4% | 6% |
| Did your political view change in graduate school? | No | 82% | 81% | 73% | 63% | 74% | 75% | 93% | 78% |
| | Yes | 18% | 19% | 28% | 38% | 26% | 25% | 7% | 22% |

In the previous survey, major differences among schools showed up in the opinions on the importance of economic assumptions and on opinions about policy issues. Table 2–5 shows the views on the importance of economic assumptions in the previous study and in this one.

Here I report only Chicago, Harvard, MIT and Stanford for the individual schools, because those were the schools presented last time. The other schools showed no major differences from the total. Students seeing the rationality assumption as very important increased from 33 percent to 68 percent at Harvard, whereas at MIT the percentage fell from 44 to only 9 percent. (Most of those moved to seeing it as important in some cases.) Harvard students also showed a significant change in their view of rational expectations, with the number seeing it as very important increasing from 14 to 41 percent, while Chicago fell from 59 to 43 percent, still larger than the average, but no longer an enormous outlier. MIT remained an outlier, with 0 percent seeing rational expectations as very important. Other schools' percentages seeing rational expectation as very important were Yale, 27 percent; Columbia, 12 percent; Stanford, 12 percent; and Princeton, 15 percent; making Harvard and Chicago the outliers.

The importance given to price rigidities went down in all schools, with all schools moving closer together. The importance of imperfect competition stayed about the same in overall importance, but there was less difference between Chicago and other schools. Behavior according to convention increased in importance, with Chicago no longer an outlier.

The differences are starker in terms of opinions about policy issues, as reported in table 2–6 (pp. 38–39).

Overall, views have moved only slightly. Fiscal policy is seen as less effective; fewer students see the market as discriminating against women; and fewer respondents believe that the distribution of income should be more equal. In terms of specific schools, we see greater movement with less variance of views than before. The percentage of students agreeing that fiscal policy can be an effective stabilizing policy increased at Chicago from 6 to 15 percent, while the percentage at Harvard decreased from 30 percent to 13 percent. The percentage of students at Chicago who believed that the Federal Reserve should maintain a constant growth of the money supply decreased from 41 to 18 percent, whereas at most other schools this percentage increased. Yale and Har-

Table 2–5: Importance of Economic Assumptions

| | Very important | | Important in some cases | | Unimportant | | No strong opinion | |
|---|---|---|---|---|---|---|---|---|
| | Then | Now | Then | Now | Then | Now | Then | Now |
| The neoclassical assumption of rational behavior of rational behavior | | | | | | | | |
| Total | 51% | 51% | 41% | 43% | 7% | 5% | 1% | 1% |
| Chicago | 78% | 79% | 22% | 21% | 0% | 0% | 0% | 0% |
| Harvard | 33% | 68% | 51% | 30% | 14% | 3% | 0% | 0% |
| MIT | 44% | 9% | 44% | 87% | 9% | 4% | 0% | 0% |
| Stanford | 58% | 54% | 36% | 38% | 6% | 4% | 0% | 4% |
| Economic behavior according to conventions | | | | | | | | |
| Total | 4% | 9% | 25% | 55% | 57% | 17% | 19% | 19% |
| Chicago | 0% | 10% | 31% | 42% | 31% | 25% | 38% | 23% |
| Harvard | 16% | 11% | 55% | 57% | 9% | 14% | 20% | 19% |
| MIT | 18% | 9% | 69% | 78% | 2% | 0% | 11% | 13% |
| Stanford | 4% | 8% | 64% | 69% | 4% | 8% | 28% | 15% |
| The rational expectations hypothesis | | | | | | | | |
| Total | 17% | 25% | 53% | 58% | 25% | 13% | 5% | 4% |
| Chicago | 59% | 43% | 38% | 48% | 0% | 7% | 3% | 2% |
| Harvard | 14% | 41% | 45% | 57% | 38% | 3% | 2% | 0% |
| MIT | 0% | 0% | 71% | 70% | 18% | 22% | 7% | 9% |
| Stanford | 9% | 12% | 53% | 81% | 32% | 8% | 6% | 0% |
| Imperfect competition | | | | | | | | |
| Total | 40% | 37% | 55% | 58% | 4% | 3% | 2% | 2% |
| Chicago | 16% | 23% | 72% | 67% | 9% | 7% | 3% | 3% |
| Harvard | 47% | 51% | 47% | 49% | 7% | 0% | 0% | 0% |
| MIT | 51% | 39% | 44% | 61% | 0% | 0% | 2% | 0% |
| Stanford | 38% | 46% | 60% | 50% | 2% | 0% | 0% | 4% |
| Price rigidities | | | | | | | | |
| Total | 27% | 14% | 60% | 65% | 10% | 11% | 3% | 10% |
| Chicago | 6% | 7% | 56% | 58% | 38% | 22% | 0% | 13% |
| Harvard | 37% | 22% | 54% | 68% | 7% | 0% | 2% | 11% |
| MIT | 38% | 17% | 56% | 70% | 4% | 9% | 0% | 4% |
| Stanford | 26% | 12% | 65% | 54% | 4% | 19% | 4% | 15% |

Table 2–5 (*cont.*)

|  | Very important | | Important in some cases | | Unimportant | | No strong opinion | |
|---|---|---|---|---|---|---|---|---|
|  | Then | Now | Then | Now | Then | Now | Then | Now |
| *Cost mark-up pricing* | | | | | | | | |
| Total | 9% | 5% | 46% | 47% | 26% | 18% | 18% | 30% |
| Chicago | 0% | 3% | 16% | 38% | 50% | 28% | 34% | 30% |
| Harvard | 7% | 3% | 48% | 49% | 26% | 16% | 19% | 32% |
| MIT | 9% | 0% | 62% | 70% | 18% | 13% | 9% | 17% |
| Stanford | 11% | 12% | 41% | 28% | 33% | 24% | 15% | 36% |

vard remained the schools with the strongest disagreement with that proposition. A similar convergence of views can be seen in the question about whether inflation is primarily a monetary phenomenon, with Yale and Chicago differing only slightly on their views on this issue. It seems that the Yale/Chicago divide on monetary policy has finally been put to rest.

Table 2–7 (p. 40) shows students' views of the importance of reading in math, sociology, and psychology by school.

MIT students saw reading in psychology as very important, but reading in math as not very important. Harvard students saw reading in sociology as very important, while Yale students did not.

### Differences among Schools on Other Dimensions

The survey asked a variety of other questions, and here I will try to summarize some of the interesting results of differences by school.

Interest in fields differed among schools. Significant differences include great interest in micro at Chicago and Yale; the most interest in international trade at Columbia; the most interest in labor at MIT and Chicago, with the least interest at Yale and Columbia. MIT students had the most interest in urban economics; macro theory was of least interest at MIT, Stanford, and Harvard, and of most interest at Columbia. Public finance was of most interest at MIT and of least interest at Columbia, Harvard, and Yale. Money and banking was of least interest

Table 2–6: Economic Opinions at Different Schools

|  | Agree | | Agree with res. | | Disagree | | No strong opinion | |
|---|---|---|---|---|---|---|---|---|
|  | Then | Now | Then | Now | Then | Now | Then | Now |
| *Fiscal policy can be an effective stabilizer.* | | | | | | | | |
| Total | 35% | 21% | 49% | 58% | 11% | 12% | 5% | 9% |
| Chicago | 6% | 15% | 34% | 60% | 44% | 13% | 16% | 12% |
| Harvard | 30% | 13% | 65% | 73% | 2% | 8% | 2% | 8% |
| Yale | 60% | 20% | 33% | 67% | 7% | 7% | 0% | 7% |
| MIT | 48% | 30% | 51% | 57% | 0% | 9% | 2% | 4% |
| Columbia | 54% | 26% | 38% | 63% | 8% | 4% | 0% | 7% |
| Stanford | 30% | 24% | 52% | 32% | 9% | 20% | 9% | 24% |
| *The Fed should maintain a constant growth rate of the money supply.* | | | | | | | | |
| Total | 9% | 7% | 34% | 22% | 45% | 50% | 12% | 22% |
| Chicago | 41% | 18% | 44% | 36% | 9% | 28% | 6% | 18% |
| Harvard | 7% | 3% | 24% | 13% | 57% | 73% | 11% | 13% |
| Yale | 0% | 0% | 21% | 13% | 64% | 73% | 14% | 13% |
| MIT | 0% | 0% | 27% | 22% | 60% | 52% | 13% | 26% |
| Columbia | 4% | 4% | 50% | 22% | 33% | 52% | 13% | 22% |
| Stanford | 2% | 8% | 39% | 16% | 44% | 40% | 15% | 36% |
| *Income distribution in developed nations should be more equal.* | | | | | | | | |
| Total | 47% | 32% | 32% | 41% | 14% | 18% | 7% | 9% |
| Chicago | 16% | 20% | 50% | 47% | 19% | 20% | 15% | 13% |
| Harvard | 54% | 25% | 33% | 48% | 13% | 23% | 0% | 5% |
| Yale | 60% | 57% | 20% | 29% | 20% | 14% | 7% | 0% |
| MIT | 52% | 39% | 30% | 35% | 9% | 9% | 9% | 17% |
| Columbia | 46% | 33% | 37% | 44% | 9% | 15% | 9% | 7% |
| Stanford | 52% | 36% | 24% | 32% | 17% | 28% | 7% | 4% |
| *A minimum wage increases unemployment among young and unskilled.* | | | | | | | | |
| Total | 34% | 33% | 39% | 38% | 18% | 23% | 9% | 7% |
| Chicago | 70% | 56% | 28% | 29% | 3% | 12% | 0% | 3% |
| Harvard | 15% | 21% | 41% | 56% | 35% | 18% | 9% | 5% |
| Yale | 33% | 33% | 27% | 53% | 13% | 13% | 27% | 0% |
| MIT | 24% | 17% | 53% | 30% | 11% | 30% | 11% | 22% |
| Columbia | 38% | 30% | 25% | 30% | 21% | 26% | 9% | 15% |
| Stanford | 36% | 38% | 40% | 35% | 19% | 27% | 4% | 0% |

Table 2–6 (*cont.*)

|  | Agree | | Agree with res. | | Disagree | | No strong opinion | |
|---|---|---|---|---|---|---|---|---|
|  | Then | Now | Then | Now | Then | Now | Then | Now |
| *Tariffs and quotas reduce general economic welfare.* | | | | | | | | |
| Total | 36% | 51% | 49% | 39% | 9% | 7% | 6% | 3% |
| Chicago | 66% | 62% | 34% | 25% | 0% | 13% | 0% | 0% |
| Harvard | 20% | 53% | 56% | 45% | 11% | 0% | 13% | 3% |
| Yale | 33% | 33% | 60% | 53% | 7% | 13% | 0% | 0% |
| MIT | 38% | 48% | 42% | 43% | 13% | 0% | 4% | 9% |
| Columbia | 38% | 30% | 54% | 48% | 8% | 15% | 0% | 7% |
| Stanford | 32% | 54% | 51% | 35% | 9% | 4% | 9% | 8% |
| *Inflation is a monetary phenomenon.* | | | | | | | | |
| Total | 27% | 34% | 33% | 33% | 29% | 20% | 11% | 14% |
| Chicago | 84% | 44% | 16% | 25% | 0% | 21% | 0% | 10% |
| Harvard | 15% | 30% | 26% | 38% | 46% | 25% | 11% | 8% |
| Yale | 13% | 40% | 40% | 20% | 33% | 20% | 13% | 20% |
| MIT | 7% | 18% | 44% | 50% | 36% | 14% | 11% | 18% |
| Columbia | 29% | 22% | 25% | 44% | 33% | 22% | 13% | 11% |
| Stanford | 23% | 28% | 45% | 24% | 23% | 16% | 10% | 32% |
| *The market tends to discriminate against women.* | | | | | | | | |
| Total | 24% | 14% | 27% | 28% | 39% | 47% | 10% | 11% |
| Chicago | 6% | 5% | 19% | 20% | 69% | 69% | 3% | 7% |
| Harvard | 44% | 15% | 20% | 33% | 26% | 43% | 11% | 10% |
| Yale | 27% | 7% | 53% | 27% | 13% | 53% | 7% | 13% |
| MIT | 24% | 22% | 22% | 30% | 40% | 39% | 13% | 9% |
| Columbia | 38% | 26% | 21% | 26% | 33% | 26% | 8% | 22% |
| Stanford | 11% | 8% | 38% | 32% | 43% | 52% | 9% | 8% |

at Harvard and of greatest interest at Princeton. Law and economics was of least interest at Princeton and of most interest at Stanford. Columbia and Chicago had the greatest interest in comparative economic systems.

The response to what skills put students on the fast track also differed by schools.[8] Stanford students saw problem solving as most important (69 percent found it very important); Columbia saw it as least im-

Table 2–7: Importance of Reading in Different Fields by School

| | Chicago | Princeton | Harvard | Yale | MIT | Columbia | Stanford | Total |
|---|---|---|---|---|---|---|---|---|
| *Mathematics* | | | | | | | | |
| Very important | 47% | 45% | 23% | 31% | 13% | 36% | 41% | 36% |
| Important | 34% | 21% | 35% | 44% | 26% | 32% | 30% | 31% |
| Moderately important | 12% | 24% | 28% | 25% | 35% | 25% | 26% | 23% |
| Unimportant | 7% | 9% | 15% | 0% | 26% | 7% | 4% | 10% |
| *Sociology* | | | | | | | | |
| Very important | 8% | 16% | 30% | 0% | 22% | 25% | 19% | 17% |
| Important | 41% | 41% | 40% | 44% | 43% | 25% | 41% | 39% |
| Moderately important | 37% | 31% | 23% | 50% | 30% | 32% | 30% | 32% |
| Unimportant | 14% | 13% | 8% | 6% | 4% | 18% | 11% | 11% |
| *Psychology* | | | | | | | | |
| Very important | 12% | 28% | 25% | 6% | 48% | 21% | 19% | 22% |
| Important | 22% | 22% | 30% | 56% | 39% | 36% | 22% | 29% |
| Moderately important | 33% | 34% | 38% | 25% | 9% | 25% | 44% | 31% |
| Unimportant | 33% | 16% | 8% | 13% | 4% | 18% | 15% | 17% |

portant (32 percent). MIT students saw empirical research as most important (50 percent); Harvard students saw it as least important (18 percent).[9] Princeton students saw excellence in mathematics as most important (48 percent); MIT students saw it as least important (17 percent). Columbia students saw having a thorough knowledge of the economy as being most important (25 percent); Yale and MIT students saw it as least important (0 percent).

Chicago students were still the most likely to use the notion of individual optimizing behavior, with 85 percent saying they used it very often, although the differences were less than before. Columbia students used it the least, with 56 percent saying they used it very often.

Students at Harvard and Yale were much more likely (75 percent) to want to be at a major university, whereas MIT and Columbia (39 percent and 46 percent respectively) were less likely, wanting instead to be at an institution involved in economic policy-making. MIT also had the largest percentage wanting to be at a good liberal arts college: 17 percent compared to an average of 9 percent. Students at Chicago and Columbia were much more likely to want to be research assistants or teaching assistants than were students at other schools, which is most likely explained by the different support levels of these programs. (Columbia has recently changed its practice, reducing the number of admitted students and providing more long-term support for a larger number of those admitted.) Chicago remains the one top school that accepts a large number of students without support, and reduces the number somewhat in core examinations, although based on discussions with faculty at Chicago, that weeding out is less than it is sometimes rumored to be. Chicago remains the largest program. Columbia, which was a large program, now has a much smaller one.

Chicago students found course work most stressful (42 percent found it very stressful);[10] this is not surprising since the core exams weed out students at Chicago much more than they do at other schools. Harvard students found it least stressful (20 percent). Chicago students also found their financial situation most stressful (18 percent); Harvard students found it least stressful (2 percent). Columbia students found the relationship with faculty most stressful (22 percent); Princeton students found it least stressful (0 percent). Most students did not find the mathematics very stressful; the most stress was felt at Stanford, Princeton, and Columbia, with Harvard, MIT, and Yale having almost no students finding the math very stressful. Columbia students found conflict between course content and interest most stressful (26 percent); Harvard students found it least stressful (7 percent).[11]

Chicago had the greatest interest in micro theory (53 percent had great interest); MIT had the least (18 percent).[12] MIT had the most interest in labor (45 percent); Yale had the least (7 percent). Columbia had the most interest in macro theory (50 percent); MIT had the least (14 percent). MIT had the most interest in public finance (45 percent); Columbia had the least (14 percent). Harvard and Chicago had the greatest interest in development (47 percent); Yale had the least (25 percent). Princeton had the greatest interest in money and banking (41 percent); Harvard had the least (7 percent). Stanford had the most interest in law and economics (26 percent); Princeton had the least (6 percent).

# Reflections on the Survey Results

Since our earlier study in the 1980s, graduate work in economics has been scrutinized and subjected to self-examination and self-criticism in a way that few disciplines have undertaken. (Krueger et al., 1991; Hansen, 1991). Yet almost none of the COGEE commission recommendations, such as making the core a concern of the entire department, or balancing the breadth and depth of the core, were specifically adopted. Nonetheless, this survey shows that economics has changed significantly since the 1980s, and graduate students today are happier with their training than they were earlier.

One reason these changes have occurred is that the way economics is done has changed, as have economists' views of themselves. Economics has become more consciously empirical than it was, and the mathematics that it uses are more likely to be applied mathematics than pure mathematics. Institutional economics has made a comeback, albeit in a different form. Rigid behavioral assumptions have become less sacrosanct, and behavioral economics and experimental economics have blossomed. While this work is not center mainstream, it is clearly at the edge of mainstream.

Technological change has helped bring about this result by making sophisticated econometrics much cheaper to do, allowing students to pull more information out of data. Methods of bringing theory to the data have increased as economists have become less rigid about their approaches to theory and to empirical work.[13] One student expressed it this way: "I think empirical work is becoming the dominant strand of microeconomics. We have the computing power, we have the datasets, we understand identification issues, and the combination of the three makes the analysis much more credible than in the past, and therefore more readily consumed by policymakers." Creativity in actually saying something—finding the "killer app" or the perfect field or natural experiment—has gained in importance, and pure technique has faded in importance. As another student put it, "Mathematical ability is great, but creativity is much more important."

The methodological debates of the 1970s and 1980s, which pitted neoclassical economics against heterodox economics, have faded, and the perception of a rigid neoclassical economics has been replaced by an eclectic mainstream whose central theme is, "What can you tell me that I don't already know?" The view of what has happened in graduate economics education was captured by a student in his responses to two questions. In response to what he most disliked about graduate school, he stated, "Being made more cynical than most would think possible. It is like seeing the inside of a sausage factory." But in answer to the question of whether economists have a relevant role in society that same student answered, "Yes, they are the only careful, structured, empirical thinkers on most economic, political, and social issues."

*Issues of Concern*

Although graduate students are generally satisfied with economics, serious issues about graduate education in economics remain open. The first is that an important reason for the more positive attitude of the students is not a change in graduate economics education, but a change in who is becoming an economist. In the early 1980s, many students went into graduate economics study thinking that it would be like undergraduate school; today almost all students know better.[14] In effect, students have been prescreened to be comfortable with the mathematics in the program. Similarly, graduate schools know better what they want and select students who are comfortable in the approach that will be taught. This prescreening, however, comes at a cost, since it likely eliminates those parts of the applicant pool who rank high on creativity and vision, but who either find the mathematics sterile or do not have the mathematical ability (Colander 1994). Mathematicians often process information differently than other people, and by filtering students through a mathematical screen, one is likely to change the nature of economics, making it harder to replicate creative economists in the style of Easterlin, North, Olsen, Streeten, Tullock, Rosenberg, Kindleberger, or Buchanan. While these are all highly analytical and sophisticated thinkers who have contributed enormously to economics, it is unclear that they would have chosen economics (or whether graduate schools would have chosen them) using the current graduate school filtering system.

A second issue is the structure of the core classes in graduate education. The COGEE report argued that these core courses should teach "those things common to all economists" and be regarded as "the concern of the entire department" (Krueger et al. 1991, 1052). Most schools have interpreted "those things common" to mean a set of common techniques; but another interpretation is that economists share a reasoning process, an imaginative combination of insights and reasoning that emphasizes intuition of how incentives matter and how institutions work. The two interpretations are, of course, somewhat connected; certainly statistical methods are common to both. But the "economic reasoning" concept of commonality relies on a less formal set of models than are often taught in the core courses of graduate school today, and emphasizes the relationship of those models to real world observations much more than does the "technique" interpretation of "those things common."

Robert Solow (1964, 7, 8) provided one justification for focusing on highly technical models in the core. He wrote, "In economics I like a man to have mastered the fancy theory before I trust him with simple theory. The practical utility of economics comes not primarily from its high-powered frontier, but from fairly low-powered reasoning. But the moral is not that we can dispense with high-powered economics, if only because high-powered economics seems to be such an excellent school for the skillful use of low-powered economics." Solow may be correct, but if that is the justification, it is worth exploring whether other screening devices could serve the same purpose.

One school, Chicago, stood out in teaching a reasoning-based, rather than a technique-based, core micro. The core micro at Chicago was more applied; it focused on giving students a sense of economic reasoning rather than techniques. The students reveled in the difference. When I mentioned the possibility of their learning more standard micro, most students strongly objected. One student stated what seemed a common view: "In micro I really like the perspective that they have here; there are a lot of schools where they just go through Mas Colell chapter by chapter. I'd much prefer a course where you don't go through a single chapter of that book." That economic reasoning approach to micro was missed at other schools. For example, one Princeton student stated, "We don't learn price theory in the first year, or get introduced to the models we use in the field courses. In applied courses we do a lot with price theory and I was frustrated that that's not part of the core anymore." Students at other schools made similar remarks. Were students to vote, they would strongly favor a core that focused on economic reasoning rather than economic technique, and which better tied in with upper-level field courses.

COGEE also argued that the core should be the concern of the entire department. In practice, however, departments seem to have allocated control of the content to a subset of individuals, and that subset has allocated control of subparts to specific individuals; there is no attempt at integration. Thus, in their core exams, students are held responsible for what the teacher of that subcourse chooses to teach. Again and again in the interviews, students remarked that what they learn depended on who was teaching that particular year. They said that if one fails the core exam, one has to retake the entire course, because the next year the content of that core would change so much.

Thus, the core is not what most outside observers would call a core. Instead, it is an introduction to the approach and techniques taken by the professors who are teaching that semester. To put it another way, the core is a more-or-less arbitrary hurdle for students. In the earlier study, we detected a strong objection among students to the requirement that they jump this hurdle. This time there is less concern about the hurdles, partly because departments have preselected better hurdlers, and partly because even those who question whether it is worth doing can still pass the exams, because the exams are structured sufficiently closely to the problem sets so that bright, mathematically oriented students who study those problems sets can pass—even if they are not totally comfortable with the techniques. One Princeton student made a typical remark: "The first year is pure theory. I frequently was doing stuff that I had no idea why I should care about it." Students are highly cognizant of how the exams are structured and can devise strategies to pass the exam at the required level, even if they are unclear about what they are learning.[15] For me, these views raise the question, Are the core courses serving the role that core courses should play?

A third issue concerns what subjects are in the core, and, specifically, with the evolution of thinking in macro, whether macro belongs in the core at all. When we did the last study, the highly technical approach to macro that now characterizes the core was not fully integrated into the core macro courses, which meant that then the core macro course still focused on macro policy. The current study shows that that is no longer the case; today, most of the macro courses never discuss macro policy, and since micro students never take advanced field courses in macro, they are taught no macro policy. The students told me that the differences in policy views on macro that showed up in the survey did not reflect what they were taught about policy in macro, since they were taught almost nothing about macro policy, but reflected their undergraduate training. When asked about survey results showing that students at his school had changed their views on policy, one student stated, "I think that in the macro course we never talked about monetary or fiscal policy, although it might have been slipped in as a variable in one particular model, but that wasn't the focus, so it didn't come from the courses." Another stated, "Monetary and fiscal policy are not abstract enough to be a question that would be answered in a macro course." In short, the macro that is taught to the students in the core has lost touch with both policy and empirical evidence.[16] Instead, students are presented with dynamic stochastic optimal control theory and Euler equations.

Macroeconomists will be quick to point out that much of the evolution in macro occurred precisely because macroeconomists were trying to bring better models to the data, and that an enormous amount of serious empirical work in macro involves that issue. My point here is not to criticize or discuss the state of macro, but only to describe the perception of macro that students get from what they are presented in the core. In micro and econometrics, the students can accept learning esoteric techniques because they hear from upper-level students that in the field courses they may use those techniques; in macro that is not the case. One Princeton student remarked, "I would still be hard-pressed to tell what any of the tools I learned in macro were for. In micro and econometrics I also initially felt that, but by the second year, things I tried to do before I came here started to make more sense. I was able to construct the models better, and I was able to apply the tools; that was not the case in macro." In many ways, macro theory today is advanced dynamic general equilibrium price theory. A strong argument can be made that macro, as it is currently being taught, does not belong in the core, and it should instead be seen as an advanced upper-level course. Eliminating macro from the core would free up resources in the core, which could be advantageously used in a number of different ways. One possibility, which would serve the same "technical hurdle" function that the core macro course does currently, would be to replace the macro core course with another econometrics and statistics course, which would provide students with more tools for bringing the models to the data. Such a course might cover various time-series, cointegration, vector autoregression, and nonparametric econometric techniques that most core econometric courses do not now cover, but which are of use in macro research.[17]

Another issue with the core concerns the breadth as opposed to the depth of the courses. The COGEE report called for a balancing of breadth and depth in the core. That clearly hasn't happened; the core focuses on depth, not breadth. The core courses provide little context for why those techniques that the students are learning are important, or why they have developed. The core courses almost never survey the field, nor do they attempt to put the ongoing debates in context. They make almost no attempt to provide knowledge of the field that would translate beyond the particular professor's approach. Students have little sense of background to the debates or the techniques and do not understand why they developed and of what use they are. Instead, the students are thrown into the particular approach, and a particular technique, and told to learn it. What the professors are doing is often interesting, and exciting, and so the students are generally comfortable with the course as long as they know that they will be able to pass the exams.[18]

## Conclusion

At about the same time that I was doing this survey, French graduate education was going through a student revolt (Fullerton 2003). The complaints of the French students were, in many ways, the same as those made by critics of U.S. education in economics in the 1980s—that the subject was taught in an unempirical manner, and that the economics they were learning lacked connection to the real world. Most graduate students in the United States were unaware of that revolt, and those who were aware of it were surprised that economics could be described as unempirical. U.S. students find their studies very empirical and are reasonably happy both with their education and with economics. U.S. students feel that they are learning useful tools and that they are entering into a profession that is respected and has something to say. The problems and stress that go along with getting a Ph. D. remain, but the stress seems to reflect a normal level of concern, not the deeper concern that I detected among the students in our previous study.

I am known as a critic of graduate education in economics, but my critique in this study is quite different from my critique of twenty years ago. Then, my critique was not only of economics graduate education but also of economics—its rigidity of assumptions, its lack of empirical grounding, and its failure to bring the models to the data in a serious way. I believe, however, that economics has changed, and it is now attempting to bring the models to the data in a much more meaningful way than it used to. Theory for the sake of theory has been reduced, but, as can happen as technology changes, the pedagogical institutional structure has not kept pace with the changing research technologies. My critique of economics now is not about economics but about pedagogy—specifically the structure of the core in graduate education. If, as the students strongly argued in the interviews, creativity and economic reasoning, not mathematics, is the core of economics then it seems reasonable that the core courses should focus somewhat more on creativity and economic reasoning and somewhat less on technique.

# Questionnaire for Graduate Students in Economics

*Background*

1.  1. Age:_____  2. Sex: _____  3. Nationality:_____

    4. Ethnic background:
    5. Are you involved in a long-term relationship?   Yes / No
    6. Do you have children?   Yes / No
    7. Do you consider yourself religious?   Yes / No

2.  1.  Occupation of mother:
    2.  Education of mother:
    3.  Occupation of father:
    4.  Education of father:
    5.  Political orientation of father (check one):
        [ ] conservative [ ] moderate [ ] liberal [ ] radical [ ] don't know
        Political orientation of mother (check one):
        [ ] conservative [ ] moderate [ ] liberal [ ] radical [ ] don't know

3.  Which undergraduate college(s) did you attend?   Name   Dates
    Undergraduate major:
    Other fields of concentration:
    Significant extracurricular activities in college:

4.  Did you begin graduate work in economics immediately after earning your B.A.?
    Yes / No
    If not, what did you do in between?

5.  When did you first consider economics as a career?

6.  At the time you were considering graduate work in economics, did you have alternative plans?   Yes / No
    If yes, what other options did you consider seriously?

7.  a. How important were the following factors in your decision to do graduate work
    in economics?
    (3-very important; 2-somewhat important; 1-unimportant)
    1. enjoyed undergraduate classes in economics                    3 2 1
    2. desire to engage in policy formulation                        3 2 1
    3. good grades in economics classes                              3 2 1

4. advice of my undergraduate teachers                      3 2 1
5. acceptance by a good graduate school                     3 2 1
6. wanted to get a job in academia, and economics seemed to offer
the best possibility                                         3 2 1
7. economics seemed the most relevant field, given my intellectual
interests                                                    3 2 1
8. political reasons                                         3 2 1
    b. What other factor was very important?
    c. Of the above factors, which (one, two, three) was/were the most important in
     your decision?

*Graduate School*

8. In what year of graduate school are you? Check one:

    [ ] first [ ] second [ ] third [ ] fourth [ ] fifth or more

9. Did you receive a fellowship for graduate school in your first year?   Yes / No
    Percentage of total financial need covered by fellowship?
    How did you finance the expenses not covered by the fellowship?

10. In which of the following activities, besides studying, are you currently engaged?
Check all applicable alternatives.
    [ ] research assistantship
    [ ] teaching assistantship
    [ ] consulting
    [ ] the writing of scholarly papers for publication
    [ ] political work
    [ ] volunteer work
    [ ] sports
    [ ] other significant activities. Please specify:

11. Please consider the following statements and compare your current opinion with
the one you held before you began graduate school. Circle the most appropriate numbers (4-strongly agree; 3-agree somewhat; 2-disagree; 1-no clear opinion).

| Current | Statement | Before |
|---|---|---|
| 4 3 2 1 | The study of neoclassical economics is relevant for the economic prob-lems of today. | 4 3 2 1 |
| 4 3 2 1 | Economists agree on the fundamental issues. | 4 3 2 1 |
| 4 3 2 1 | We can draw a sharp line between positive and normative economics. | 4 3 2 1 |
| 4 3 2 1 | Learning neoclassical economics means learning a set of tools. | 4 3 2 1 |
| 4 3 2 1 | Economics is the most scientific discipline among the social sciences. | 4 3 2 1 |

12. Can you think of any elements of graduate school that have been, or are currently,
stressful for you? Circle one: (4-very stressful; 3-stressful; 2-moderately stressful; 1-not
stressful).

course work                         4 3 2 1
your financial situation            4 3 2 1
relationships with faculty          4 3 2 1

relationships with students            4 3 2 1
doing the mathematics                  4 3 2 1
finding a dissertation topic           4 3 2 1
maintaining a meaningful life outside  4 3 2 1
graduate school
conflict between course content and    4 3 2 1
your interests

13. What do you like most about graduate school?
What do you dislike most about graduate school?

14. Where have you learned most about economics? (Rank the top three starting with "1.")
   [ ] in the classroom
   [ ] in seminars
   [ ] by reading assigned readings on your own
   [ ] by reading unassigned readings on your own
   [ ] in discussions with other students
   [ ] in your job as a research assistant
   [ ] teaching a section of principles or being a teaching assistant
   [ ] other. Specify:

15. Rate the following fields with respect to your degree of interest. Circle one. (3-of great interest to me; 2-of moderate interest to me; 1-of no interest to me).

| | | | | | |
|---|---|---|---|---|---|
| micro theory | 3 2 1 | macro theory | 3 2 1 | econometrics | 3 2 1 |
| intern. trade | 3 2 1 | public fin | 3 2 1 | mon & banking | 3 2 1 |
| labor | 3 2 1 | ind. organ. | 3 2 1 | law & econ | 3 2 1 |
| urban econ | 3 2 1 | econ devel | 3 2 1 | comp econ systems | 3 2 1 |
| hist of thought | 3 2 1 | political econ | 3 2 1 | | |

In which fields are you, or will you be, specializing?

16. Which professors in the graduate program are at the moment most important for you? (Please give name and field, and specify briefly the reason.)
   1.
   2.
   3.

17. How important to your development as an economist would you, if you had the time, consider readings in or discussions about topics in the following fields? Circle one. (4-very important; 3-important; 2-moderately important; 1-unimportant)

| | | | |
|---|---|---|---|
| mathematics | 4 3 2 1 | computer science | 4 3 2 1 |
| physics | 4 3 2 1 | political science | 4 3 2 1 |
| sociology | 4 3 2 1 | psychology | 4 3 2 1 |
| philosophy | 4 3 2 1 | history | 4 3 2 1 |

18. Do you have frequent interactions with graduate students or scholars in other disciplines? Yes / No
If yes, are those interactions primarily intellectual or social?

19. What has been, or probably will be, the major factor in your choice of the dissertation topic? Check one.

[ ] the suggestion of a teacher
[ ] the desire to understand some economic phenomenon
[ ] the desire to get the dissertation done, and thus the feasibility of the topic
[ ] the application of certain mathematical or econometric techniques; the economic topic is of secondary importance
[ ] other. Specify:

20. a. Indicate your political orientation:
    [ ] conservative [ ] moderate [ ] liberal [ ] radical
    [ ] politics are unimportant to me
    b. Did your political views change in graduate school?   Yes / No
    c. If yes, in what way?

21. If you had to do it over again, would you go to graduate school in economics?
Yes / No / Unsure
Would you go to the same graduate school?   Yes / No / Unsure
If not, why?

*About being an economist*
22. Which economists (dead or alive) do you respect most? Please specify the characteristics that you admire in each of them.

1.        Characteristics:
2.        Characteristics:
3.        Characteristics:

23. Do you consider the role that economists currently have in society relevant? Circle one. Yes / No / Uncertain
Why?

24. Which characteristics will most likely place students on the fast track? Circle one. (4-very important; 3-moderately important; 2-unimportant; 1-I don't know).

| | |
|---|---|
| being smart in the sense that they are good at problem solving | 4 3 2 1 |
| being interested in, and good at, empirical research | 4 3 2 1 |
| excellence in mathematics | 4 3 2 1 |
| being very knowledgeable about one particular field | 4 3 2 1 |
| ability to make connections with prominent professors | 4 3 2 1 |
| a broad knowledge of the economics literature | 4 3 2 1 |
| a thorough knowledge of the economy | 4 3 2 1 |

Other (specify) and comments:

25. What is your idea of a successful economist? (Specify the characteristics.)

26. Will you pursue an academic career after graduate school?  Yes / No / Unsure
If no, or if unsure, what other career might you pursue?

27. Where do you hope to be fifteen years from now?
[ ] at a major university
[ ] at a good liberal arts college
[ ] at a major research institution
[ ] at an institution that is indirectly involved in economic policy-making
[ ] in the private sector
[ ] other. Specify:

*About Economics*

28. Rank the following types of articles according to your interest. The journals are mentioned to give further indication of the type that is meant. (1 is most interesting, 2 is second, etc.)
___ an article on pure theory (cf., *Journal of Economic Theory*)
___ an article on pure econometrics (cf., *Econometrica*)
___ an article that combines theory and econometrics (cf., *AER*)
___ an article in applied economics (cf., *Brookings Papers*)
___ an article in nonconventional economics (cf., *Review of Radical Political Economics*)

29. Do you agree with the following propositions? Circle one. (4-I agree; 3-I agree with some reservations; 2-I disagree; 1-I have no opinion).
4 3 2 1    Fiscal policy can be an effective tool in a stabilization policy.
4 3 2 1    The Federal Reserve Bank should maintain a constant growth of the money supply.
4 3 2 1    The distribution of income in developed nations should be more equal.
4 3 2 1    A minimum wage increases unemployment among young and unskilled workers.
4 3 2 1    Tariffs and import quotas reduce general economic welfare.
4 3 2 1    Inflation is primarily a monetary phenomenon.
4 3 2 1    Wage-price controls should be used to control inflation.
4 3 2 1    Worker democracy will increase labor productivity.
4 3 2 1    The market system tends to discriminate against women.
4 3 2 1    The capitalist system has an inherent tendency toward crisis.

30. How important do you consider the following assumptions or perspectives for an economic analysis? Circle one. (4-very important; 3-important in some cases; 2-unimportant; 1-I have no strong opinion).
4 3 2 1    the neoclassical assumption of rational behavior
4 3 2 1    economic behavior according to conventions
4 3 2 1    the rational expectations hypothesis
4 3 2 1    imperfect competition
4 3 2 1    price rigidities
4 3 2 1    cost markup pricing
4 3 2 1    the goal of a capitalist firm is to extract surplus value from workers

31. Do you use the neoclassical notion of individual optimizing behavior when you think or talk about non-economic issues?

[ ] very often       [ ] infrequently       [ ] never

Your name (optional):

If you are willing to be interviewed in-depth, please give your address, telephone number, and convenient times to call you.

David Colander

# Methodology of the Questionnaire

The questionnaire was distributed in 2001–02 at Princeton University and during the 2002–03 school year at the other schools. The total number of respondents was 231 from an estimated population of 800–900, a response rate of approximately 27 percent, normal for this type of survey. The survey was identical to our 1985 survey and took students anywhere from fifteen minutes to more than an hour to complete. The distribution of respondents by school was Chicago 26 percent, Princeton 15 percent, Harvard 18 percent, Yale 7 percent, MIT 10 percent, Columbia 12 percent, and Stanford 12 percent. The distribution by year was first year 22 percent, second year 25 percent, third year 19 percent, fourth year 14 percent, and fifth year or more 20 percent.

The academic coordinators at the various schools distributed the survey. It was placed in student mailboxes, and students were asked to return it to a central point. Students were reminded to varying degrees by email from the academic coordinators to fill in the questionnaires, and the differing tenacity of the academic coordinator in reminding students likely accounts for some of the different number of respondents by school.

As we stated in the previous study, there is a potential for bias in the surveys: technically oriented students were probably less likely to answer questionnaires, as were foreign students. Other biases are also possible. For example, there is a social dynamic in answering questionnaires in which students' interactions with other students leads to subgroups of students participating more than other subgroups. For example, a former Harvard student told me that in our 1985 survey, radical Harvard students made a concerted effort to get other radical Harvard students to respond, thereby influencing the results. To check for such biases, I asked students in the interview about particular results that seemed as if they might reflect such a bias, and did not find any obvious outliers. Still, care must be taken in using these data as anything other than a general indication of the nature of graduate education and how schools differ.

Interviews were conducted with students who agreed to be interviewed and who gave their email address on the questionnaire. They were contacted and a date was set up for the interview. Although the interviews were taped and transcribed, anonymity was promised to all interviewees. Students were interviewed three or four at a time in interviews that were approximately an hour in length. During the interviews, I asked students about the questionnaire, graduate economic education, economics, and differences between their schools and others. I had a number of set questions but allowed each interview to evolve on its own.

Response rate to the interviews differed by school and varied from three to ten participants per school. No attempt to ensure a random selection of students to interview was made, although in all interviews, I asked the students if they felt they were representative of the views of the larger student population. One obvious difference between this interview process and the last is that I did all of the interviews this time, whereas in our earlier study, Arjo Klamer did a number of them.

# Some Additional Tables upon Which the Discussion Is Based

Table C–1: Relevance of Economics by Gender

| Economics relevant | Total | Male | Female |
|---|---|---|---|
| Yes | 73.13% | 72.20% | 75.38% |
| No | 7.49% | 6.18% | 10.77% |
| Uncertain | 15.86% | 17.29% | 12.31% |
| NA | 3.52% | 4.33% | 1.54% |

Table C–2: Relevance of Economics by Year

| Economics relevant | 1st year | 2nd year | 3rd year | 4th year | 5th or more |
|---|---|---|---|---|---|
| Yes | 65.31% | 82.1% | 70.45% | 78.79% | 68.89% |
| No | 6.12% | 7.10% | 4.54% | 9.09% | 11.11% |
| Uncertain | 22.45% | 8.90% | 22.72% | 9.09% | 15.56% |
| NA | 6.12% | 1.90% | 2.29% | 3.03% | 4.44% |

Table C–3: Relevance of Economics by School

| Economics relevant | Harvard | Chicago | MIT | Princeton | Yale | Columbia | Stanford |
|---|---|---|---|---|---|---|---|
| Yes | 77.50% | 75.41% | 86.96% | 69.70% | 62.50% | 60.71% | 73.07% |
| No | 0.00% | 13.11% | 4.34% | 12.12% | 0.00% | 7.14% | 7.70% |
| Uncertain | 15.00% | 9.84% | 8.70% | 12.12% | 37.50% | 28.57% | 15.38% |
| NA | 7.50% | 1.64% | 0.00% | 6.06% | 0.00% | 3.58% | 3.85% |

Table C–4: Elements of Stress

| Stressful elements | Not stressful | Moderately stressful | Stressful | Very stressful | NA |
|---|---|---|---|---|---|
| Coursework | 8.4% | 25.1% | 31.7% | 33.0% | 1.8% |
| Your financial situation | 46.3% | 32.6% | 11.9% | 8.4% | 0.9% |
| Relationship with faculty | 32.6% | 33.5% | 23.8% | 9.3% | 0.9% |
| Relationship with students | 63.44% | 24.67% | 9.69% | 1.32% | 0.88% |
| Doing the mathematics | 35.7% | 30.8% | 21.1% | 11.5% | 0.9% |
| Finding a dissertation topic | 17.6% | 19.8% | 32.2% | 27.8% | 2.6% |
| Maintaining a meaningful life outside school | 25.55% | 29.07% | 22.03% | 21.15% | 2.20% |
| Conflict between course content and your interests | 31.7% | 33.9% | 17.6% | 15.4% | 1.3% |

Table C–5: Elements of Stress by Gender

| Stressful elements | Not stressful | | Moderately stressful | | Stressful | | Very stressful | | NA | |
|---|---|---|---|---|---|---|---|---|---|---|
| | Male | Female | Male | Female | Male | Female | Male | Female | Male | Female |
| Coursework | 9.9% | 4.6% | 29.0% | 15.4% | 34.6% | 24.6% | 25.3% | 52.3% | 1.2% | 3.1% |
| Your financial situation | 47.53% | 43.08% | 28.40% | 43.08% | 11.73% | 12.31% | 11.11% | 1.54% | 1.23 | 0.00% |
| Relationship with faculty | 36.42% | 23.08% | 33.95% | 32.31% | 22.22% | 27.69% | 6.17% | 16.92% | 1.23% | 0.00% |
| Relationship with students | 69.1% | 49.3% | 21.1% | 33.8% | 8.0% | 13.8% | 0.6% | 3.1% | 1.2% | 0.00% |
| Doing the mathematics | 38.89% | 27.69% | 33.95% | 23.08% | 19.14% | 26.15% | 6.79% | 23.08% | 1.23% | 0.00% |
| Finding a dissertation topic | 20.37% | 10.77% | 19.14% | 21.54% | 31.48% | 33.85% | 26.54% | 30.77% | 2.47% | 3.08% |
| Maintaining a meaningful life outside school | 25.31% | 26.15% | 27.78% | 32.31% | 24.07% | 16.92% | 20.37% | 23.08% | 2.47% | 1.54% |
| Conflict between course content and your interests | 31.48% | 32.31% | 37.04% | 26.15% | 15.43% | 23.08% | 14.81% | 16.92% | 1.23% | 1.54% |

# Further Results from the Survey

QUESTIONNAIRES AND SURVEYS are faulty sources of data: questions inevitably have implicit values within them, the options allowed within the questions are limiting, and there's no guarantee that people are answering truthfully. Having been trained as an economist to doubt the results of surveys, I approached the survey reported in the last chapter skeptically. I used it nevertheless, because it is a source of quantifiable information, and for any information to get a hearing by the economics profession, it must be quantifiable.

To help respondents flesh out their numerical choices, and to help me interpret the numerical results, I invited written comments on any question. I also included a number of questions that required written answers. In this chapter I present a representative sampling of the responses.

## On the Relevance of Economics

One of the general questions I asked was to explain whether economics was seen as relevant or not. As I reported in the last chapter, of those who responded, 75 percent found it relevant, 8 percent did not, and 17 percent were uncertain. At the end of that question I asked them to explain their reason for choosing the answer they did. Below, in table 3–1, is a sampling of their responses.

## Ranking Economists

Another of the general questions asked was, "Which economist (dead or alive) do you respect most?" This question was deliberately vague since

Table 3–1: A Sample of Responses on Relevance

- Yes, both governments and society in general are recognizing the importance of economic factors.
- Yes, but not relevant enough; people should listen more to economists.
- Yes, economics, broadly defined, encompasses every decision we make.
- Yes, economists are an important voice in the policy process.
- Yes, economists are ideally equipped with tools that are useful in analyzing social activities.
- Yes, economists are listened to by the media much more than are other academics.
- Yes, economists are often the ones who realize that policies affect others besides the ones directly affected.
- Yes, economists are the only careful, structured, empirical thinkers on most economic, political, and social topics.
- Yes, economists debunk myths and depoliticize topics of importance by being objective and rigorous (when we do it right).
- Yes, economists generate the ideas that politicians turn to when things go badly.
- Yes, economists have a good understanding about how markets and incentives work. Used carefully, this can be helpful.
- Yes, economists know a lot about how society works. We just need to be more assertive and clear in conveying our ideas to the general public.
- Yes, economists serve a crucial role in providing clarification of issues, both technically and in the policy debates end of it.
- Yes, I think (at least in the United States) that economists have useful things to say about society but that many are dishonest in their research because they are pushing a political agenda.
- Yes, of all the academic fields, economics is the most important and influential for society at large. It provides a rigorous evaluation of many important policies and programs.
- Yes, people listen to economists, perhaps too much.
- Yes, politicians listen to what good economists think.
- Yes, the major policy questions are fundamentally about economics or about strategic interaction of optimizing agents.
- Yes, there are a lot of economists out there doing great things.
- Yes, they have an important role, but it is often abused.
- Yes, through the World Bank, IMF, etc., we pretty much rule the world.
- Yes, unfortunately. Economics has a relevant role, especially in underdeveloped countries. In these societies there is a great desire for economic growth and this makes economists important. However, my view is that economists don't have a good understanding of what causes growth.
- Uncertain. I think the role of economists is mysterious to most people in the United States.
- Uncertain. Economists have become too influential, and standard economic thought tends to obliterate fundamental human features such as altruism and love.
- Uncertain. Good economists can make a difference in policy, but there are rare instances of this occurring. The greatest fight for economists is the struggle against bad economic thinking permeating society at large.
- Uncertain. Lobbies can do more than economic models to influence policy.
- Uncertain. Only those at the top of their field have much real impact on policy issues.
- Uncertain. The reliance on mathematical rigor, while academically helpful, may make incorporating economic theory into policy more difficult than necessary.

Table 3–1 (*cont.*)

---

- Uncertain. Economists help to shape the "factual debate" as opposed to the "political debate."
- Uncertain. They talk about everything, but I am not sure they are aware of the social impact of their suggestions.
- Uncertain. While not true of everyone, many economists undervalue the contributions of other disciplines and don't effectively engage in the policy-making process.
- Uncertain. Economics is more important than other professions, but more than half of the work economists do is completely irrelevant to actual issues, and economists are bad policy implementers.
- Uncertain. Economists tend to consider themselves more than what they really are.
- Uncertain. In areas where economists have relevant things to say (mostly microeconomics), they are largely ignored.
- Uncertain. On the one hand, economists are involved in a lot of practical policy-making; on the other hand, people "outside" think completely differently than we do and do not believe what we say. It feels like we are saying "the earth is round," while the crowd insists "can't you see it's flat."
- Uncertain. Some are relevant but most are unable to explain new developments in the economics profession.
- No, most are unfamiliar with reality.
- No, normal people solve crosswords; economists write papers (of which 80 percent are never read).
- No, too hard to model such dynamic systems. Failure to come up with any concrete solid answers.

---

I wanted to see how students would rank living vs. dead economists, and as was the case last time, living economists were mentioned significantly more than dead economists. The respondents chose live economists by a wide margin, and their choices were often of professors at their school. So there was a wide diversity of responses. The top five most respected economists this time and last are presented in table 3–2.[1]

As you can see, the choices of most respected economists varied significantly from school to school, but in terms of the overall ranking, Becker, Lucas, and Friedman moved into the top five, and Arrow, Samuelson, and Marx moved out. (Paul Samuelson was sixth this time.) The only two that were named in both surveys were Adam Smith and J. M. Keynes.

This overall change in ranking can be explained in a number of ways. First, Chicago is much more heavily weighted this time because of the better turnout, which explains much of the upward movement of the three Chicago economists. Gary Becker was also teaching a highly popular micro course at Chicago this time, which may help explain his increase in popularity at Chicago compared to last time. Second, Ken Arrow has retired from Stanford and is less active, which moved him away from teaching and from the spotlight. Similarly with Samuelson,

Table 3–2: The Five Most Respected Economists in Early 2000s

| | Stanford | Columbia | Yale | Chicago | MIT | Harvard | Princeton | Total |
|---|---|---|---|---|---|---|---|---|
| Becker | | 3 | 1 | 29 | | 3 | 3 | 39 |
| Keynes | 3 | 7 | 2 | 3 | 4 | 3 | 6 | 28 |
| Lucas | 2 | 4 | 1 | 15 | | 4 | 1 | 27 |
| Smith | | 2 | | 7 | 3 | 5 | 5 | 22 |
| Friedman | 1 | | | 14 | | 4 | 3 | 22 |

The Five Most Respected Economists in Mid-1980s

| | Stanford | Columbia | Yale | Chicago | MIT | Harvard | Total |
|---|---|---|---|---|---|---|---|
| Keynes | 7 | 11 | 6 | 0 | 17 | 17 | 58 |
| Arrow | 23 | 0 | 3 | 0 | 0 | 9 | 35 |
| Samuelson | 7 | 0 | 0 | 4 | 10 | 5 | 26 |
| Marx | 5 | 0 | 3 | 0 | 5 | 10 | 23 |
| Smith | 5 | 3 | 0 | 8 | 2 | 0 | 18 |

who while retired in our earlier study, was still somewhat more active then than he is now. Marx leaving the list reflects a movement away from radical ideas, a movement seen in the survey results. So I am not surprised by these changes. The only somewhat surprising result is that Keynes has remained the second most respected economist, even as what is known as Keynesian macroeconomics has faded from the teaching of economics. He was the only economist listed at all schools.

Looking at the individual schools, Columbia ranked Joe Stiglitz (who teaches there) first and Keynes second. Stanford ranked Ken Arrow first and Keynes second. Princeton ranked Keynes first and Adam Smith second. Harvard ranked Paul Samuelson first and Adam Smith, Paul Krugman, and Amartya Sen tied for third. Chicago ranked Gary Becker first, Robert Lucas second. Yale ranked Paul Samuelson first with Amartya Sen and Keynes tying for second. MIT ranked Keynes first and Adam Smith second.

I also asked students to explain why they respected the economists on their lists. The following is a representative sampling of the responses.

**Becker**
• choice of problems
• important source of bringing new topics to the attention of economists

- economic intuition—actually believes in economic theory
- creativity, moral courage, persistence, humility
- committed to intellectual honesty
- imaginative
- brilliant
- great teaching, very approachable
- deep thought about human behavior
- uses economics to answer meaningful questions
- challenges conventional wisdom

**Keynes**
- broad intellectual interests
- treated economics as something more than an intellectual game
- the best economist ever, had the ability to rewrite the subject alone
- prescient and generally awe-inspiring
- developed theory relevant to the real world
- because in the long run we're all dead, and economists still need to be periodically reminded of that
- his intellect and engagement in political affairs
- influence of his work
- addressed vitally important issues
- willing to fight classical establishment

**Smith**
- inspiration for so much
- great vision
- all we're doing is confirming mathematically what he said
- had a moral defense of the market system like no economist since, especially not today's economists
- incredible insight
- breadth of interest
- ground-breaking, seminal thought
- all ideas in economics can be found in the *Wealth of Nations*

**Lucas**
- an eye for the most important problems
- serious research economist
- able to think deeply about any topic
- able to define a problem clearly
- interested in big questions
- intellectual consistency
- intellectual drive
- originality of ideas

**Friedman**
- linking empirical evidence with coherent theory
- ability to explain power of markets to non-economists
- concerned about theory, data, economic thought, and methodology
- willing to stand up for good ideas even if they're unpopular
- answered questions about the real world in a convincing way
- genius as an academic, brilliant as a policymaker

- able to spread ideas to nonscholars
- for changing my view from being a Keynesian to a capitalist
- original ideas
- ability to go against institutions and shape world's economic thought
- complete: technical ability and intellectual depth

## Likes and Dislikes

Another of the general questions I asked was what the students liked and disliked about economics and their school. This question was designed to capture the mood of graduate students and to see if it differed by school. Table 3–3 is a representative sampling of the various responses, organized by school.

Table 3–3: What the Students Liked and Disliked about Graduate School by School

### What Chicago students like

- being challenged beyond my perceived limitations; doing something I believe is important
- the intensity and seriousness of the atmosphere
- the intense intellectual environment
- meeting great brains (e.g., professors and fellow students)
- everything
- the other students and the work that professors do
- coursework with excellent learning experience; ability to make my own schedule
- the focus on science, not politics
- opportunity to immerse myself in the subject matter and learn it thoroughly
- opportunity to learn from professors and other students
- once one has survived to ABD stage, the freedom to set one's own curricular and extracurricular path
- learning, intellectual stimulation
- one learns a set of sharp tools with which one can potentially answer any question
- environment: lots of interesting people (faculty and students), workshops; sometimes you learn something beautiful
- being able to be taught by professors who are best in their fields and to be able to learn from them by talking or working with them; being around very competent fellow graduate students as well
- learning economics, having more knowledge and thinking ability on economic issues
- interaction with faculty, learning from very good people
- freedom to do whatever you like
- the possibility of being creative in your research
- the rigorous treatment of economic issues
- intellectual atmosphere
- so much to learn. . . . It's great if you like economics; I love that the faculty here is so good
- independence, doing what you like the most
- the impression that I have to learn how to "do" economic theory, instead of just "studying" it

Table 3–3 (*cont.*)

- freedom to choose what I work on/think about; discussions about proper methods of inquiry and about substantive problems
- study with top students from all over the world—great minds, great thoughts; inspirations from faculty (their ideas, thoughts)

*What Princeton students like*

- the intellectual growth, opportunity to concentrate on study, peer association
- generally high quality of teaching, very good scholarly atmosphere
- friendships with other students
- for me, it was the first time of only studying, and this is very valuable to me; stressless lifestyle, in which main concern is doing well in exams; owning my time is a definite plus
- the opportunity to do research in my field of interest, having the best preparation possible
- stimulating environment—it's not a job, it is studying, learning
- still being a student and learning
- the food
- flexibility
- opportunity to learn, meet interesting people
- playing hockey; people are well educated (can talk about econ at an intellectual level)
- conducting my own research
- intensity of learning
- being challenged
- exposure to wonderful and stimulating people and their ideas (both teachers and students)
- interacting with students who have common interests/enthusiasm for the subject; teaching and advising undergrads
- it's not manual labor
- quality of professional environment
- intellectual advancement
- lots of free time to explore what I find interesting
- lifestyle—the flexibility of schedule
- collaborative environment (no competition), no pressure
- the intellectual freedom (and challenge) to think about any problem
- freedom to manage my time, study what I want to study
- being paid to study
- talking to and working with bright, motivated teachers and peers; the second-year courses have been a great experience as well

*What Harvard students like*

- having fellow students willing to talk nonstop about economics
- it makes you grow intellectually; you get to hang out with very smart people who constantly challenge you
- I love the flexibility to work on whatever I find interesting
- freedom to think about and pursue interesting ideas; introduction to new research as well as a longer-term perspective on the field
- nothing

Table 3–3 (*cont.*)

- learning lots of fascinating things; working with extremely bright fellow students and faculty
- opportunity to learn with/from such impressive faculty/students
- amazing faculty
- not a real job
- doing independent research
- freedom to work on things I liked
- intellectual freedom and brilliant colleagues
- seminars, exposure to new ideas
- the possibility to do research that is interesting to me and to take classes that I like
- the people, both faculty and students; great learning experience
- the set of tools I have acquired are applicable to many situations
- the intellectual environment; talking to faculty, peers; seminars
- talking with my advisors and learning directly from the very best in the field
- the professors, the freedom to set your own schedule (I worked for two years before school)
- intellectual stimulation
- the other students; interacting with them
- the opportunity to have access to the frontier of economic research, and the interaction with people who are as interested in economics as I am, and the access to top scholars and events even in other areas
- intellectual environment, research
- great ideas and great people
- fieldwork in developing countries, tailored to my interests
- seeing new ideas and new research; interaction with faculty
- I am learning a lot
- the chance to meet so many incredibly intelligent professors and students; the quality of my work has increased significantly because of this interaction
- I can explore my intellectual interests, while being my own boss
- the lifestyle

*What Yale students like*

- chance to talk to brilliant people, attend conferences, etc; manage my time, find people to relate with
- time to read on topics of my interest
- being around (generally) more intelligent people; taking courses that are (generally) not trivial and patronizing
- being taught to do significant research; being introduced to research frontier
- I like the intellectual atmosphere and our access to professors, many of whom are very intelligent; as well as the attitudes of the other students and the subject matter, which is difficult and interesting
- doing research, talking about important issues, being with very smart people, no fixed schedule (waking up at 11 a.m.), feeling I'm learning every day and I'm understanding better what's going on
- the fact that we can spend our time thinking about better ways to approach different problems and maybe provide some solutions
- due to the pace of the program I have no choice but to understand and realize my focus "in real time"
- learning the details of theories superficially covered in undergrad courses

Table 3–3 (*cont.*)

- stimulating intellectual environment
- exciting environment
- offers academic career possibility

*What MIT students like*
- doing research in my fields of interests
- freedom to work on what interests me most; fantastic classmates and peers
- engaging in my own research under the guidance of experts in the field
- the opportunity to study a subject that I find extremely interesting
- interacting with students and faculty; freedom to do what I want (after coursework)
- the job opportunities; my classmates
- actually doing research
- the intellectual stimulation
- being a student again—flexible schedule
- intellectual atmosphere; great coffee-table conversations about any topic; diverse international background among classmates
- the chance to pursue my own intellectual interests
- classes, problem-solving
- all the new tools I'm learning
- access to excellent advisors/peers, intellectual environment
- lifestyle
- hang out with nice people doing fun work
- fellow grad students
- the health care
- the essence of being free to think about economics and being surrounded by other people who also have the same goal and approach it in different ways

*What Columbia students like*
- the intellectual freedom
- the freedom, the opportunities it creates, the contact with brilliant people, the challenge, and the financial situation
- independence when coursework ended (intellectually, personally)
- intellectual environment, international community of students
- to be in an environment whose main aims are research and education
- intellectual adventure
- you can research whatever you want
- the opportunity of being able to meet other students; the opportunity of finding out what economics is really about; the opportunity to meet a couple of faculty members who have greatly influenced my life
- faculty seminars and the chance to hear really excellent/rigorous analyses presented
- learning new theories
- leading to academic career
- independence, financial security, fellow students
- freedom to explore whatever topics interest me
- focusing on my intellectual interest
- academic freedom

# FURTHER RESULTS FROM THE SURVEY

Table 3–3 (*cont.*)

- formalization of arguments; enjoyable learning milieu, classmates
- financial support
- the feeling that you are at the frontier of research and in contact with very clever and interesting people
- not much responsibility, having a lot of time
- intellectually challenging
- the fact that with economics I acquired tools to analyze the world
- I could deepen my understanding of basic concepts; discussion with faculty about research topics provides me with a couple of new perspectives
- the possibility to study a wide array of topics
- exposure to interesting people and ideas
- the freedom and flexibility

*What Stanford students like*

- freedom to manage my own time; freedom to write and read
- intellectual community
- intellectual depth
- freedom to study what I wish
- the intellectual environment
- the people here
- intellectual environment
- edification into the depths of previously assumed/ignored cases
- California
- learning new concepts and new views on things I've seen before; being taught by the best
- learning about the field
- time flexibility
- being on a campus and on academic schedule
- the collection of intelligent, focused minds
- intellectual challenge
- the environment full of freedom, in which I can study whatever I want
- flexibility; intellectual stimulation, coffee
- I can do whatever I want; if I'm not productive, I can take off and watch movies, or go snowboarding
- freedom to study what I want; freedom to plan my schedule how I want
- I've enjoyed the classes, especially the attention to detail that was often put aside in undergraduate classes; I've also enjoyed finding out about the diverse interests of classmates
- the academic environment; being around others who are motivated to better our understanding of economics
- flexible work hours
- research, thinking about how to approach questions of social interest

*What Chicago students dislike*

- I care about ideas—I'm not just a math nerd; often during the first two years the emphasis is more on math skill than economic thinking or good ideas—but that is in the short-run, so I continue to hope that good ideas (pluotechnical skill) win out in the long run
- the useless time pressure they put on you; economics is understanding, not learning by heart
- the loss of perspective on the real world and what is really important in life

Table 3–3 (*cont.*)

- writing for publications and meeting the deadlines
- social life; money; unnecessary rudeness; conflict with "reality"
- it is temporary
- problem sets in the first year
- being broke
- difficulty interacting with faculty; difficulty organizing time efficiently
- the detachment from "real world" issues
- lack of balance—here as a first year student you almost focus solely on completing homework assignments with practice problems, not research
- the pressure you have to find topics for research
- too strong incentives during course work; lack of interest/support from faculty during dissertation stage
- difficulty of surviving to ABD stage
- postponing life outside school
- the core exam at the end of the first year
- have no one to ask questions
- the first two years are very schoolish; then total freedom with little specialization
- that you have to be very very good for professors to pay attention to you
- feeling humiliated quite often
- always thinking about work
- the pressure to do a good thesis
- stress about finding a job; sometimes economics is a bit distressing; the "academic game" is not very relevant
- being stressed about coming up with a good thesis topic and research idea
- it's too hard, there's no time for social/personal life
- the first year—very stressful
- deadlines, being evaluated
- social life
- the stress
- I hate the core exam
- competition, high pressure, unreasonable expectations
- competition with students; everyone believes he or she is better or the best
- distance from faculty, and their absence of interest
- omnipresence, arrogance, lack of real friends
- conflict between course content and your interests
- too demanding, I cannot do anything else
- I found the dissertation very limiting, restrictive, and even boring; I found it hard to interact with professors (probably my fault)
- the competition among students
- the solitude of doing research if you don't team up with other students
- sticking to someone else's interests (in academic terms)
- not much; sometimes it's too much math, but I like math more and more; first year and the core exam are stressful; no life at the moment

Table 3–3 (*cont.*)

## *What Princeton students dislike*

- the atmosphere
- too much intellectual homogeneity; lack of opportunity to explore and study outside of very narrow bounds
- method of teaching in most courses is still having a teacher reproduce papers on board
- overemphasis on methodology
- having to do coursework in not-so-interesting topics
- first year doesn't allow for independent thinking, they just throw a lot of information for us to digest, but that's the way it has to be
- it is more stressful than an actual job
- stress
- the first-year exams at Princeton University (i.e., extreme stress)
- culture
- lack of structure
- narrow-mindedness; meet uninteresting people
- living in Princeton—I am a big-city dude, I need restaurants, bars, women, clubs, etc.; people are not open-minded (most students have the same conservative and boring backgrounds—they are too focused on silly subjects, as opposed to being happy and enjoying life; although very educated, most are not smart)
- the first years
- being somehow brainwashed
- not having a personal or private life
- lack of help in finding a "structured" path to a dissertation
- poor standard of living, social isolation
- it's not a vacation
- human beings here are no better than in any other crappy place
- poor social life—very narrow social circle
- pressure to perform to have a permanent place to be
- the stress (of research now, of coursework in first two years)
- too many problem sets, this means no time to study (which seems strange for somebody who chooses to study as a career); a lot of algebra, intuition is too naïve (it would make sense to have both); many early deadlines along the year that gives you little time for thinking about something on a wider perspective (i.e., thinking about research)
- time constraints
- spartan lifestyle; overemphasis on problem solving at the cost of explaining fundamental concepts
- the focus on publishing
- time pressure and stress to finish for job market in time
- it is not tailored to students' backgrounds
- right now—general exams; last year—macro; in general—homesickness, lack of sleep

## *What Harvard students dislike*

- finding a thesis topic is stressful (but also very exciting!)
- stressful environment, a lot of pressure

71

Table 3–3 (*cont.*)

- the stress about the job market
- competition among classmates, particularly the fact that Harvard lets in many of their own undergrads; the stress of coming up with solid, original research ideas
- course work unrelated to my interests, unsociable peers; I am bad at it
- uncertainty, especially about what efforts to devote to various parts of the program; feeling dumb (seriously)
- uncertainty about own ability to build relationship with faculty and do important work
- "Problem sets will dull your mind—destroy the potential for authentic creativity"
- finding good topics to work on is hard
- not sure. Will know better once I leave
- first-year work does not leave a whole lot of time to do your own exploring into your fields of interest
- need to focus on only one topic
- no structure
- bad classes
- the stress of finding a dissertation topic, and not having enough guidance
- feeling lost—not being sure I belong here
- the stress and workload
- the ventilation in our computer lab, the lack of intellectual history in our training
- sometimes it's difficult to study something that most people either don't understand and/or don't find interesting
- tough question. I am really enjoying my time. At the beginning, it was probably that I was pretty much the guy with the least math skills
- not enough hours in a day to do all the work
- loneliness
- the pressure to compete with other students
- being away from my family
- financial stress, nearly no life out of school (i.e., becoming one-dimensional)
- I never feel like I can really take a break
- that jarring post-orals twist when one is supposed to become a "researcher"; I haven't gotten over that yet
- lack of "moral support"
- implicitly competitive among students; not enough attention from faculty
- the transition from coursework to research and the limited opportunity to do stuff outside of the department
- nothing in particular, maybe being far from home and own language
- first two years are hard. I didn't know where I was, if I was absolutely stupid or not
- setting own schedule; not "applied" as much as I'd like
- there is always more work than can be done; you can't feel like you've accomplished all you needed to in any one day
- the uncertainty regarding one's future success

Table 3–3 (*cont*).

## *What Yale students dislike*

- if not being one of the top guys makes you lose your confidence, then it sucks. I've found little guidance in terms of approaching academic life and work, and it can turn very stressful
- stress in first year; maintaining a meaningful life outside graduate school
- stupid problem sets that are just algebra exercises; macro lecturers who cannot explain formally what they are trying to do with their algebra
- stress of upcoming job market
- the problem sets and the fact that we have so little choice in the first year—we still have to learn all this micro and macro that we won't probably use
- little social interaction among people; researchers are not socially skilled, in general, and I miss that
- I still feel like a pupil
- difficulty meeting people outside of economics
- being forced to take classes you don't like

## *What MIT students dislike*

- classes are excessively challenging
- no structured routine (after course work is over)—hard to get used to
- enduring coursework in classes unrelated to my interests, particularly in the poorly taught classes
- the lack of time to do other things apart from working
- coursework not related to my interests; doing research just for the sake of it
- asshole faculty; being made more cynical than most would think possible, seeing the inside of the sausage factory; having your best ideas crapped on and then seeing someone else go far with them
- the lack of guidance in the first two years; the mismatch between class lectures, class homework, and class exams; the way grades are based on one 1.25-hour exam
- peer group rarely extends past others in our program
- slow pace of progress and daily life in front of a computer; being removed from the issues I feel passionately about
- first two years it was exams, now it's deadlines for presentations; also hard to see some classmates become unhappy over the years (who should not have gone to grad school)
- limited attention from professors
- I'm not convinced I'm doing anything that matters outside of the ivory tower of academics
- the constant challenges/difficulties of learning the tools of the trade
- some coursework requirements outside of my fields of interest
- the job market
- wondering whether my research will really matter
- matching dissertation research with the needs of "the market" rather than solely with my interests
- I feel out of place
- the hypocrisy of economists treating economics like an "objective science"—e.g., constraining results to fit known "laws" that in fact have never been demonstrated—when in reality economics is based on a set of at-best questionable assumptions that are heavily biased in favor of certain implications; as a corollary, the unfounded egos of the professors
- the amount of coursework (though I still am grateful to be forced to do it)

Table 3–3 (*cont.*)

## *What Columbia students dislike*

- the uncertainty about grades, then about the research topic, then about the job market
- no personal life; too much pressure from the school to "revolutionize" economics, little support from the faculty, but high expectations
- first-year exams and professors
- stress and feeling of uselessness
- the need for personal connections
- exams
- the disconnect from real life; distortion (severe) of private life; department politics
- finding an advisor
- meaningless politics
- the first year; I was miserable; the fact that most of faculty don't care about students; they make you feel that you're wasting their time; there is no support from the department; if you openly manifest that you're not sure about pursuing academia, then they wouldn't support you at all
- to work alone all the time; little chance to talk to other students and faculty about research; little chance to work with something different
- lack of support and connection between grad students and faculty as a whole
- people are boring, including me
- coursework, meaningless math
- lack of advisor support
- tests in the first year
- workload
- consciousness of separation of the "academic" from other shades of reality
- no professors in the field of my interest
- the isolation from other people that sometimes research brings about
- when you don't have a topic to work on
- irrelevant definitions cramming
- I expected a more intellectually stimulating environment, but students are not as smart as I hoped; professors won't spend time with us
- in the second year I was required to take a couple of courses that were redundant to my research
- the toughness of academic research; both in finding a topic of study and an advisor
- compulsory, theoretical classes with little relevance to current real economic problems
- the insulation from the "real world"

## *What Stanford students dislike*

- relationship with faculty
- lack of time
- macroeconomics is religious indoctrination; in general, not feeling like I will ever figure out the material
- no choices in first year
- workload
- freedom to study what I wish
- the college bureaucracy

Table 3–3 (*cont.*)

---

- the focus on theory, not empirics
- too much technique
- isolation
- atmosphere, research, esoteric nature of much work, inability to apply much research; ignorance of real-world applicability; lack of balance; being treated like a peon
- first year = boot camp
- the feeling that I always have to be working
- low income
- everything having to do with economics
- competing with students already possessing master's knowledge
- pressure, working too much, disinterested faculty
- nothing
- ineffectiveness/irrelevance of so much of what we do
- at times, the (mostly informalized) pressure to succeed and the stress that accompanies it can be practically unbearable; there are no points for models that almost converge
- uncertainty about when and how to finish the degree; dislike my current research topic; RA job can be tedious
- it would be nice to spend some more time on applications during the first year
- it sometimes seems like we are pressured to appear to know more than we actually do; and thus, important questions may not be asked in classroom/seminar/discussion situations because of fear of being too basic
- feeling the need to work constantly
- the comps

---

Definite themes come through in this listing of what students like and dislike that transcend individual schools. Almost universally the students like the freedom and intellectual challenge, the flexibility, and the interaction with students and faculty. Overwhelmingly, the students liked what they were learning, and felt that they were learning something. There were, however, some differences among schools. Students at Harvard, Princeton, Stanford, and MIT mentioned lifestyle as something they liked, but one did not see lifestyle mentioned by students at Chicago, Yale, or Columbia. At Chicago, in particular, there seemed to be much more focus on the intellectual atmosphere and the intensity with which economists approach study that the students liked, more so than other factors.

There were also definite themes in what the students disliked. This included isolation, theoretical classes with little relevance, the difficulty of interacting with faculty, the first-year boot camp atmosphere, time pressure, the stress, the problem sets, the lack of a social life, and the

75

difficulty of finding a dissertation topic. Stress seemed more of a concern at Chicago, Yale, and Columbia. In the case of Chicago this is not surprising, since moving to the ABD stage is less likely there than it is at most other schools.

## What Makes a Successful Economist?

Another general question I asked concerned the students' views of a successful economist. In table 3–4, I list responses by schools. As you can tell by reading through the comments, the students have a varied view of what it means to be a successful economist. Some focused on external success—finding a good job, publishing in the right journals. Others focused more on internal success—being creative and making a contribution to social goals. Many of the comments concerned relevance of one's work. These responses for the most part seemed positive and indicative of honestly wanting one's work to have policy relevance.

Table 3–4: What Makes a Successful Economist

### *Stanford*

- not too many compromises
- well-published, often talked about, cited, invited to conferences; thinking of new things, happy
- publishes, teaches
- someone who publishes a lot of correct/rigorous papers on important topics
- one who is able to use formal theory successfully to predict empirical facts, and then use this formal theory to find welfare-maximizing policies or institutions
- someone who makes relevant and informed policy decisions
- an intellectual with broad knowledge and good technical skills; should be able to contribute to public debates
- influential, insightful
- one who can make contributions that help us understand economic behavior and can teach the subject well
- someone whose research expands knowledge into new territory, and is recognized for this
- someone who is doing something they are interested in
- writes frequently, is published and cited; knowledgeable in two to three core areas; adequate lecturer
- tenure at a top ten school
- makes and develops rigorous models, therefore rational and logical; loves the job as an economist, therefore passionate and loves people

Table 3–4 (*cont.*)

- quick witted, deep thinking; focused
- tenure, a family
- someone who tries to answer the important questions with solid techniques
- solid grasp of mathematics; creative in approach to problems; makes respected and influential contributions to his/her field
- a successful economist is one who has made a contribution to the understanding of economic forces. . . . this contribution may be made in journal publications, teaching, or through public service; a successful economist also must be honest; this includes not manipulating data or statistics to prove a certain point and not claiming to have proven results that are more general than what is actually shown in his or her research
- respect from others in field, publications; what's the definition of "successful"?

*Columbia*

- a successful economist should always search for answers in the data and have a multitude of approaches from sociology, psychology, and econometrics in addressing their research questions
- advances boundaries of knowledge that is useful to both academics and policy
- somebody who can introduce new ideas to the profession
- able to explain real-life phenomena in the simplest way possible—to grasp the most important ingredients of a problem; able to offer advice on how to tackle problems that stem from inefficiency of arrangements
- smart; writes lots of papers; takes care of students
- an individual who publishes a lot in top journals but is not necessarily a good professor and/or is not necessarily successful at other aspects of life (don't agree with this, but I think it's like that)
- curious, rigorous analytically, resourceful, relevant, creative
- well motivated and perseverant
- someone who actually analyzes issues of socioeconomic importance
- has innovative and insightful ideas; turns common sense into a useful mathematical model
- hard to describe; in general, economists need to strike a good balance between teaching and the real-world problems, and formulating theoretical models
- achieves good policy for society, and his teachings are applicable to making good policy
- has command over tools, organizing principles of economics, but is able to reach into other fields rather than restrict himself/herself to overstretching "economic" arguments
- publishes influential papers
- aims at answering important questions; answers them in a simple way; good communicator: knows how to translate his/her ideas to any audience
- writes a few, good, influential papers; not necessarily mathematically sophisticated
- someone without inferiority complex and marginally socially integrable
- those who write original papers that will be cited by future economists
- those who can inspire a discussion in academia
- someone who has grasped theory and applied it to real public policy recommendations
- someone who is able to carry out independent research on practical problems and is able to communicate his results to a wider public

Table 3–4 (*cont.*)

## MIT

- good academic job; lots of good publications
- performs rigorous research that sheds light on issues relevant to society
- someone who is able to provide good policy guidance on specific issues; the advice/recommendations should ideally have strong theoretical basis and some recorded empirical evidence
- two definitions: (1) conventional—publishing lots of papers in top journals; (2) fulfilling whatever your personal goals are
- someone who can identify interesting problems and propose good solutions for them; someone who is both a good researcher and a good teacher
- someone who gets published in good journals and gives interesting talks
- one who gets tenure (I do not interpret "successful" necessarily to mean "good")
- someone whose work endures more than twenty years (even if name doesn't); something that makes it to textbooks is likely to endure, or "popularization" literature; another type is someone who affects specific policies by empirical studies
- original thinker; conducts research relevant to those outside of discipline; engaged with professionals outside of discipline
- someone who sees the connection of the ideas in a broad variety of fields
- teaches and researches issues relevant to the everyday person's welfare; understands the fundamental processes of human behavior and economic reality; research and theories empirically based and supported
- ability to tie economic theory to empirical problems, and to communicate those results effectively
- analytical ability combined with strong intuition and a good deal of wit
- published, tenured, engaged
- one whose research is policy relevant; answers important policy questions
- does policy relevant research
- (1) draws cautious conclusions, informed by a reading of the literature as well as their own results, and not by ego; (2) well-read outside of economics, offering explanations drawn from other disciplines respectfully, even when they aren't empirically testable. (3) chooses topics based on social relevance, not the desire to use fancy econometrics, a cute trick, or to hop on a trend; (4) careful in their empirics and clear in presentation
- one whose understanding is not just deep but also broad, not just technically but also in terms of the economy, society, and human behavior more generally.

## Yale

- can "find" interesting topics, attack them in a novel and professional way, and produce output effectively
- does research that addresses important issues instead of pursuing minor extensions to existing models
- someone whose name is associated with or comes up when talking about a certain theory/area
- one who publishes a substantial number of papers, based upon the merit of those papers and their usefulness to economics; or an economist who works for an important banking, consulting, political or other firm, or who teaches and does research at a liberal arts college

Table 3–4 (*cont.*)

- in academia: someone who influences other economists and advances science; outside academia: in policy-making, someone who "improves the world"
- someone who has a good understanding of the underlying process in different situations and is able to communicate them well
- sees new phenomena/problems and (ideally) is able to analyze/solve them; has a broad picture of his field; deep understanding/intuition
- someone who understands theory well enough to apply to reality
- well published in his or her fields; sought after as a consultant by firms, governments, or NGOs.

*Harvard*

- famous (among economists), known for particular contributions, tenured at a prestigious university
- someone who is open to new ideas, engages and makes a contribution
- novel, quirky way of looking at the world and seeing new interesting phenomenon to explore; clear, logical thinker; good writer, effective communicator; good at packaging ideas; good at collaborating/working with others
- combines theoretical insight with clever method of empirically proving
- someone who has produced useful and insightful work in his/her field, and who understands the field well enough to be able to interact with others and contribute toward their research
- widely cited work; challenges accepted ideas (successfully)
- their work is interesting and relevant
- has changed the way economists think about an interesting and important topic
- someone who writes a paper that will be on a course reading-list ten years from now
- someone who comes up with good and relevant questions to explore and a novel approach to tackle them
- respected by successful economists
- publication in top journals
- raises a simple but hard question; build or begin a theory that seems relevant; empirically prove something or solve some question; apply successfully academic economics in real life
- good theoretical background (not necessarily theorist); good knowledge of empirical evidence and real-life problems (not necessarily an empiricist)
- can model any problem theoretically, so it can be tested empirically
- has a university position, with research mix of academic and policy-oriented subjects
- able to say something meaningful about any economic topic; aware of other approaches to a problem; communication skills; problem-driven, not method-driven; does not hide behind math
- publishes frequently on important topics
- one who understands economic phenomena and models deeply, to the point of being able to explain it clearly; one who influences profession with his/her ideas, as measured by the number of citations; one who is bold to make out-of-sample predictions (and gets them right!)
- does interesting research; makes a difference in the field
- has the creativity to come up with new insights and has a mastery of the necessary technical tools; aware of the economic relevance of what he/she studies
- comes up with (relatively) new ideas, which must rely on broad but sharp principles; ability to communicate these ideas

Table 3–4 (*cont.*)

- a person who understands something important about the world and is able to communicate that understanding to others (that's a clear definition of "success"; I have much more trouble defining "economist")
- (1) publishes frequently in top journals; (2) does work that is either directly relevant to real issues or can be used by people doing directly relevant work; (3) ideally works across subfields, disciplines, and methodologies
- expert in one field, knowledgeable across fields; affects public policy
- academic at one of the top ten to twenty-five programs
- influential, innovative, nonconformist, refined, "clean," articulate
- someone able to put his ideas on paper in a convincing, attractive, and helpful way; good papers shed light over many topics, and they are usually simple
- performs careful, original research that is widely read and cited; produces students who go on to successful research careers themselves; meaningfully communicates ideas of economics to students who are not Ph.D.'s
- economists can be successful in many ways, e.g.: (1) tenure at a good university and an impressive list of publications; (2) success in the public arena: Fed, IMF, WB, Treasury, etc.

*Princeton*

- Paul Krugman; outspoken, part of society, opinionated
- one who can use a large set of tools (math, history, empirics) to analyze questions of relevance and who can effectively communicate both to his peers and to the general public
- someone who says something new and important (substantial)
- expands knowledge of a relevant topic
- being able to offer a solid explanation of any relevant economic problem imposed
- I think there are no specific characteristics common among all economists
- someone who greatly contributes through either publications or through personal influence on policy decisions
- human, well rounded, aware of history, clear on the role of economics, the inefficiencies of economics, the limits . . . ; concerned with the impact of the discipline on policy, on political culture-social organization
- has influence, enjoys the work
- someone who links insights in many different (sub)fields
- inspires other minds; does work that is both pleasing and practical; understands the big picture; has some $$
- someone who credibly identifies causal impacts of what he or she is studying, and who asks interesting questions
- being able to influence economic thought
- publishes in top journals, tenured at a top ten school, interested in explaining relevant phenomena, and is a good teacher

Table 3–4 (*cont.*)

- (1) has a very good knowledge of social, political, economic context in which he/she is doing research; (2) very good technical skills coupled with intellectual integrity (knows that you don't send a paper for publication if you have an endogeneity problem and can't solve it); (3) broad interests (not limited to a specific field)
- able to clarify an issue on a topic that is of practical interest and make recommendations that can have real benefits
- frequently published and cited
- Angus Deaton
- involved in real-world problem solving; ground-breaking research
- tenure at a top five university
- someone good enough to be known and respected outside of academia
- innovative, rigorous, connected with reality; able to communicate to a larger audience; able to suggest new institutions that work well
- he does research in the academy, but he's not completely disconnected from the real world (not just technicalities, but can also answer questions like what to do for unemployment, etc.); he's able to stimulate students, making them more interested in research in economics, giving something more than the material he's supposed to teach
- somebody who can enjoy the freedom of research without being enslaved by it
- someone who can simplify the real world and put it in a model
- no clear idea, maybe there are different ways to be a successful economist
- impact on the questions and ways of thinking and understanding in their field; legacy of students
- one who has made a lasting and significant contribution toward the evolution of economic theory and/or the approach to policy issues
- developing ideas that lead to important advances/changes in the way we think about economics; applying economic knowledge/ideas to improve the world/society.

*Chicago*
- applies economic analyses to issues both within the context of research and in their lives in general; believes, at some level, in markets; realizes that math is the "tool," but that good ideas are more important; honest
- someone who provides compelling insights and evidence to important social problems and consequently influences the behavior of key decision makers (e.g., policymakers or consumers) in a positive way; also, someone who teaches other people how to do this
- a man who understands abstractly the reality of things
- someone who doesn't merely use old theories, but makes us think about new ones
- knowledgeable, open-minded, expert in certain fields, writes important publications and has some impact on the society (including both government and laymen)
- innovative but not necessarily prolific; answers policy questions
- (1) has a thorough knowledge of the economy; (2) jumps easily between theory and practice; (3) has ability to communicate

Table 3–4 (*cont.*)

- someone who applies economic analyses in ways that haven't been considered before and derives solutions to problems that increase aggregate welfare in some reasonable sense
- makes new contributions to knowledge; understands the "world" (meaning that he or she gets the big picture, not only marginal mathematics); relates it to everyday life and tries to "teach" it to nonscholars
- someone who is good at applying theory to important, real-world problems, is good at teaching, and is still a kind, moral person
- one who is able to successfully explain (and perhaps solve) an economic phenomenon or problem; but he needs to be able to explain it to non-economists too
- someone who has a sense of what is important in a phenomenon and has a strong analytical capacity
- deep objective—not in love with a theory; original, maybe even unconventional
- makes path-breaking theoretical contributions; gives birth to a fertile empirical strategy
- someone who can do economics that is valuable in some way to those outside the discipline
- creative, relevant, influential in real-society problems
- has tenure at a good university (top twenty); (average) one publication every three years in *AER, JPE, Econometrica, RES, JET*
- being able to develop new tools (or models) to minimize the chance of misinterpreting the data and have those models fit with empirical data as much as possible
- useful for society, through research or good applications of existing knowledge
- an economist whose research can contribute to increase the social welfare
- one who asks interesting, relevant questions and succeeds at answering them using rigorous methods
- creative, smart
- someone who publishes one paper per year in a top journal
- original ideas, excellent research, rigorous scholarship, and a good teacher
- being able to model and observe phenomena in a sensible, clear, and useful way
- an economist should relate his ideas with real situations, motivated by empirical findings, be able to model his/her thoughts in a comprehensive way, and most of all be able to raise interesting questions
- not too math-oriented; developing models in line with reality (being intuitive) and being nice to people (students, other professors, etc.), i.e., offering encouragement
- being able to (1) pick an interesting economic phenomenon; (2) analyze it in a careful, systematic, independent manner; (3) get meaningful theoretical and empirical results
- someone who can write down models that explain something unexplained so far and then test it with the data
- someone who aims at understanding relevant problems/questions; a link to reality is important
- creative, technically capable, rigorous
- respected by his peers, able to choose where to work
- one whose position (in academics, government, or industry) allows him to use economics for the improvement of society, and who makes good use of this opportunity

Table 3–4 (*cont.*)

- one who gets things published, hence spreads his ideas and vision; and who answers questions relevant in practice, i.e., with important policy implications likely to affect people's lives
- economist who can write down a simple model and empirically test it with identification
- cares about people
- critical and original reasoning; highly productive; influential in the profession
- (1) stop emerging problems of society; (2) apply economic analysis; (3) communicate suggested solutions effectively to non-economists
- creative, working on topics that truly interest him

## Conclusion

The foregoing selection of comments gives you a good sense of the views of the students and should fill in some of the holes in the questionnaire. Combined with the interviews, I think they give an insightful picture of who graduate students in economics are and what they think. As you can see, they are far from monolithic; they have many different approaches to economics and see it in many different ways. For the most part they are positive on the profession, but they are open to questions about its relevance and its importance.

# How the Views of the Original
# Survey Respondents Have Changed

To supplement the survey of current students, I also surveyed respondents of the original survey in the early 2000s, when they were in their late 30s and early 40s, and hence in the prime of their careers. Since the earlier surveys were anonymous, but respondents could voluntarily include their names, I did not have a large sample. I gathered the names of those respondents who voluntarily listed their names on the previous survey and who said that they would be open to further contact.[1] The purpose of the study was to capture the respondents' reflective views of the profession and their graduate school experience, along with how they have changed in fifteen years. To encourage participation, the survey was relatively short. To facilitate comparisons, it repeated a number of the questions asked in the previous survey.

The division of responses by school in this survey differed from that in the original survey. In the 1985 survey (conducted in 1985, published in 1987), the percentage division of respondents among schools was: Yale, 7 percent; MIT, 22 percent; Columbia, 12 percent; Chicago, 15 percent; Harvard, 22 percent; and Stanford, 22 percent. In the current survey the percentages were Yale, 5 percent; MIT, 16 percent; Columbia, 5 percent; Chicago, 13 percent; Harvard, 29 percent; and Stanford, 33 percent. As you can see, the representation of Stanford and Harvard rose while the representation of the others fell. To insure comparability of this subgroup with the original study, I checked the previous surveys of the subgroup, and where relevant differences exist, I present both the subgroup responses and the original survey response.

Despite the limitations of surveys in general, and of this survey in particular, I believe that results offer important insights into the economics profession, which are in large part descriptive of how economists feel about their profession. This follows because the results confirmed many of my priors gathered through conversations with economists, and through the osmosis inherent in being active in the profession.[2] Given the inherent weaknesses of surveys, and of empirical work in general, these broader checks are a necessary component to the degree of belief that can be given to the results. I believe, as was the case with the previous survey, when it was later expanded upon by the COGEE Commission with a much more detailed and scientific survey, that the results will not significantly change.

## Profile

The composite economist represented in this survey is a thirty-nine-year-old male who works in academia. In the survey, 88 percent of the respondents were male; 12 percent female. In the original sample 19 percent were women, which suggests that women have tended to leave economics at a greater rate than men; this is consistent with general data that the percentage of women declines as economists move up the ladder.

The respondents are primarily academics, with 62 percent in academia (13 percent in liberal arts schools and 49 percent in universities), 25 percent in government, and 13 percent in private business. This is consistent with where, fifteen years ago, the original sample thought they would be now. (In the original survey 53 percent were planning to pursue an academic career, 33 percent were planning to go into policy-related work, 17 percent into business, 8 percent into research institutions, and 2 percent into journalism.) Those in academia are primarily full and associate professors, although some have adjunct and temporary positions. Those in business and government vary in their positions from CEOs and high-ranking political appointees to staff economists. Most have had more than one job in the past fifteen years.

While the aggregate numbers remain comparable, many did not end up where they thought they would. For example, in the previous questionnaire one third of those at a university had indicated another preference as to where they would like to be.

## Political Orientation

The political orientation of this subgroup in graduate school was 50 percent liberal, 20 percent moderate, 5 percent conservative, 20 percent radical, and 5 percent other. (This was slightly different than the entire original group, which was 47 percent liberal, 22 percent moderate, 15 percent conservative, 12 percent radical, and 4 percent other.) The political orientation of the subgroup has changed toward conservative in the new survey, with 55 percent considering themselves liberal, 18 percent considering themselves conservative, 11 percent considering themselves libertarian, 7 percent considering themselves radical, and 9 percent considering themselves other. (The choices given respondents were different in the two surveys: "moderate" was not given as an option in the second survey, but "libertarian" was.)

The movement toward conservatism can be better seen in answer to the question regarding which way they believed they had changed their political views. Twenty-seven percent said that they have become more conservative, and 11 percent said they had become more liberal, with the remainder unchanged. A typical comment of those who said they had become more conservative was, "Fifteen years of teaching (and some research) on economic development have left me more skeptical than previously about the merits of 'statist' or even 'activist' government policy."

These data are consistent with George's Stigler's (1975) observation that economics tends to make individuals more conservative. Of course, aging has also been associated with conservatism, and in the past fifteen years there has been a definite swing toward conservatism in the general population, and so the effect of being an economist on becoming more conservative is not definitive.

Liberal economists were relatively more likely to be in government than in academia. (Of those economists who had positions in government, 73 percent listed themselves as liberal whereas 47 percent of the economists in academia considered themselves liberal.) Radical economists were found mostly in academia.

## Views of Successful Economists

For the most part the respondents had a mature understanding of success and saw it as multifaceted. A number noted that there were many possible ways to be successful and it depended on what one did. The question, "What is your idea of a successful economist?" brought forth comments such as the following: "someone able to apply economics to answer interesting questions and communicate effectively"; and "Someone who makes careful, creative contributions to knowledge or social policy; reflective, open-minded, rigorous, and flexible." Another wrote, "someone who doesn't care about getting prizes or editing journals, who helps to understand how the real world works." Several respondents were more direct. One wrote, "Alas, I've been conditioned to believe that 'successful' = 'lots of publications.' " Another wrote, "Academic success: achieve tenure, continue publishing, become an administrator."

In response to the question regarding which economist they most respected, the top nine choices were, in order of number of times mentioned, Kenneth Arrow, J. M. Keynes, Paul Krugman, Larry Summers, Adam Smith, Robert Solow, John Stuart Mill, Paul Samuelson, and Robert Lucas. Their choices in the original survey were quite similar and included all except Krugman and Summers, who were both too young to be considered in the earlier survey. Marx dropped substantially in the rankings; in this subgroup he was selected by eight of the respondents last time, and by only one this time.

The fact that Keynes stands so high even though Keynesian economics is not significantly taught today suggests that Keynes's approach to economics remains influential at least among those who learned it in graduate school. What students liked about Keynes in both surveys was his scope of vision, his political influence, his practical passion, and his real-world success, which are very similar characteristics to those given in the earlier survey.

# Views of Graduate Education

One of the much remarked-upon findings of the first study was the dissatisfaction with the state of graduate education. That dissatisfaction was somewhat reduced, or at least modified, in the recent study. While twice as many respondents had a negative view of graduate school as had a positive view, there seemed to be a greater acceptance that this is the way it is. Perhaps from the vantage point of a teacher, as compared to that of a student, people are more accepting of, and less dissatisfied with, the institutions of graduate school, although they still recognize the problems. There was a sense that professors know that they are not doing as good a job teaching as they could be doing, but that they also recognize that the incentives for success are not to improve their teaching significantly, or to spend the time changing the institutions to make them better, but are instead to do research.

Typical comments to the question regarding older respondents' view of graduate school included the following: "I love teaching and grad education. I think our students learn a great deal. But I think often grad teaching is poorly focused and lazily executed. I don't think my views have changed much since grad school"; and "The importance of institutions and policy is too often neglected, as is history of thought"; and "It is about the same or a little worse in terms of overemphasis on technical/mathematical material." A couple of respondents remarked that some programs had changed and that "more emphasis is placed on empirical work and on linking students with faculty earlier and more systematically." Another comment was, "There is still an overemphasis on technique at the expense of insight, but in many ways the discipline seems to have broadened and become more diverse and creative in recent years."

A large number of respondents outside academia refrained from answering the question about graduate education. Many of them pointed out that they were so removed from it that they felt unable to make relevant comments. It simply is no longer part of their lives, and they do not follow it carefully. Not surprisingly, those who did comment felt that "not enough emphasis was placed on 'practical' economics." One respondent stated, "It seems to be more systematic and more difficult, but it is fraught with similar tensions." Another stated, "My view is that graduate education has improved, but the gap between the graduates and practitioners has gotten worse. Ph.D. programs are great preparation for teaching, but a mixed preparation for other careers." Another response was, "The training I received on thinking clearly and problem-solving has been very relevant. The specific content of my economics training has been less relevant."

One academic respondent summed up the views of many with the following long, insightful statement.

> My current view is similar to what I thought as a graduate student. Graduate economic education is aimed at preparing students for academic careers. In writing papers for publication in scholarly journals, academics are trying to solve the following problem: show that starting from a set of not completely implausible assumptions can lead one to an interesting (i.e., novel or counterintuitive) result. No one else (i.e., private sector economists, government economists, policymakers, economics undergraduates) has that as an objective. Thus, unless and until they adopt this objective as their own, the people listed in brackets above find much of academic economics misdirected, irrelevant, or esoteric. This leads to some understandable frustration. Nonetheless, having a large group of people pursue this objective has (perhaps inadvertently) generated techniques and insights that are valuable outside academia. If I knew how to make academic economics more directly relevant to what non-academics are interested in, I would push for some changes. But I don't know how to do that. Indeed, there may not be any way of doing that.

## Changing Views of Economics and of the Profession

While the respondents' view of graduate economics education has not changed significantly, their view of the economics profession has become more positive. The same respondents who had negative comments on graduate education were much more positive about the economics profession and about the relevance of their graduate training for their current jobs. When asked, "How relevant would you say your graduate school training is for your current job?" 70 percent felt it was very relevant, and none felt that it was not especially relevant. Government economists were more likely to answer "reasonably" rather than "very" relevant, while academic economists were much more likely to answer "very" relevant. It seems that those who stay in the profession learn to appreciate their training, especially if they are in academia.

89

One student wrote, "I was an extremely skeptical graduate student, but have found the economics I learned a very powerful tool in all my work." Only 2 percent said they would not do it again, with 20 percent unsure. This compares to 6 percent in the first survey who said they would not do it again and 21 percent who said they were unsure.

To get a sense of their changing views of the profession, four of the questions asked were almost identical to those asked in the earlier survey; the following sections present the answers to those questions.

*Economists' View of Economics as a Science*

Table 4–1 considers the opinions of students about economics as a science. It has four separate response sets: (1) what the respondents said in the original study, (2) what the subset of respondents said in the original survey, (3) what the subset of respondents thought that they had answered on the original study, and (4) what they believe now.

It shows that there was significant change in how much agreement the respondents believe exists. Whereas originally only 4 percent of the subgroup strongly agreed and 58 percent disagreed that economists agree on fundamental issues, now 17 percent strongly agreed and only 20 percent disagreed. There are probably two reasons for this change. First, today economists do tend to agree more; the major divisions in macro that characterized the 1980s have ended. Second, graduate school is a time where many different views are tried out, and so disagreement probably seems greater in graduate school.

A somewhat smaller movement occurred in whether the respondents saw a sharp line between positive and normative economics, with an increase from 4 percent to 15 percent in those who strongly agree, and a decrease from 60 percent to 46 percent who disagree. Similarly, there was an increase in the percentage of those who strongly agreed that economics is the most scientific of the social sciences, from 20 percent to 35 percent. Interestingly, their perceptions of how scientific they remembered thinking economics to be in graduate school were much higher than what they had actually said as grad students.

There were some differences between academic and government economists in what they thought in graduate school about the strength of their beliefs concerning the relevance of neoclassical economics in

Table 4–1: Opinions of Economics as a Science

| | What the sample said in graduate school | | | | What the subgroup said in graduate school | | | | What the subgroup thought they said in graduate school | | | | What the subgroup says now | | | |
|---|---|---|---|---|---|---|---|---|---|---|---|---|---|---|---|---|
| | Str Agr | Agree Smw | Dis Agr | No Op | Str Agr | Agree Smw | Dis Agr | No Op | Str Agr | Agree Smw | Dis Agr | No Op | Str Agr | Agree Smw | Dis Agr | No Op |
| Neoclassical economics is relevant for the economic problems of today. | 34% | 54% | 11% | 1% | 47% | 47% | 4% | 2% | 39% | 46% | 4% | 11% | 54% | 39% | 7% | 0% |
| Economists agree on the fundamental issues. | 4% | 40% | 52% | 4% | 4% | 31% | 58% | 7% | 9% | 54% | 22% | 15% | 17% | 61% | 20% | 2% |
| There is a sharp line between positive and normative economics. | 9% | 23% | 62% | 6% | 4% | 29% | 60% | 7% | 13% | 39% | 33% | 15% | 15% | 33% | 46% | 7% |
| Learning neoclassical economics means learning a set of tools. | N/A | N/A | N/A | N/A | 33% | 42% | 16% | 9% | 35% | 43% | 11% | 11% | 33% | 52% | 15% | 0% |
| Economics is the most scientific discipline among the social sciences. | 28% | 39% | 19% | 14% | 20% | 33% | 29% | 18% | 43% | 33% | 13% | 11% | 35% | 39% | 17% | 9% |

graduate school. Forty-three percent of future academic economists, but only 18 percent of future government economists in the subgroup, thought they strongly agreed that neoclassical economics was relevant in graduate school. (In actual fact 36 percent of future government economists strongly agreed.) Their current views are quite different: 61 percent of academic economists and 54 percent of government economists strongly agreed that neoclassical economics is relevant. Those from the earlier study who became government economists did, however, see economics as less scientific; 32 percent of future academics strongly agreed with the proposition that economics was the most scientific of the social sciences, whereas 0 percent of the future government economists agreed. This somewhat evened out with 44 percent of academics and 27 percent of government economists strongly agreeing with the proposition now.

## Economists' View of Economic Assumptions

Table 4–2 reports the respondents' views about the importance of various economic assumptions. It reports three separate sets of responses: (1) what the respondents in the original survey said in graduate school; (2) what the subgroup said in graduate school; and (3) what the subgroup says now.

Table 4–2 shows less dramatic changes than table 4–1, but it still shows a slight increase in the number seeing the neoclassical assumption of rational behavior as very important, and for the subgroup it shows a decrease from 13 percent to 4 percent of those who saw economic behavior according to conventions as very important. Those who view the rational expectations hypothesis as very important increased slightly. The importance given to assumptions of price rigidities, cost markup pricing, and extracting surplus labor declined. The latter is consistent with the elimination of Marx as one of the most admired economists.

The questions about neoclassical assumptions provoked a number of written comments that suggest that there has been an opening up of the profession. Two such comments were, "What we do today is largely model 'neoclassical,' isn't it? But, more open today than fifteen to twenty years ago"; and "Clearly, neoclassical economics is a set of

Table 4–2: Importance of Economic Assumptions

| | What the original survey said in graduate school | | | | What the subgroup said in graduate school | | | | What the subgroup says now | | | |
|---|---|---|---|---|---|---|---|---|---|---|---|---|
| | Very imp. | Mod imp. | Unimp. | Don't know | Very imp. | Mod imp. | Unimp. | Don't know | Very imp. | Mod imp. | Unimp. | Don't know |
| The neoclassical assumption of rational behavior | 51% | 41% | 7% | 1% | 51% | 36% | 9% | 4% | 61% | 35% | 2% | 2% |
| Economic behavior according to conventions | 4% | 25% | 57% | 15% | 13% | 56% | 7% | 24% | 4% | 63% | 13% | 20% |
| The rational expectations hypothesis | 17% | 53% | 25% | 5% | 11% | 51% | 27% | 11% | 15% | 59% | 22% | 4% |
| Imperfect competition | 40% | 55% | 4% | 2% | 33% | 56% | 4% | 7% | 39% | 52% | 9% | 0% |
| Price rigidities | 27% | 60% | 10% | 3% | 22% | 56% | 13% | 9% | 11% | 72% | 15% | 2% |
| Cost-mark-up pricing | 9% | 46% | 26% | 18% | 7% | 42% | 31% | 20% | 2% | 43% | 30% | 24% |
| The goal of a capitalist firm is to extract surplus value from workers | N/A | N/A | N/A | N/A | 4% | 29% | 51% | 16% | 2% | 11% | 74% | 13% |

tools—but it's a lot more than that, too. Since grad school, I think there have been two trends: one, to admit more non-neoclassical elements into economics; and second, to extend neoclassical analysis to a broader range of areas and disciplines outside of economics." So while economics is still the same as it was, it seems that the respondents believe that it is more open to new ideas and more inclusive of broader issues than it was previously.

There were some differences between government and academic economists in their responses to these and other questions, with academic economists exhibiting much more disagreement in their answers to the questions. For example, for academic economists 19 percent saw rational expectations as very important, 50 percent saw it as moderately important, and 31 percent saw it as unimportant. For government economists, 9 percent saw it as very important and 73 percent saw it as moderately important (18 percent had no opinion). I suspect that this smaller amount of disagreement among government economists reflects the fact that government economists spend less time in technical modeling and thus do not form such strong opinions about particular assumptions.

*Perceptions of What Makes a Successful Economist*

Table 4–3 reports the respondents' views of what skills put students on the fast track in graduate school today, and of what puts economists on the fast track at their jobs. It also compares those responses to those in the original survey and to what the subgroup believed in graduate school would put them on the fast track. Thus, there are four sets of responses in the table: (1) what the original survey results were, (2) what the results for the subgroup in the original study was, (3) what the subgroup thinks would put a student on the fast track in graduate school today, and (4) what the subgroup thinks would put an economist on the fast track in their jobs today. The answers are somewhat expected but are nonetheless interesting.

Being smart in the sense of being good at problem solving remained the element of success that respondents saw as most important. The respondents in their current jobs give this an even higher ranking in

Table 4-3: Perceptions of Success

| | What the survey thought would put someone on the fast track in graduate school (1985) | | | | Would put someone on the fast track in graduate school (1985) | | | | What the subgroup thought would put someone on the fast track in graduate school (today) | | | | What the subgroup thought would put someone on the fast track in their jobs | | | |
|---|---|---|---|---|---|---|---|---|---|---|---|---|---|---|---|---|
| | Very imp. | Mod imp. | Unimp. | Don't know | Very imp. | Mod imp. | Unimp. | Don't know | Very imp. | Mod imp. | Unimp. | Don't know | Very imp. | Mod imp. | Unimp. | Don't know |
| *Being smart in the sense of being good at problem solving | 65% | 32% | 3% | 1% | 58% | 36% | 2% | 4% | 87% | 11% | 0% | 2% | 67% | 28% | 2% | 2% |
| *Excellence in mathematics | 57% | 41% | 2% | 0% | 53% | 40% | 4% | 2% | 83% | 15% | 2% | 0% | 22% | 59% | 17% | 2% |
| *Being very knowledgeable in one particular field | 37% | 42% | 19% | 2% | 44% | 38% | 13% | 4% | 30% | 43% | 26% | 0% | 35% | 46% | 17% | 2% |
| *Ability to make connections with prominent professors | 26% | 50% | 16% | 9% | 36% | 44% | 13% | 7% | 39% | 50% | 11% | 0% | 17% | 46% | 30% | 7% |
| *Being interested in, and good at, empirical research | 16% | 60% | 23% | 1% | 11% | 60% | 24% | 4% | 20% | 59% | 17% | 4% | 46% | 39% | 11% | 4% |
| *Having a broad knowledge of the economics literature | 10% | 41% | 43% | 5% | 9% | 44% | 36% | 11% | 13% | 37% | 46% | 4% | 24% | 39% | 35% | 2% |
| *Having a thorough knowledge of the economy | 3% | 22% | 68% | 7% | 0% | 22% | 71% | 7% | 4% | 20% | 67% | 9% | 28% | 35% | 24% | 13% |

their advice to graduate students than they did when they were in graduate school, with 58 percent seeing it as very important in graduate school and 87 percent seeing it as very important for graduate students today, and 67 percent seeing it as very important for their current jobs. Problem solving is clearly a central element in what economists do and in how they perceive themselves.

The nature of those problems, however, changes significantly as economists progress in their careers. In graduate school 53 percent saw excellence in mathematics as very important and today, in their advice to graduate students, that percentage increased to 83 percent. As it applies to their jobs today, however, the percentage who saw excellence in mathematics as very important fell to 22 percent. It seems that graduate school has a mathematical filter: both in the jobs and in graduate school, problem-solving is important; but in graduate school the problem-solving is more mathematical.

The ability to make connections with prominent professors was seen as much more important in graduate school than on the job, as could be expected. More interesting is the major change that occurred in respondents' opinions about the role of being interested in, and good at, empirical research. In graduate school, 11 percent strongly agreed that this was important; on the job, 46 percent strongly agreed that this was important. The importance of empirical work is seen as greater on the job than in graduate school today, with only 20 percent of the respondents strongly agreeing that it is important in grad school today. So there has been some movement toward the empirical skills, but mathematical skills continue to predominate as the most important in graduate school. This difference probably reflects the difficulty of supervising empirical work; empirical work remains a skill that needs on-the-job training.

Two of the most cited statistics from our original study were the importance given to a broad knowledge of the economy and the importance given to having a thorough knowledge of the economy for getting on the fast track. In that original study, 3 percent believed that having a thorough knowledge of the economy was very important, and 10 percent of the respondents considered having a broad knowledge of the economics literature as very important. (These responses were similar to those of the subgroup, with 0 percent and 9 percent respectively thinking that a thorough knowledge of the economy and a broad knowledge of the economics literature are very important.)

The respondents continued to hold these same beliefs for graduate students today: 4 percent saw having a thorough knowledge of the economy as very important and 13 percent saw having a broad knowledge of the economics literature as very important. On the job, however, the importance of both of these skills increased significantly, with 24 percent of the respondents seeing a broad knowledge of economics literature as very important and 28 percent seeing a thorough knowledge of the economy as very important. Still, even in their jobs, 35 percent see having a broad knowledge of the economics literature as unimportant and 24 percent see having a thorough knowledge of the economy as unimportant.

Consistent with this change, the kinds of journals that the subgroup prefers to read have changed. Less technical journals such as the *Journal of Economic Perspectives* and journals of applied economics such as *Brookings Papers* tied as running the articles they are most interested in today. Other skills that respondents mentioned in written comments included the ability to write and speak effectively, persistence, ability to work hard, creative thinking, and organization.

Not surprisingly, the importance given to various factors depended on the jobs that the respondents hold. Seventy-one percent of academics see being smart in the sense of being good at problem solving as very important, while only 54 percent of business economists see it as very important. There was a similar difference for excellence in math. Twenty-eight percent of academics see it as very important; 8 percent of government economists see it as very important. Being knowledgeable in a particular field is seen as very important by 39 percent of academics, while only 8 percent of government economists see it as very important.

The relative rankings were reversed for valuing knowledge of the economy: 75 percent of government economists see having a thorough knowledge of the economy as very important, with only 18 percent of academic economists seeing it as very important. Similarly, 34 percent of academic economists see having a broad knowledge of the economy as unimportant, whereas 0 percent of government economists see it as unimportant.

*Opinions on Policy*

Table 4–4 presents economists' opinions on policy over time. It consists of three sets of responses, (1) the original survey responses; (2) the subgroup's responses in the original survey, and (3) the responses of the subgroup in the current survey.

A number of changes show up in table 4–4. In graduate school, 40 percent of the respondents agreed without reservation that fiscal policy can be an effective tool, while now only 20 percent agreed without reservation. Given that in the original study the students were less positive on fiscal policy than the profession was (35 percent saw it as effective compared to 65 percent of American economists who at the time saw it as effective, these changes suggest that fiscal policy's effectiveness continues to decline in economists' view.

A second change worth noting occurred in respondents' views about the distribution of income. In graduate school, 53 percent of the subgroup agreed without reservation that the distribution of income should be more equal; today 30 percent agree without reservation. Their views on the minimum wage did not change significantly: the number believing without reservation that it increased unemployment increased only slightly, from 29 percent to 33 percent. This is much less than might have been predicted from the earlier study, where fewer believed that the minimum wage increased unemployment (34 percent of the original respondents saw it as increasing unemployment without reservation, compared to 68 percent of American economists at the time believing without reservation that the minimum wage increased unemployment. It seems that, perhaps because of recent empirical work by Card and Krueger (1997), the respondents' views on the minimum wage have not changed as much as might have been predicted.

There was, however, a significant rise in the percentage of respondents (from 36 percent to 61 percent) who agreed that tariffs and import quotas definitely reduce economic welfare. This was much closer to the movement toward conservatism that could have been predicted from the difference in views between graduate students and the profession that showed up in the earlier study, where in graduate school 36 percent of the respondents saw it as definitely true, while 81 percent of

Table 4–4: Opinions on Policy

| Economic opinions | What the survey said in graduate school | | | | What the subgroup said in graduate school | | | | What the subgroup says now | | | |
|---|---|---|---|---|---|---|---|---|---|---|---|---|
| | Agree | Agree with reservations | Disagree | No opinion | Agree | Agree with reservations | Disagree | No opinion | Agree | Agree with reservations | Disagree | No opinion |
| Fiscal policy can be an effective tool in stabilization policy. | 35% | 49% | 11% | 5% | 40% | 40% | 9% | 11% | 20% | 50% | 22% | 9% |
| The Federal Reserve Bank should maintain a constant growth of the money supply. | 9% | 34% | 45% | 12% | 9% | 40% | 42% | 9% | 9% | 22% | 54% | 15% |
| The distribution of income in developed nations should be more equal. | 47% | 32% | 14% | 7% | 53% | 29% | 13% | 4% | 30% | 35% | 24% | 11% |
| A minimum wage increases unemployment among young and unskilled workers. | 34% | 39% | 18% | 9% | 29% | 38% | 22% | 11% | 33% | 45% | 11% | 11% |
| Tariffs and import quotas reduce general economic welfare. | 36% | 49% | 9% | 6% | 36% | 44% | 4% | 16% | 61% | 35% | 0% | 4% |
| Inflation is primarily a monetary phenomenon. | 27% | 33% | 29% | 11% | 22% | 36% | 31% | 11% | 52% | 26% | 17% | 4% |

Table 4-4 (cont.)

| Economic opinions | What the survey said in graduate school | | | | What the subgroup said in graduate school | | | | What the subgroup says now | | | |
|---|---|---|---|---|---|---|---|---|---|---|---|---|
| | Agree | Agree with reservations | Disagree | No opinion | Agree | Agree with reservations | Disagree | No opinion | Agree | Agree with reservations | Disagree | No opinion |
| Wage-price controls should be used to control inflation | 1% | 17% | 73% | 9% | 2% | 18% | 73% | 7% | 0% | 2% | 96% | 2% |
| Worker democracy will increase labor productivity. | 13% | 40% | 22% | 24% | 11% | 51% | 22% | 16% | 7% | 20% | 37% | 37% |
| The market system tends to discriminate against women. | 24% | 27% | 39% | 10% | 22% | 36% | 38% | 4% | 11% | 33% | 48% | 9% |
| The capitalist system has an inherent tendency toward crisis. | 8% | 23% | 59% | 13% | 9% | 27% | 56% | 9% | 7% | 17% | 61% | 15% |

the broader profession saw it as true. In graduate school, where one learns the models, one sees the ambiguities in theory; in practice one sees the way tariffs work.

Liberal policy views—support of wage price controls, worker democracy, and the belief that the market system discriminates against women—decreased in importance, which is consistent with the movement toward conservatism that I remarked upon earlier.

## School Differences

There were insufficient responses to report percentage differences among schools in this survey. Thus I do not report in tabular form the division of responses by school. I will, however, briefly list those differences that appeared substantial, although I caution the reader that these are based upon limited information.[3] I have checked the responses both with the original sample and with the subsample, to eliminate subsample bias. Some substantial school differences are

- Stanford graduates saw economists disagreeing on fundamental issues more than graduates from other schools.
- MIT and Stanford graduates saw economics today as more primarily model building than did Harvard and Chicago students.
- Harvard and Chicago graduates felt the strongest about the importance of empirical research.
- MIT graduates saw being knowledgeable about one particular field as especially important compared to graduates from other schools.[4]
- Stanford graduates saw a broad knowledge of the economic literature as less important than did graduates of other schools.
- MIT and Chicago graduates saw a thorough knowledge of the economy as relatively less important than did other graduates.
- Stanford graduates saw the assumption of rational expectations hypothesis as least important; Chicago graduates saw it as the most important.
- Chicago graduates continued to see economics as the most scientific discipline compared to other graduates.
- Chicago graduates continued to have the strongest belief that inflation is primarily a monetary phenomenon.
- Chicago graduates remained the strongest in their belief about the ineffectiveness of fiscal policy.
- Chicago graduates were the strongest in their belief against the distribution of income in developed countries being more equal, with Stanford students the strongest in their belief that income should be more equal.

101

- Chicago graduates had a much stronger view that the minimum wage increases unemployment and that tariffs and import quotas reduce economic welfare, with all Chicago students strongly agreeing.
- MIT graduates were the strongest believers that the market system tends to discriminate against women.

## Some Thoughts on Implications for Graduate Study of Economics

As I discussed in the introduction, our original study provoked much discussion in the profession. It played a role in the establishment of the COGEE Commission (Hansen 1991; Krueger et al. 1991), which studied the role of graduate economic education. The same view of the lack of connection between the economy and the work one does in graduate school that existed in the 1980s shows up in the recent survey of the subgroup, but there is far less concern about changing it. This partially reflects the change in perspective from student to professor, but it also, I believe, reflects the fact that there actually is less concern. In response to the ferment of the 1980s, while there was much discussion, there was little in the way of change. As discussed above, some schools slightly modified their programs; others introduced some additional counseling in the initial year. But there was no revolution in graduate economic education; if anything, the profession continued in the same direction it was going in the past, with increased amounts of mathematical and theoretical work in the first two years.

One of the changes that I believe has occurred is in the selection criteria of who goes on to graduate school. Before, a good undergraduate who was interested in policy, but not particularly interested in the fine points of theory or of math, would often consider graduate economics as a career; today this happens far less frequently. The majority of students entering graduate economics programs have significant mathematical training, and are entering graduate school with a good understanding of what they will be experiencing. Information about the character of graduate education in economics is better diffused; thus the shock for students is less. Those who have chosen economics are happier with their choice. In short, the students have changed to fit graduate school, rather than graduate school changing to fit a broader student policy interest. The result is that fewer U.S. students have gone on to graduate school, and many more beginning graduate students have significant training, such as M.A.'s in mathematics. These changes have made for less dissention in the U.S. profession.[5] This in turn has led to an easier environment within which to teach, and that easier environment, in my view, accounts for the more positive view of the profession, even though graduate school has not changed.

The cost of this structure is that there is a mathematical filter on who enters graduate school, which changes the mix of individuals who become economists. The intelligent generalist with good insights and sensibility is weeded out.[6] Graduate school is a defining experience. It shapes the way students think and it teaches them the problem-solving techniques that are the essence of the way an economist thinks. One does problem solving in both graduate school and in the real world, but in graduate school the problem solving is more mathematical.

As students get into the profession, they recognize the importance of institutions and of literature—life does not center around problem sets—and they learn on the job. Perhaps that is the way it has to be, but there seemed to be a hope expressed by the respondents that there was a better way.

My particular view is that there remains a need for more diversity in graduate economic training, perhaps with some schools focusing on preparing students to work in government, policy research institutions, and teaching in liberal arts schools, and others on preparing students to do pure theory. At the top schools this has not happened; all seem to compete on one dimension. This continues because, despite the faults of graduate education in economics, it seems to be working acceptably. Regardless of the continued concerns with the state of graduate education, the respondents were happy with their training and with the current state of the profession.

There was, however, underlying concern about whether economics is attracting the top students, but it is a concern that goes beyond economics. One of the respondents to this study put it as follows:

Look, by every available measure I have done well. I am paid well. I can publish most of my research. I get to teach good students. I live in a nice place. That said, I recognize two things are also true: there is really no essential difference between me and hundreds/thousands of others who work as hard, but who do not have what I have—so I am quite lucky. Comparatively speaking, academic life stinks, but its most redeeming feature is the freedom. Yet, it is hard to look a bright kid in the face and recommend this job. Sure, it might work out, but for most people I am not so sure. And here is what really gets me. Our job is so much better than the other social sciences. Economics is a very good discipline at the elite level; not so for most other fields. Generally, when I look at academics, especially economists, I do not see a bright future. It is worrisome. Entrepreneurial people get tenure, then burn out. The profession does not reward enough to keep scholars going. Also, the culture of the profession can stifle creativity. It is hard for us to grow with this culture.

The reality is that economics must compete for students within the academic institutions that exist today, and given those institutions, my best undergraduates almost inevitably choose business. The best ones can get over $100,000 a year in starting salary, and have enormous job potential. It is quite hard to convince them of the value of an academic life, especially if it involves two years of work quite unrelated to the economy.

## Conclusion

Let me conclude by briefly summarizing the major findings of this chapter. Overall, the economists I surveyed are generally satisfied with their career and with the training that they received in graduate school. They have become somewhat more conservative, and they see economics as more of a science than they did when they were in graduate school. Their views of many policies have changed, and in general they have become less activist and more market-oriented. The majority, especially those in policy positions, has become less interested in theory and more interested in empirical work.

The respondents do not feel that graduate school has changed—they still see it as too technical and too mathematical in the early years—but they do not convey the same urgency toward change that they expressed in the earlier study. The respondents have also broadened their perspective, and they now recognize the importance of institutions, and of knowledge of the economy, more so than they did in graduate school. There is much on-the-job training that goes on, especially for government and policy economists, and the views of government and policy economists differ from those of academics.

Thus, my interpretation of the broader issues addressed by the survey is that the economics profession has evolved since the first survey, in response to the graduate school ferment in the 1980s, albeit not in the way that many of the reform-minded economists had hoped that it would.

# PART II

Conversations with Graduate Students

THIS PART CONSISTS of the conversations with groups of students at six of the seven schools in the survey. Participation was voluntary, and the students are not necessarily representative of their schools. (At most schools I asked students to comment on the degree to which they saw their views as representative.)

The editing of the conversations has been minimal and the conversational quality of the interviews has been maintained. Editing consisted of smoothing sentences here and there to facilitate reading, and the cutting of some discussions that seemed extraneous or repetitive. The names of the students have been altered to shield their identity, and some highly identifying statements have been eliminated.

For me, these conversations fill in the gaps in the survey; they give the reader a very good sense of graduate students' views and help put the survey results into perspective. The conversations are independent, and readers can pick and choose among them, although most readers have found that once they have read one, they have wanted to read others because they give the reader a glimpse of graduate school that non-economists, and even economists not involved in graduate school, seldom see.

# Harvard Interview

*This interview was conducted in Cambridge at the seminar room in the National Bureau in April 2003. It is with seven Harvard students who are in their second, third, and fourth years of study.*

**Do you consider yourself a representative sample, and if not, how do you deviate from the mean student here at Harvard?**

*Gordon*   I think the location of this interview (at the NBER) gives you the bias. We're all at the Bureau, so no one here does pure theoretical economics. It is also slanted to those who like labor economics; and there are way too few international students.

*(others concur)*

*Naomie*   Today is Easter, so religious Christians are also underrepresented. There is also an overrepresentative number of women. In my class there are about 25 percent women. The overrepresentation of labor and women go together.

**How many international students are there in the program?**

*Angella*   It varies by class, but probably one third to one half of the students are international.

**In our previous study of graduate education, we entitled the chapter on Harvard "Diversity and Skepticism?" Do you think that this is still an appropriate title for Harvard?**

*John*   What was meant by "diversity"?

**"Diversity" referred to the significant number of students with radical points of view.[1]**

*Gordon*   What does "radical" mean?

**We meant that there was a wider range of student views at Harvard than at other schools. In the last survey, Yale had the largest population of radical students, whereas Harvard had a wide mix. MIT and Stanford were relatively-neutral and Chicago was significantly to the right. This was in the early-to-mid 1980s.**

*Naomie*   The radical part definitely does not fit, but the diversity part does. I expected that when I went to grad school that everyone would be in a very narrow band—center-to-center right, and I don't think that that's true; the students' political views are diverse, although I think the whole political spectrum may have shrunk since the previous study.

**How about your professors?**

*John*   There is a fair amount of political diversity. Ben Friedman is a hard-core Democrat. Greg Mankiw and Robert Barro are hard-core Republicans. But I don't think the faculty is particularly diverse in terms of the methods that they use. With the exception of Steve Marglin, who is definitely on the outside, I think that by and large all the professors use the same methods, and think about economic issues is a similar way. They just come to different conclusions.

**So there's no one pushing, say an agent-based modeling, complexity, or a computable economics approach?**

*Dan*   There is a bit of dabbling in it. Simulations are being incorporated in research more and more. Learning and game theory are used a lot. Most faculty still follow a more classical approach to modeling.

*Gordon*   The professors take incremental steps away from the standard approach, not radical jumps. Most professors deal with their models.

*John*   I think the place where Harvard differs most from other graduate programs is that it has a lot more students working on behavioral economics and a lot more faculty who are sympathetic to behavioral economics.

*Dave*   I agree. The primary way in which Harvard is probably different than other graduate programs is that Harvard is more focused on psychological and behavioral issues.

*Gordon*   There was some discussion of complexity organized by someone in the political science department. So it is around. Some faculty are interested in networks.

*Naomie*   I also think that there is more discussion of qualitative methods in social science here than at other programs. For example, there might be a pairing of economics with sociology. There is also more interest in the institutional structure. For example, in his dissertation here Steve Levitt did work on how drug-selling works, and how their operations work. Not that that many graduate students are taking up on it, but if a graduate student wanted to he could.

**Last time, one of the quotes from the graduate students was that "sociology" is a dirty word. Is that no longer the case?**

*Rich*   I think what people are saying now is that sociology is an interesting field—it's just that sociologists don't know how to do it.

*Naomie*   That's a bit strong. Larry Katz says that within sociology there are two camps—the quantitative and the qualitative camps. The quantitative people are just doing bad, non-identified economics. They should go away. Anyone who is interested in quantitative sociological questions should come to an economics department. But the qualitative sociology—that's what we don't know what to do. That's what missing from some of our models and needs to be integrated into them. We should be talking to ethnographers. So there is a distinction. I think "ethnography" is not at all a dirty word, but is very highly valued.

*John*   There are also tons of people who are doing sociological type work. In our department there is Ed Glazier and Andre Schleifer, among others, who have whole sections of their papers that are sociology or history. They are quite open to a narrative-based discussion.

*Gordon*   People in the department are searching for understanding; there is a lot of applying economic methods to sociological problems.

**What would you describe as an economic method?**

*Gordon*   Putting it down in math, and then really trying to identify something that really comes out of that model—looking for a correlation among the variables.

**Does a formal model have to have micro foundations?**

*Gordon*   Usually it does, although a lot of times it is a partial equilibrium, or very reduced form, model. I think that the focus in labor economics, or in any applied micro field, is really nailing something empirically. And that is not something that is really stressed by sociologists. I am a friend with some sociologists, and it is interesting how they use a different approach to choosing areas to work on than do economists. Economists tend to avoid topics that are really difficult and really hard to solve, because there is no good way of getting at the problem; sociologists do not. For an economist there is no sense writing another paper on compensating differentials, because there is no good way of identifying compensating differentials. Unless an economist can think of some clever new approach, or can figure out a randomized experiment, which can shed quantitative evidence on the problem, they avoid it.

Sociologists have a different approach. They choose topics by what they are interested in—what they consider a serious sociological problem. They get some data and look at it. They are not as concerned about whether they will be able to nail the topic empirically. It's weird because it's a question of your audience. If you are writing for other sociologists who are not going to hold you to that high empirical standard, then the sociologists' approach makes sense. Why bother with the difficult empirical issues as long as you can get your work published, and this is the best you can do with the tools you're given. As long as everyone is okay with it, then fine.

*Prakash*   The sociologists tend to think that our questions are very narrow and not very interesting and that the models that we create do not explain very complex phenomena.

*John*   You asked a question about micro foundations. In our class, for example, there are one, maybe two, people out of thirty who worry about such things. I remember quite distinctly a conversation with Ed Glazier when I came here to visit before I enrolled. He said that it is really questionable to require students to take two semesters of macro now that macro is just another subfield of micro. This turned out to be an accurate reflection of the status of macro at Harvard now. It is the equivalent to IO.

**Do you think Harvard is different than other places, or do you see this as a general trend in the profession?**

*Rich*   I think it is a general trend in the profession.

*Prakash*   I think it is different for foreign students—I'm one of the few foreign students here who does micro. The reason for the difference is probably because in developing economies they need macroeconomists.

**Could you describe the typical progression for a student at Harvard?**

*Naomie*  It's different for different people. People come into the program with significant different backgrounds. Some people have masters degrees but they don't skip the first year. They might take fields at the same time they are taking their core courses. They take their generals and their orals in quick succession. Others who don't have a masters generally take longer. They tend to put their orals back further and further. Among this last group the median time that they take their orals is September or October of their third year.

**After orals do you turn to writing your thesis?**

*Gordon*  A lot of third years do nothing.

*(laughter)*

*Dave*  By about the end of first year or the beginning of second year, there is a very strong impression that classes should be a smaller part of what you do, and that you should be getting down to working on your thesis. First year is devoted to working hard in classes. Then there is a very long period of time devoted to doing things like taking orals, taking classes, and teaching. You have to get all this stuff out of the way at some point.

**Is there a lot of pressure about whether you are going to pass the orals?**

*Gordon*  Does anyone know anyone who did not pass his or her orals?

*All*  No.

*Rich*  But people take them very seriously. They do so because it is a big signal for you—how the faculty will think of you. But compared to the generals where you were completely anonymous by construction—we all were given a number in our exam book—orals are clearly a hurdle that people just want to pass.

**How do the generals work in relation to the core courses? Are they designed by the same people who do the core courses, or are they designed by the department?**

*Dave*  They are designed by the people who taught the course, so they are basically a year-long final. Each person who taught a part of the core course prepares that section of the generals; as the people teaching change, the generals change. So there actually is a decent amount of variation in what we call generals.

**But it's pretty much expected that people will pass the generals?**

*Angella*   No, some people fail them the first time, but they take them again later in the summer, and at that point just about everyone passes.

*Prakash*   Not this year. Some failed a second time.

**What happens to them if they don't pass a second time?**

*Prakash*   I think one person did leave.

*John*   But overall I think people who leave the program leave voluntarily. They decide they don't want to do this.

**Any reaction to the Ec 10 controversy?[2] It sounded like the undergraduates were unhappy with the coverage of the material in the course.**

*Angella*   I think that the undergraduate students wanted changes in the way it was taught, but I don't think it had to do with the politics.

*Rich*   This was a particular group of undergraduates who were also actively involved in other kinds of protests.

*Angella*   The material that is covered in Ec 10 is pretty standard.

*Rich*   I think the protest was misplaced. It does seem to be a small group of people who have a political agenda, farther from the center from where Ec 10 is taught, who want an undergraduate course that offers different perspectives on economic theory. I think that actually is quite important. As graduate students, we are required to take a type of mini-course that includes alternative perspectives. The undergraduates don't have any-thing equivalent. But perhaps the energy is misplaced in trying to fault Ec 10 as giving a slanted viewpoint and necessitating another alternative perspective.

*Gordon*   We have a pedagogical problem in that the simple models don't fit well empirically and have normative implications that are far to one side of the subject. I think Ec 10 teaches the simple models because they can be reduced to graphs and have historical importance. Then later on, the course does secondarily address situations that don't fit the models.

*John*   If you were to do a survey of the students at the end of Ec 10 and ask them about the normative issues, and what the politics of the course was, you'd get a set of answers that would not match the views found in a similar survey of the faculty of the department; you'd find that 90 percent of the faculty don't hold the normative judgments that the students come away from the course with. What happens is that you learn some basic ideas in Ec 10 and then you spend the rest of the time learning the nuances. For example, the students learn models in which price controls and regulations are bad, which obviously is not always true. But you have to start somewhere. My view is that there is a little bit too much of a tendency to sell the models as policy-relevant than there should be.

*Angella*   At the beginning there tends to be a big emphasis on efficiency rather than distribution issues, because it is much easier to talk about efficiency than it is to get into the difficult issues of distribution. In terms of what students believe at the end of Ec 10, I actually had one student say that if there is only one thing that she can conclude from Ec 10, it is that she is never going to support having subsidies for anything.

*John*   I don't agree that there is something inherent in the models that is necessarily normative. It depends on how your section leader presents the material. There are things you can emphasize in the traditional theory that give you a liberal policy prescription. So I think that a big part of the conservatism comes from the parts that the professor in Ec 10 emphasizes. He talks about the bad effect of minimum wage laws on unemployment. I don't think he mentions the Card and Krueger work that empirically shows that this may not be true. That's his choice.

**In terms of graduate courses what are the hardest and easiest courses?**

*Rich*   For a liberal arts graduate who hasn't seen a lot of the math that you get in the first year, the micro sequence is hard.

*Prakash*   I think most people would agree that micro is harder than macro.

*Rich*   I think there are differences of opinion. There are some people who have never had macro before and they found macro harder.

**What do they cover in macro?**

*Naomie*  They start with the IS/LM model and then cover all the new Keynesian work, monetary policy, growth, political economy models, and finally some international models with the professors each teaching their specialty.

*Angella*  In our year we didn't have any international; well I guess there was a guest lecturer, but what's taught depends on who is teaching that year.

**Are they trying in the core courses to give you an overview, or are they teaching what they are working on?**

*Gordon*  I think the macro course is more an overview, but it is an overview where they want to bring you to the forefront of theory. However, the overview you get depends on who is teaching the course; so, in fact, it is more of a topics course.

*Rich*  I think they attempt to make it an overview, but in the end they tend to emphasize what they know. In micro the different parts are more connected because the teaching is centered around a central model. Different professors are selected to teach because they do work on parts of the model, but the parts are tied together. This makes it so that there is a lot more continuity from year to year.

**I don't detect that there is a lot of pressure here in terms of workload. What would you say the workload is? And how does it compare to other disciplines?**

*Rich*  I think the workload associated with courses here is much less in economics. I think the workload, however, is very peer centered. Everything is centered on getting you off to do your thing.

*Naomie*  I agree with that. I think one of the questions on your survey was how important is it to becoming an economist to understand the literature in your field, and I think that is not so important in economics. That's one of the reasons why the second-year courses are less important than research. To learn everything in IO or to learn everything in labor doesn't end up getting valued. In other programs, such as political science, I think that it is more valued. In those fields students can take their whole third year studying and reading before they take their comprehensive exam, reading 200 books per field. So when they finish, they know their field. That's not something we're encouraged to do. I think it is a bit unfortunate. You're pushed to research right away, and you don't know what has been done.

116

*Prakash*  Although in some subjects, the professors want you to know the field
when you take your orals from them. I feel that the idea of the orals is
to have a broader sense of our field, and not the specifics that you and
your professors are working on, so when you go on the job market and
you say "I am a labor economist," that it means something—you know
the labor literature and can teach a course in labor economics.

*Naomie*  I think that that's true, and I think that my field courses have been
great. I'm looking forward to studying for orals. But everyone passes
orals, and there's not a lot of pressure. There's not a sense that this is a
big hoop that you have to jump through.

*Gordon*  Yeah, everyone passes, but if you just pass, they will write you off as
someone that they're not going to pay attention to for the next three
years. Then you might as well have failed and left the program. Whereas
in generals, all you have to do is to get over the hurdle and you can
forget everything that you've learned, and nobody really cares.

Taking my orals in public finance and labor, I covered all the major stuff.
The courses presented all the basic public finance theory since the 1950s,
and the professors made it clear that they wanted us to know it. I really
got a sense of what the field was. That's why I took public economics
over development; I felt like the development sequence was neither here
nor there—there was no sense of knowing the field when you were done
with it. In public finance there was a clear set of papers and results that
you were expected to know.

*Naomie*  In development I did as much reading as I could, and it ended up
being a lot. I feel that most of the other students in the class didn't do
that. I don't know whether that's fair, but it seems like general knowledge of the field counts for so little that's there little incentive to do it,
and that many students end up cutting corners.

*Gordon*  I certainly read most of what I read for the orals after classes were
over. During the year you try to keep up and go to seminars, and then
you pick a month before the orals and read everything on the syllabus.

*Rich*  It varies a lot by field. Some fields define a set of knowledge to know
while others do not.

**In terms of math, did most of you feel prepared when you came in?**

117

*Gordon*   I think that we all felt prepared to pass generals. But I also think that there certainly is a sense that the people who had more math had a much easier first year.

**Could you tell who were going to be the stars from the beginning?**

*Gordon*   I would have to say no. There are a lot of people who were very good at math, but who were not stars.

*Rich*   There were a few people coming into the program who had already done significant class work and significant research, and you knew would do well. But the first-year success is not a good indicator; it is so much about math. But for those students who come in with both math and research, it is quite clear that they are likely to be a star.

*Angella*   But other than that, I don't think that there is a close connection between how well people did in the first year and how they ultimately do.

*Naomie*   I would also say that math per se is not as important the first year as was analytical and logical thinking. I never had real analysis, and I took the math for economists course in the first year, but I found that I didn't really need the math. You learn the five tricks of the math as it applies to economics and that's it for the math. For example, in the game theory and information theory that we did in micro, logic was more important than high-powered math. It was more whether you liked to do those puzzles when you were eight years old—the puzzles that asked: Whose house was Stella in, and questions like that.

*Prakash*   However, there are some things you can't do unless you have a really strong math background.

*Gordon*   And there is a bit a premature selection. I don't think that there is anyone who comes into the first year having never seen graduate micro or taken advanced math classes like real analysis, who does theory. The overwhelming number of those who do theory are those who have done a lot of math before they come here. And that in some sense may be a shame, because what you need to be a good theorist may be creativity, not whether you can do hard math.

*Rich*   It is tough right now for highly trained mathematical students coming in. I sense from watching some of them that they feel, okay I'm really good; now this must lead to something I can do in a research area. But about the only area they can go into is micro theory. They can really struggle finding a research topic to use their math skills on.

*Gordon*   So the math hurdle is bad because it keeps some people who would have been good at economics out of economics, but it is also bad because it keeps some who might have been good theorists out of theory.

**We never got an estimate of the hours a student would work. Would a first year work forty or fifty hours a week?**

*Prakash*   It's hard to put it in those terms.

**We've got to quantify.**

*(laughter)*

*Prakash*   Fifty, including class time.

*Dave*   In the second year it is a bit more studying, but less class time. And in the third year it varies significantly. If you have a project going, you can work up to eighty hours a week.

**If you were asked to summarize what they are trying to teach you here, what would you say?**

*Rich*   How to get a good academic job.

**How do you get a good job?**

*Rich*   You write a good job market paper.

**How does a good job market paper differ from a good paper?**

*Prakash*   A good job market paper shows that you have the ability to use the tools well. So if you are doing empirical work, you have to show that you can nail it down empirically. It's not the question you have; it's a demonstration of your ability to use the tools.

*Gordon*   In a good paper you're interested in what the paper says; in a job market paper you're interested in the abilities of who wrote the paper, and that's very different.

119

*Prakash*   It goes back to the question of choice of topic—the decision not to work on something because I'm not going to be able to nail it in the nine months that I have.

*Dave*   It's funny; you hear professors talk about starting to collect data three years ago when they had a conversation with someone. For a job market paper we can't do topics like that. If we do such work, it has to be in the background as we work on a paper that can be done in less than a year.

*Prakash*   The other thing is that you have to be careful about choosing to write in a very narrow field. For example, I was told that I shouldn't write on one topic because it would put me in the education field. If you write too narrowly, you will no longer be considered a labor economist.

**How do the top graduate schools differ?**

*Dave*   It's hard to say. We don't really get a lot of insight into what goes on at other schools.

*Naomie*   On the job market, if there is an MIT person and a Harvard person, the MIT gets enormous direction in how to write a paper and do it well; the Harvard person is given as much freedom to think about an interesting question and really attack it on his or her own. True, sometimes it means you fail and strike out, but you can learn from that. I think going to MIT is safer. I think people on the job market know that, and so [if] they see someone from MIT who has a good randomized experiment, they know that they worked on it closely with some of the professors there, so it is hard to know which is their contribution and which is the professor's. But that is MIT in particular.

*Gordon*   I have some good friends at Princeton, and that information, and information about job market candidates, gives me some sense. At Princeton there are very particular ways of doing things. For example, if you do macroeconomics at Princeton, you are doing Woodford's macroeconomics;[3] if you are doing microeconomics, you are doing Pesendorfer-type work. I think the general thing about Harvard is that it is extremely broad. It has a big faculty, which means that there are many different types of work that you can do here. I think that makes it very different. You can do Chicago-style economics at Harvard if you want to. But if you are at Stanford Business School and you're doing micro, you will be limited.

*Dave*   For the quality of students that it gets coming in, I don't think that Harvard students do as well on the job market as one might expect.

Although Harvard pretty much gets the students it wants, it is not at all clear that Harvard students have been outperforming students at other top programs.

**Why is that?**

*Gordon*   I think the stereotype is that Harvard students are not pushed. Because of that, they aren't trained as well; their fundamentals aren't as good; they do too many things.

*Dave*   That creates a sense that Harvard produces a few people who do very, very well; if you are extremely good anyway, you can really do well at Harvard, whereas people in the middle fall into the generalist category, and don't do as well as they might with more direction.

**Where do most people go when you graduate, and what are the faculty pushing you toward?**

*Gordon*   Certainly, they are pushing us toward graduate academic jobs.

**What if you said that you wanted to become a liberal arts professor? How would the faculty respond?**

*John*   I think that to the degree that our advisers have an actual stake in how we do, they want us to follow in their footsteps. So, for most people who got a job at a liberal arts college—they'd say, well that's the job you got. If someone were to say, I got this job at Chicago and I got this job at Amherst, and I really love teaching and I'm going to Amherst, your adviser would sit down with you and have a heart-to-heart talk.

*Prakash*   If you want to have your adviser's attention on your thesis, you shouldn't say that you want to work at a liberal arts school or at a policy institute. Of course, you don't have to tell him.

*John*   If you take the ranking of jobs according to the standard ranking, I don't know if I've ever heard of someone who got a good academic job but who instead went into the private sector or the World Bank; there are a few people who don't apply for academic jobs at all.

*Prakash*   That is not particularly true in finance; many of the finance specialists would go to Wall Street over an academic job. It doesn't happen with other fields so much.

121

*Naomie*   Some people have geographic constraints, which plays a central role in their choice.

*John*   I think most people coming into the program are planning to be university professors. I think that if you said on the application that you really wanted to work at a teaching college, you wouldn't get in.

**What if you said you wanted to work in public policy?**

*All (in unison)*   You wouldn't get in.

*Rich*   You'd be wasting their resources because they are supporting you.

*Naomie*   On my application I said that I wanted to teach writing as part of what I did. True, I left it very ambiguous how I would do that, but I got in.

**Have any of you heard of the Cambridge controversy?[4]**

*John*   I think so; didn't it have something to do with a mass exodus of radical economists twenty-five years ago, or something like that? Why do you ask?

**Because it was one of the topics that was significantly discussed in the earlier interviews, and I was wondering about whether you still learned anything about it.**
(*The others all agree that they are unfamiliar with it.*)

**How many of you are associated with the NBER? Does it significantly influence your work?**

*Gordon*   It is a huge, huge benefit for people in public finance and labor. There are three reasons why. The first is office space that we don't get in the department. Second is the access you get to professors in your field. Actually, the majority of them are in their offices here more than they are in the offices in the department. Third is access to the conferences. I've met pretty much all the major professors in my field at the major universities that I would love to teach at. This is an enormous advantage. Getting a job is not only about the quality of your work; it is about whether people like you and will want to hire you.

122

*John*   Going to conferences is separate from having office space. Students in relevant areas get invited to conferences who don't have offices here. I would also add another advantage, which is having people who are interested in the same thing around that you can talk to.

*All*   We agree with that; that is invaluable.

**Does it create a subset of students at Harvard, which might be differentiated from the subset of students not associated with NBER?**

*Naomie*   There are also MIT people here, although the NBER is predominantly Harvard.

**How about international students at the NBER?**

*Gordon*   Although foreign students make up about a third to a half of the student body at Harvard, at the NBER, they make up probably more about 20 percent.

*Prakash*   It also depends on how you count foreign students—foreign born, or coming from non-U.S. schools. A lot of foreign-born students here have gone to school in the United States.

*John*   It is definitely true that there are certain cliques, but there is some crossover. There are also students who are primarily working on their own; they are more isolated. NBER people tend to be more explicitly empirical, and the non-NBER students tend to be more theoretical.

*Prakash*   In my year most of the foreign students interact a lot with other foreign students, and not so much with American students. To get space in the NBER you have to work closely with one professor. I feel like in general it is harder for foreign students to do that.

**Do foreign students generally do better or worse than U.S. students?**

*Prakash*   There is no correlation; it is very idiosyncratic.

*Rich*   Foreign students probably have advantages and disadvantages. The advantage is that foreign undergraduate programs tend to be a lot less liberal artsy; a foreign student will concentrate almost entirely on economics. One foreign student I know told me that he took four non-

123

economic classes in his undergraduate education. In my whole undergraduate career I took a total of six economics classes. So there is certainly a structural break there. The big disadvantage of being a foreign student is language. If you go on the job market and do not speak English very well, it hurts your presentation and it hurts your chances on the job market.

*Prakash*   Also, although it may be a smaller number than in the past, some foreign graduate students want to go back home.

*Naomie*   Another advantage of foreign students is that they generally have a better math background.

**What would you say makes a successful economist?**

*Dave*   There are lots of different ways to be successful. There are some economists who have one really incredible idea; there are others that are really good at math.

*John*   You can just look at the faculty. They are all successful economists and they are so different from each other. You can have lots of different role models.

**When Arjo and I did the previous interview, there was much discussion of competing views. There were Keynesians and New Classicals in macro. In micro there were structuralists and reduced form advocates. There were a lot of debates raging. Do you feel that that has carried through? Or would you see economics as a more unified field today?**

*John*   I think it is a lot more unified than it was earlier. Certainly in macro you might learn about debates in the history of thought, but when it comes down to doing the research and doing the paper, people are using the same language and models.

*Rich*   I think we're lucky in this at Harvard. At other schools, there tends to be a focus on one approach rather than another. Here anyone in the department talks to anyone else.

*Dave*   To be fair, we are getting only a partial view of how people do economics. There is a sorting of who does what. It is hard for us to tell what's going on at different schools. As you take different classes, you may have a different take on how you do research.

*Naomie*　I was recently looking at a course that was the same course that I had taken a couple of years ago. When I looked at it, it was enormously different. We didn't cover many of the same papers. In the classes it is seldom mentioned that here's one view, and here's another.

*Prakash*　There are many debates going on at a larger level, but our field classes don't introduce us to them. The sense we get is that people pretty much agree on things.

*Rich*　There are disagreements, but when I think of intellectual debates, there aren't many.

*John*　One example might be in psychological economics—Harvard, MIT, and a couple other schools are heavily into it, while other schools don't do it at all.

*Rich*　I haven't had a lot of contact with other schools, but my feeling is that it is hard to find people who argue that rationality is empirically descriptive of how people behave, and that psychological foundations are not important. The debate is about whether the kind of stuff people are doing in behavioral economics is useful.

*Naomie*　The structural/reduced form debate is still raging in labor economics, except that reduced form is more focused on key experiments.

**Any issues that you would like to bring up?**

*Gordon*　Maybe the one comment I would like to make is that there are probably lots of other economists who are not as successful or not as well known or as successful as Harvard economists. The difference is a matter of devotion to the field. People who are on the faculty have to give up some family life because they spend an enormous amount of time working on economics. There is a serious commitment, and by that I mean emotional commitment to the field, of the faculty here. These people are totally absorbed in what they do. I think that might be the connecting theme, even though there are all kinds of different styles.

125

# Princeton Interviews

## Princeton Interview I

*Two Princeton interviews are presented in this section. Both were conducted in the graduate student lounge in April of 2002. The first is with one first-year student and two fifth-year students.*

**You all filled out the questionnaire. What did you think about it?**

*Sylvia*   I thought it was interesting; some of the questions were dated, but that was interesting in its own right. I think I was the only person who knew what Marxist economics was. I remember struggling with the question "If I had it to do over again, would I?" I answered I wasn't sure, but I leaned toward no.

*Jeff*   I answered yes; I would definitely do it over.

**Do you feel most of your fellow students would say, "Yes, they'd do it over again"?**

*Jeff*   My peer group would, but probably only half of my class would.

**Why wouldn't you do it again?**

*Sylvia*   Even though I came in with a good knowledge of what to expect, I did not recognize that the costs would be as severe as they were. It's not only the difficulty of the work; it's the isolation. I'm very happy I've gotten these tools, and I have a chance of eventually influencing public policy. But the cost has been so great that I think that I could have done just as well with a different degree.

**What would you have done instead?**

*Sylvia*   That's hard to know. Perhaps law school or a public policy degree. Although you certainly don't get the same skills; if you get a good public policy degree, you get some other skills that you don't get in economics.

**In the program do you think the push has been toward public policy or toward theory?**

*Mario*   Definitely toward theory. There is very little talk about policy. In part it has to do with what you specialize in. I suspect that Sylvia has done much more public policy than I have, but that's because she was interested in that. In the first year, there is almost no discussion of policy. I don't think we are meant to be the people who are going on and influence policy. They give us the tools, but it takes an extra effort to do policy.

*Sylvia*   You don't see people who combine the two any more. Maybe Alan Blinder did a good job back in his day, but now you see a real split. After the first year, I've done nothing but applied research on public policy issues.

*Jeff*   The first year is pure theory. I frequently was doing stuff that I had no idea why I should care about it. But the second year, at least with the classes I've taken—public finance, labor, and econometrics—the applied stuff dominates; there's almost too little theory.

**How do the first-year courses tie into the second-year courses? Are the tools used in the first year relevant for the second year?**

*Jeff*   I would still be hard pressed to tell what any of the tools I learned in macro were for. But in micro and econometrics, by the second year, things I tried to do before I came here started to make more sense. I was able to construct the models better, and I was able to apply the tools.

*Mario*   I found that too.

*Sylvia*   I was originally going to say that it was orthogonal. But when I reflect on it, there were some tools, but there were also problems. For example, at Princeton we don't learn price theory in the first year, or get introduced to the models we use in the field courses. In applied courses we do a lot with price theory, and I was frustrated that that's not part of the core anymore.

**What is the core here?**

*Sylvia*  It's micro, macro, and econometrics of course, but micro isn't price theory. We spend a lot of time talking about preferences and game theory. Then there's a segment of general equilibrium theory and a segment on information theory.

*Mario*  I think that that is idiosyncratic to us. The way it is supposed to be is tastes and technology in the first quarter, then game theory, general equilibrium, and then informational theory. The teachers we had put a lot of emphasis on the foundations, how do you translate preferences into utility functions, rather than working with particular utility functions. For people going on into micro theory, that's helpful, but for the majority, it is problematic.

**Is the focus of the program on theoretical issues, or on applied policy?**

*Jeff*  I get the impression that there isn't a stronger emphasis on one of the two, but that relative to other universities they might be more separated.

**How did you choose Princeton?**

*Mario*  Because I didn't get into MIT. I realized that the criteria that I was using to judge schools had nothing to do with the correct criteria. I looked at the faculty and the money they were giving me. Princeton gave me less money than some other schools, but when I averaged the two I chose Princeton.

*Jeff*  I chose Princeton because when I came to visit, the people I met seemed more interested in economics rather than just getting ahead in the world. They weren't bitter like some of the people at Chicago.

**What do you mean bitter, and whom do you mean—students or faculty?**

*Jeff*  I mean students; the faculty thought it was great. The students who weren't bitter seemed very cutthroat. By "bitter" I mean that they weren't happy to be alive.

*Mario* I don't think that's the case here. Well, maybe in the first year, but in general I don't think the climate is cutthroat.

*Sylvia* I agree; I'm ready to go; don't get me wrong. As to why I came here, my undergraduate advisor had come to Princeton. I did get into MIT, but I had better information about this place. I knew there was an excellent labor group, and that the faculty outnumbers the students. So I knew I'd get a lot of attention—sometime more attention than I want.

**Did you have good information about what graduate school would be like before you came in?**

*Mario* I didn't even know that graduate school existed when I was in college. I thought that it was great that Gregory Chow was here, but once I got here, I realized that he isn't the type of guy who is going to have any influence on any graduate student's life. This should have been obvious to me. But it wasn't.

*Sylvia* I had read your book and I had also heard a lot from my adviser and other alums. Everyone had said, it's horrible; it's worse than you can imagine. And I couldn't imagine it. I was surprised by the level of emotional torture that I experienced in the first year; it was worse than anything I expected. I remember one of my advisors telling me that it took her five years to get over the damage done to her in grad school. There are just not words to express it.

**Is there another way to do it?**

*Mario* I agree with what Sylvia said. For me it was actually the reverse. My first year was probably my best year here, just because I learned so much. It is also clear that I had done a masters before, so I definitely had an advantage. I did work very hard and it was stressful. But I found a nice social environment in the study groups that we formed.

*Jeff* I started getting interested in graduate school very early in my undergraduate career, so I talked to a lot of professors, and I had done some work for some graduate students. So I had a pretty good idea of what I was getting into. It was still painful.

**Is the pain worth it? I gather Jeff and Mario would say yes, and Sylvia would say no.**

*Sylvia* I would say maybe, probably.

129

*Mario*   There is another type of pain that develops. I didn't agree with Sylvia about her statement about the first year. It is other stuff that makes it tough.

*Sylvia*   Do you think that that's because I'm in an area where I'm constantly interacting with my advisors?

*Mario*   That's part of it, but another part is that we just have different comparative advantages. My comparative advantage, given my history, was in taking exams. Sylvia's comparative advantage was in being an economist. So I guess we switched. In the first year, you were miserable; now I am miserable. I'm just not very good at doing the type of thing you need to do to get research done.

**Do you have much contact with students in other disciplines—sociology or political science? Is the first year different in those fields than in economics?**

*Jeff*   In my first year I lived in graduate housing, so I had a little bit of contact. I got the impression that the math graduate students were under no stress. It could be that they are geniuses too. I knew a poly sci guy, and I believe their stress is a bit less, but it is the same type of thing.

**Do graduate students talk a lot about policy issues?**

*Sylvia*   Yeah, we talk about it almost all the time.

**I understand that Alan Blinder put a question on the generals one time asking what GDP was, and other such issues, and that the students got really upset because they didn't know any of it.**

*Jeff*   I would have to admit that my knowledge of basic macroeconomics is very poor. I was able to learn math, and set up an equation of something I didn't understand. So that I could pass the exams, but I don't really have a good feeling for the foundations of macro. That may be more specific to me than it is to others. But occasionally in our "spare" time (that's in quotes for the tape recorder) we do talk about policy issues.

*Sylvia*   Particularly since Paul Krugman is here now and everyone reads his column. That gives us something to talk about.

*Jeff*   About how Republicans are terrible.

*(laughter)*

*Sylvia*  At least at Princeton, the people who are interested in policy are the micro types.

*Mario*  I agree; I don't think that macro types talk much about policy at all. Personally, I'm interested in politics.

**You have Alan Blinder here, and Ben Bernanke here.**[1] Both follow politics and economic policy rather carefully. Do such approaches get integrated into your courses?

*Jeff*  Not in your first-year courses. Policy does get integrated into your second-year courses like public finance. Two-thirds of public finance was almost pure public policy. And there's a lot of that in labor too.

*Mario*  I guess it very much depends on what you mean by "policy." Here policy is synonymous with micro people. Policy might mean what one teaches in Ec 101 [the principles course at Princeton], and that's not what people here mean by policy. If someone were to ask me, if we increased the interest rate by twenty-five basis points, what effect it would have, I wouldn't know.

**What would be the best background for going into graduate school?**

*Jeff*  Lots of math.

*Sylvia*  A double major in math and economics.

*Mario*  I agree with that somewhat. I took a look at the courses that they offer here in math at the undergraduate level and I wouldn't have taken any. One of the things I was thinking I could do when I came here was to take some math courses, but I didn't find any that would be particularly useful for what I needed to do.

**Could someone who knew little economics, but was a superb mathematician, do extremely well in the program?**

*All (in unison)*  Yes.

*Jeff*  I think there's a lot of stuff—such as micro theory—that is more math than economics.

*Sylvia*  Before I came I worked in policy, so I got a broad sense of what economists can do in the real world. And that's when I figured out that I
wanted to be a labor economist. I had minored in math as an undergrad.
I wish I had taken a few more courses; but I think the grounding in the
real world would be helpful for someone who is going to have to struggle
through the math.

**There's been a greater focus on rational expectation in the past twenty years.
What is your view on rational expectations?**

*Mario*  I am a big fan of rational expectations.

*Jeff*  I don't know if I have a view. It was something that I learned; I don't
follow one side or another.

*Sylvia*  That's something they talk about in macro?

**How would you describe the economic method to somebody?**

*Mario*  Oh goodness. I think that for me it is just trying to be careful about
what you do.

**How would you differentiate economics from philosophy or some other field?**

*Mario*  Yes and no. I mean to the extent that when I studied philosophy, every
philosopher was trying to dispute what the previous philosopher had
done. To that extent I think economics is different from philosophy. In
economics we start from the assumption that there is a set of phenomena
out there that we can explain logically with a model. You try to be careful
about what the agents in our model do, and what their objectives are.
  I can compare myself to a sociologist, which I know a little bit about
because I am planning to marry one. I think that the big difference
between economists and sociologists is that sociologists give a lot of
emphasis to being comprehensive in their description of the phenomena. They say the world is very complicated; therefore our theories need
to be complicated and bring in a lot of these things that we see. You
can't abstract from anything. The economists are the other side of the
spectrum. They are very willing to make abstractions, abstractions that
often come back and hurt them. It keeps them from even trying to explain some phenomena because they think they are too complicated.
  Sociologists often end up being extremely ineffective because it is
not clear what their assumptions are. So when they come to different
conclusions it is difficult to reconcile them. Because economists start

from common ground, it is easier to reconcile conclusions, or see why they differ.

*Sylvia*   If someone were asking me what the economic method was, I would also emphasize that we try to make simple straightforward assumptions, and predict what behavior would be in response to different incentives.

*Jeff*   It involves an empirical component.

*Mario*   In my field, there is much more emphasis on building up the theory and having objects that you can talk about and understand. Unfortunately, we often forget about whether it actually works in the real world.

*Sylvia*   I was thinking more about what it meant to be rational from the perspective of a micro person. Actually, in micro we do have a fair amount of discussion of when people appear to behave irrationally. They teach Kahneman and Tversky's work. One of the professors in the labor section said that what we are trying to do is work the invisible handshake in with the invisible hand. Orley Ashenfelter refers to that stuff as wackonomics. But I think people are trying to take seriously some of the psychological assumptions, and build into the models the fact that people don't always behave like our models suggest. We want to make the irrational rational.

*Mario*   I think people still start from the assumption that it is rational in some sense. It's just that they have to find the sense in which it is rational. It's the new behavioralist approach. You still have people who maximize something, but it is more complicated than simple rationality.

**The core of economics is sometimes referred to as greed, rationality, and equilibrium. You've said that rationality has been modified somewhat. How about greed and equilibrium? For example, when a person is sharing something he or she might not take full strategic advantage of the situation.**

*Sylvia*   I was thinking about our first year when our professor had us play the gift giving game. The right equilibrium was to split the amount 50–50, but we kept screwing up time after time. We couldn't get that equilibrium because up to that point we had been so interested in maximizing our own framework. A lot of the research I am doing now looks at whether women are more generous toward children than men are.

**How about equilibrium?**

*Mario*   I think in macro it is very important. Actually in a book I'm reading now, there is a footnote explaining equilibrium in a sticky price model. The author said that some people might think that this is disequilibrium because prices are not adjusting continuously, and that in a certain sense the market is not in equilibrium. But he sees it as in equilibrium because the first order conditions are satisfied. I don't think I've ever come across a paper here that talks about disequilibrium behavior. But if you are a labor economist who is interested in running a regression to tease out some relationship, I'm not sure you think a lot about what an equilibrium is. It is a much more theoretical concept.

*Jeff*   You always have it in the back of your mind: Is there going to be a general equilibrium?

**If you were describing the profession today, what different approaches would you describe?**

*Jeff*   The more recent stuff seems a lot more specialized than the older stuff. The older stuff seemed to know a lot more about this great thing called economics. Now people build careers on one question.

*Sylvia*   Well, there's reduced form versus structuralist. Although in our minds there's only one approach there. (*laughter*) I've been told that if you went to my next institution where they are much more structuralist, that there's a steep learning curve. It's a whole other world that I didn't know much about.

**Can you be more precise by what you mean by "structuralist" and "reduced form"?**

*Sylvia*   By "structuralist" I mean modeling things in a manner that the underlying structure is clear. By "reduced form" I mean just running a regression without having a clearly specified model. You search around for natural experiments. The criticism of the reduced form approach is that you have a black box, and it isn't clear what one has found.

*Mario*   In macro I would say that 90 percent of macro economists agree on a general approach. A small group, that I associate with Minnesota rather than Chicago, has a different sense of what doing macro is. For them it means a lot of theory. They are not very much interested in policy questions. I think that they see themselves as being separate from the rest of the profession, and doing the right thing. But I don't think that there is a freshwater/saltwater division any more.

**So you would say that Princeton falls into the same type approach that is used by most schools—Chicago and Minnesota excepted.**

*Sylvia*   Penn would also be an outlier.

*Mario*   The differences are not that great. We hired someone from Chicago last year. There would be little difference between Princeton and the Cambridge schools.

**Would you say that there is any specific political orientation here?**

*Sylvia*   It's certainly not apolitical. I think we have a lot of Democrats in the department, and there are a few Republicans. But we would lean toward liberal. That is, liberal for economists, not liberal for academia.

**What do you mean—liberal for economists?**

*Sylvia*   I think everyone here basically believes in the economic method. We had a prominent conservative on campus the other day, and there wasn't that much fighting. The fighting comes in terms of the political implications of your research. I do a little bit of work with an interdisciplinary group on campus and the economists are generally the most conservative people in the room.

*Mario*   I totally agree.

**How many hours a week do you generally work?**

*Jeff*   In the first year we work all the time. Well maybe 70 or 80 hours a week. In the second year I worked less until about February; then we had our papers, so I worked more. I'm hoping to get to the third year. (*laughter*)

*Sylvia*   That's about right. In the third year, I put in 50 or 60 hours a week.

*Mario*   In the third year I was also teaching. I definitely didn't do less work as far as my research was involved.

**If someone came and said that he or she would like to go teach at a good liberal arts school, how do you think the faculty would respond?**

(*laughter*)

**Why are you laughing?**

*Mario*  Because I know Sylvia has a very good story.

*Sylvia*  It depends on what your gender is.

*Mario*  I definitely know one person—a male—who was told to forget about it. He was a good teacher; he liked teaching, and he was pushed away from that by the placement direction. And there was a female who wasn't interested in going to a liberal arts college, and they suggested it for her.

**Was this difference an example of different attitudes toward women and men, or was it for other reasons.**

*Sylvia*  I think it was an outlier, but it was a very unfortunate case. The male took a job at a top school where he will unlikely get tenure, but will make a gazillion dollars. I think it depends on who you are. We've seen plenty of people go to good liberal arts colleges.

**When you first come in, would they see teaching at a liberal arts school as a legitimate goal? Or would they try to discourage you?**

*Sylvia*  I wouldn't tell them that that was your interest until after your letters of recommendations were sent.

**There are not very many women in the program.**

*Sylvia*  There were more a few years ago.

**Would you say they are making an attempt to bring in women?**

*Sylvia*  I think that if you ask them they would say that it is a non-issue.

**What's the biggest failing of Princeton as a graduate economics school?**

*Mario*  Job market placement. We have a top faculty. I think it is the best program nowadays. Harvard and MIT get better students than us, but there is a greater disparity between placements than there is in who comes. So there is something, and I think that that something is after your

generals. The program at that point is not very effective. It is very different across areas. Some sections are much better than others.

**Is it fair to say that Princeton is actually four or five different schools?**

*All (in unison)* Yes.

*Jeff*   Even physically, it is different. Each section is in a different place.

*Mario*   My feeling is that the best students in the first year often lose themselves.
There's too little direction for many. I don't think this happens in other
schools.

**So you are suggesting that the skills you need for the first two years are quite
different than the skills you need in the later years?**

*Mario*   That's true, but there is a basic set of skills and interests—being quick,
and I think that the program is supposed to build on those things. My
impression is that it isn't doing a great job at that. How much do you
think an economist is value added, and how much is pure talent?

*Sylvia*   I think it's mostly value added.

*Mario*   Otherwise it doesn't explain why people spend so many resources training economists. If that's the case, then I'm not sure the program is adding as much as it should. If you had asked me ex ante but after the exams,
who do you think the good economists are going to be, I would have
had a good idea of who the good economists were going to be, and they
would not necessarily be the ones who did best on the exams. And it's
kind of weird that they did turn out to be those. That means that in the
years that we spent here the department didn't add much.

*Sylvia*   So you're saying that the rankings you made were almost completely
orthogonal to how people did on the exams.

*Mario*   It was completely clear then that other than passing, doing well in the
first year did not make a big difference.

*Sylvia*   I would be tempted to say that one of Princeton's biggest failings is that
we're not well-rounded economists. Everything I learned about GDP, I

learned before I came here. I think I learned nothing of practical value in macro in the first year.

*Mario*   Had you taught Ec 101 you could answer that; I taught 101 for three semesters so I know that stuff.

**If you had some advice for someone coming into graduate school, what would it be?**

*Mario*   My advice would be not to think about exams. I actually told this to the first-year students when they came. You must think from the very beginning that you're here to become an economist and you're here to do research. If you have an extra hour, should you spend it learning a little bit more for the exam, or should you spend it thinking what you want to do? I would suggest thinking about what you want to do—to make sense of what you are doing. It's important to pass the exams. It helps to get decent grades, but it is much, much overvalued.

*Jeff*   I don't think I have anything significant to add to that.

*Sylvia*   I would say know why you are coming in, and what you want to do with it.

## Princeton Interview II

*The second Princeton Interview is with three fourth- and fifth-year students and, like the first, was conducted in April of 2002 in the graduate student lounge at Princeton.*

**Any comments on the questionnaire?**

*Steve*   It was familiar from your book.

*Ellen*   I never read the book and I hardly remember the questionnaire.

*(laughter)*

**Was graduate school what you expected?**

*Ellen*   It wasn't really a shock. Maybe the math was a bit higher level than I thought it would be. I thought I was good at math before I came here, and then I discovered that I was wrong; I now recognize that I am at best competent at math on a good day. But other than that, it was just a lot of material. It was the fire hose method—wherein information is poured in with a fire hose, and there is just a small hole that lets it into the brain. So it is learning at a maximal rate.

*Lucy*   Having read your earlier book, I expected to be miserable and I was miserable. But I knew what to expect.

*Steve*   I think I was pretty prepared for the same reason. I knew the first year would be the hardest. But a lot of people were totally overwhelmed.

**How would you describe your pre-generals course work?**

*Ellen*   The core classes are micro, macro, and econometrics. I'd say that the micro especially is very theoretical. We use a lot of real analysis. Actually, all of it is very theoretical. We don't get to applied stuff until the second year. For me the first year was pretty much math. I didn't do a lot of economics my first year. I had to rediscover economics in my second year.

*Steve*   Actually the department is currently discussing revamping the graduate program because the first-year program is very theoretical, which some people really like, but which empirical people don't like too much. It's actually kind of pivotal. Some of the theoretical micro professors are brilliant, but there is a question of balance between theory and applications.

**How about macro? Are the same issues relevant there?**

*Lucy*   The macro problem sets were as intense, or more intense. The same issues apply—if you can do the formulas, you can do the problem sets.

*Ellen*   It was the same for me; the macro courses were hard and not much use. I think a lot of the applied faculty and students feel that way too.

*Steve*   One thing that has made me feel better is that it sounds as if the faculty have the same debates over the program as do the students. In macro, there is also a feeling that the applied work doesn't fit with the theoretical work. Even some of the macro students don't like the theoretical focus because it doesn't fit in with their later, more applied work.

**Are many people focused on macro?**

*Steve*   Not a lot of them.

**We have three U.S. students and no foreign students here. Is that representative of the class?**

*All* (*in unison*) No.

*Steve*   Our class was about half and half, but more generally, about a quarter of the students are U.S. students.

**If you were advising someone to come to graduate school in economics, what would you tell them to do as an undergrad?**

*Ellen*   Real analysis.

*Steve*   I second that.

**Would you do it again?**

*Ellen*   I would go to graduate school again; I don't think that I would like the idea. Maybe I would choose my undergraduate courses a bit differently.

*Steve*   I worked for a few years in finance before coming. I did this as a career change, because I want to have an academic career. People ask, would I go back to Wall Street, and that would be just ridiculous. Graduate school is to give you academic training to be an academic economist. It gives you somewhat the training you need, but also the union card needed to get a job as an economist. I feel terrible for people who go on to consulting or Wall Street jobs. The Ph.D. economics program is not the training they need. A masters program would make much more sense.

**When you came in was it clear who was going to be on the fast track?**

*Ellen*   I wouldn't say it was very clear, although I attempted to avoid my classmates. I was never in the loop of who did well.

*Lucy*   I'd say the first-year performance was entirely clear. Most of the foreign students had had a course using Mas Collel. Even if it was not as high a level, having been through it before meant that they did well in the problem sets. But that changed. The superstars now are not the ones who necessarily did well in their first-year classes.

*Steve*  When we came in our first year it was all about grades. Then once you pass generals, it's all about getting a good job market paper; then it's all about your research. So if you are doing a theory area, there is probably a correlation, but if you are doing applied work, there is little correlation. A lot of professors told us, "Look, you've got to pass the generals, but don't worry much about how well you do." We didn't believe them, but they were right.

*Lucy*  That's right. The empirical people weren't too worried about theory.

**How would you distinguish an applied person from a theoretical person?**

*Ellen*  If you work with data.

**You mean theoreticians don't work with data?**

*Ellen*  They work with data to show how to apply their model that they created in their head. I wouldn't expect any nonparametrics in a theory person, for example. An applied person would ask, "What does the data tell us?" I guess the difference is your starting point.

*Steve*  I kind of object to the definition of applied as empirical, although I admit it is widely used. I'm very applied; I'm not theoretical, but I don't have any empirical part for the dissertation yet. There can be applied theory that is not empirical. You're taking general theory and applying it.

**Is what you are saying is that "applied" can mean taking theory and using it to design an institution or an optimal contract?**

*Ellen*  That's not what I mean as applied. I guess if you were to design a contract or an auction, that would be applied.

**What's the difference between an economist's and a sociologist's methodology?**

*Ellen*  The distinction between an economist and a sociologist is that we believe a utility function exists that people maximize; sociologists would fundamentally disagree with that.

**Do you believe that there is a utility function that people maximize?**

*Ellen*  Well yeah, I mean I've heard it said that the lifetime income hypothesis is good at predicting the consumption of economists, and not of anyone else.

*Lucy*  When I took my first undergraduate economics course, I was turned off by the whole idea, but now it really makes a lot of sense.

*Steve*  I don't believe that I've got a utility function that is anything like we study. I think it is more something that would be described by the new behavioral economics. Using its assumptions, economics is good at providing logical and clear approaches to public policy debates; a lot of other fields are not clear.

**So if you were telling people which social science had the best approach, what would you say?**

*All*  (*in unison*) Economics.

*Ellen*  I would say that economics is the only one of the social sciences that uses statistics; I don't see other social sciences trying to prove the statistical significance of something.

**What do you think of Deirdre McCloskey's challenge of statistical significance tests?**

*Lucy*  I've heard that but I haven't actually read it.

*Ellen*  I don't understand what you are talking about. So what's wrong with statistical significance tests?

*Steve*  The panic sets in.

**Her point is that statistical significance is arbitrary and does not necessarily measure economic significance.**

*Ellen*  Well of course, you want to look at the size of the coefficient too.

*Lucy*  That's obvious.

*Steve*  I think just in general that if you want to think about policy, economics is most useful. Law is being taken over more and more by economics. It's not just the utility functions or the statistics; it's the simple arguments that economics makes that all economists would agree with that are powerful.

**One of the criticisms of economics is that it does not appropriately integrate institutions into the analysis. How would you react to this?**

*Ellen*  How would you define institutions?

**Defined however you want it.**

*Steve*  Economists teach what they know and they primarily know basic things. It is only recently that we're getting more institutions into the theory. I think it's right to criticize economics as an academic discipline.

*Ellen*  I wouldn't say that institutions are absent from what we do. In labor economics people look at what happens to wages and say, "Institute a collective bargaining arrangement." I would call that institutional.

*Lucy*  I agree—especially on empirical work. You really have to integrate institutions into your project.

**Is there an economic approach, or are there many?**

*Lucy*  What do you mean?

**When I did the first study, there would have been a number of approaches that students were familiar with, although they did not necessarily study them. There would have been a radical approach, an Austrian approach, and a Keynesian approach, and a new classical approach in macro.**

*Lucy*  There's just mainstream now.

*Steve*  I went into one of the top macro/monetarist professor's office and asked him about the various approaches in macro. He just didn't understand my question. Macro now is a blend of various approaches. Everyone assumes that you have to take a micro foundations approach as much

as possible. It's acceptable to have certain features that are Keynesian—
sticky prices, but one wants micro foundations for it.

*Ellen*   I guess since the Lucas critique, macro is done with micro foundations. Agents have to be rational, but I wouldn't assign that to a school of thought. People might tweak rationality, but they accept it.

*Steve*   The behavioral work is hot now and some students see the need to do that for the job market.

**Alan Blinder is here. Have many of you had courses with him?**

*Ellen*   Alan Blinder is one of two people who I knew before I came here. I thought that was a big thing; I was impressed by his being here when I was applying.

*Steve*   I find him very interesting. He's great to talk with about what's going on in the world, and he's widely respected, but the students who are doing macro wouldn't want to choose him as their advisor.

**Why wouldn't they want to?**

*Steve*   He's not doing technical current cutting-edge research. The same would be true with Ben Bernanke, who was recently nominated to the Fed Board. Several people have him as an advisor, but he's not doing cutting-edge work.

**So professors become obsolete very quickly in their role as advisors of graduate students in dissertations.**

*Ellen*   In macro that's probably true, or in theory. But I'm in neither.

*Steve*   That's not necessarily true. I'm thinking of someone like Blanchard. He's still relevant at MIT.

**How do you choose a dissertation advisor?**

*Steve*   Most people want a tenured professor because your advisor is central to getting a job. There are some people who are known as being good advisors.

*Ellen*   What I thought about was my advisor's ability to push me on the job market. You want someone who can pick up a phone and call these places and get you an interview.

*Steve*   In empirical there are older professors who make very good advisors.

**What kind of jobs do they direct you to? If someone came in and said, "I'd like to go teach at a liberal arts school."**

*Steve*   I know somebody who said that to the placement director and the placement director said, "No you don't really want to do that. You want to go for a more research-oriented job."

*Lucy*   There was a female student who was pushed the other way. Is that a female/male issue?

*Ellen*   Nobody pushed me to do anything really. I guess my advisors expected that I would go for an academic job. But they didn't put any expectations on me.

*Steve*   I get the idea that if they don't think you are going to do well on the research university front, they will push you to something else. But in terms of the environment of the place, I didn't feel an enormous push toward an academic job. I see people going openly for consulting jobs. But I'm doing finance, and that may be different.

*Lucy*   I think I would hide it.

*Ellen*   I went on one consulting interview and I didn't tell any of my advisors. That sends a bad signal—a signal that you are not interested in doing something serious.

*Lucy*   I mentioned to one of my advisors last year that I might be interested in policy research, which I really am interested in, and she was definitely dismissive. So I think at the beginning they steer you toward an academic job; at the end, that may change.

*Steve*   I don't think any of this is obvious in your first couple of years here. I came here to become an academic, and it seemed like the first couple of years at least half the class was talking about how much money you could make in consulting. At the time I remember wishing we had more

145

of an environment focused on getting an academic degree. I think a few years ago our placements weren't as good as they are now. Back then our faculty wasn't pushing as hard as they are now to do well in the academic job market.

**How many hours a week do you work?**

*Ellen*   All the time. Doing economics is the default activity.

**What do people do if they are married?**

*Ellen*   Take longer. They have no life, too. A couple of the foreign students left their wives back in their country.

**Do you think economists work harder than other graduate students?**

*Ellen*   That's really hard to judge.

*Steve*   I don't think other departments have two years of as solid work as does economics. We definitely work the most hours our first year. Once you're past generals you can decide if you want to have more of a life.

**What's the hardest part of graduate school?**

*Ellen*   I think eventually the long hours start to wear on you. When I was an undergraduate, working to two or three in the morning was no problem. Then as I moved through my twenties, you get tired of being a student.

*Lucy*   I'd say it's the stress, or the emotional trauma. The first-year courses are highly stressful.

*Steve*   We're all U.S. students. I know that there are some foreign students who, even in the first year, spend six or seven nights a week in the pub, so there's definitely a range.

**How about the easiest part of graduate school?**

*Ellen*   I have complete control over my own time.

*Steve*   Summers are nice; you can do what you want.

*Lucy*   I'd say everything; we're well taken care of. There's enough money; there's subsidized housing.

**Any final comment for someone thinking of going on in graduate school?**

*Ellen*   One piece of advice that I've given to prospective students is that if they want to gauge how happy grad students are, they should look and see if they are attempting to form a union. At Yale they are trying to form one; here they are not. If you have to form a labor union to get something out of a university, that's not a nice place to be.

*Lucy*   I'd say two things. First, don't come as a default. Make sure that economics is what you want to do, because it is miserable.

**Do you mean miserable the entire time?**

*Ellen*   The first year is miserable. In the second year you can choose the courses you want to take.

*Lucy*   But unless you really love economic research, you're never going to be happy enough to put up with what you have to. A second piece of advice is not to be afraid to ask for help. I was hesitant to ask for help. I thought I had to have really polished work before I could show it to a professor. Now I realize that they just want to help us as much as possible.

*Steve*   I agree with that. The other thing I'd advise is to take real analysis.

*Lucy*   And take as many graduate-level courses as possible.

147

CHAPTER SEVEN

# Stanford Interview

*The interview was conducted on a Saturday afternoon at Stanford University Economics Lounge in July 2004. Three students were present, a third year, a fourth year, and a fifth year.*

**Could each of you tell me how you came to Stanford?**

*Adam*   I was interested in graduate school since my sophomore year in college. I considered doing graduate work in political science or economics, but decided on economics. I applied to all the best schools; among these, Stanford was one of my first choices because of its strength in Industrialization Organization.

*Greg*   I followed a rather different route. I knew I wanted to go to graduate school for a long time; the only problem was I did physics and math as an undergraduate. Somewhere about my junior year I decided that economics was a lot more fun, so I switched over to doing economics. I applied to a whole bunch of graduate schools; it was pretty much a shot in the dark. A couple of them accepted me, and since Stanford was strong in the theoretical type of stuff that most interested me, it was an easy choice.

*Kurt*   I decided on graduate school shortly after I started taking economics classes. So I took the classes I knew I had to take to get into a graduate economics program.

**How much math is necessary for somebody to take?**

*Adam*   It depends on whether you mean: to get in or to do well?

*Greg*   You could take the math at the same time as you are taking the economics, but that is a lot more painful. Since I already had done math as an undergrad I already had all the math, and more, that I needed, so I am not the best person to ask for this.

*Adam*   I think basic calculus and linear algebra are necessary. You have to know what a matrix is and how to invert it. You also have to know what a density function is. You don't need to know anything really complicated, but you need to know those things comfortably.

**Students at Princeton had one piece of advice for the students coming in: take real analysis. Would you agree with that?**

*Greg*   That's extreme; it certainly won't hurt you. It seems like a good idea, but it depends on what you want to do. I found a lot of the stuff I learned when I took real analysis useful, but I'm interested in theory. If you are planning to do statistics for the rest of your life, it's probably not all that useful.

*Adam*   I think that actual concepts in a real analysis course are necessary, but all that's really necessary is an undergraduate course in real analysis, not a graduate course. Certainly you should know how to find maximum functions; you should know they exist in closed intervals and all that good stuff.

**Can you describe the program here? What's the normal progression for a student?**

*Kurt*   The first year you take the core courses.

*Adam*   You take microeconomics for a year, macroeconomics for a year, and econometrics for a year. You could fit in an elective if you wanted to hurt yourself, but it is not advisable.

*Greg*   I did take an elective.

*Kurt*   I think it would be a better idea if more people did. I took an elective my first year.

*Adam*   I think both your experiences are extreme; that's not normal behavior.

*Greg*   If you come in with a lot of math it'll help; the problem sets become significantly easier because you already know the tools. While it is true that they will teach you all the real analysis you'll need in your first micro course, if you already know it, it makes your first-year micro course a lot easier.

**When do you take comprehensives?**

*Adam*   You take comprehensives in micro, macro, and econometrics at the end of your first year.

**Are they true comprehensives, or are they essentially course exams?**

*Kurt*   They are essentially course exams, written by the faculty teaching the course.

**What percentage of the students passes the comprehensives?**

*Greg*   There are two different types of comprehensives. There's the micro and macro comprehensives that you really should pass the first time through. I would say about 90 percent pass their first time, although it depends on who is teaching the class and what the students are like. Comprehensives are also given in September of the second year, so students who fail the first time around can study through the summer. Almost all students pass by the second time around. If you don't pass it the second time, there is something seriously wrong.

**And then there's the econometrics comprehensive?**

*Adam*   Traditionally econometrics is seen as the hardest exam, although maybe it is less so now. It's the one that's optional in a sense that you can retake it year after year after year. I know of one student who is finishing his sixth year who hasn't passed it yet. It can be the kind of thing that drags on and on forever. Once you've shown that you don't like econometrics, the desire to go take a first-year course with a bunch of people younger than you in the program is pretty low. So it can become a problem.

*Greg*   The people teaching may be different from when they took it, which means that the exam can change. However, it has more content than other courses, so it changes somewhat less.

**Can you tell right at the beginning who the top students are going to be?**

*Adam*  Yes and no. There was one guy who was clearly the top student; he graduated in four years, and was the top student on the market. I'd say that in my class that was pretty much the case, so I'd say yes.

*Kurt*  But there is a difference in screening. It is not necessarily the people who do well in first-year classes who will become the top students. There is a difference in how students do in first-year classes and students who do well after that.

**At other schools students mentioned a fairly big difference between students who do well in the first-year classes and those who could find good dissertation topics.**

*Adam*  In my class that was only true of Asian students. For non-Asian students, I think that is not the case. Smart people generally do well across the board.

*Greg*  I don't actually have much knowledge about what we are going to look like on the job market. It seems pretty constant in my class who's been at the top.

**What do you do in your second and third years?**

*Kurt*  In your second year you take classes in your area; you do your field courses; in your third year you choose a dissertation topic and you attend workshops.

**When are students supposed to choose a dissertation topic?**

*Kurt*  By the end of the third year you should know what your dissertation topic is. It varies a lot from person to person. A lot of people don't get a lot out of their third year.

*Greg*  For me the third year was productive. I hadn't taken much economics coming in, so I used that third year to extend my knowledge of economics. I have one or two things submitted to the journals now.

*Adam*  That's not the norm. I think a lot of students don't complete all their courses in their second year. Maybe in the future they will, because they are moving to a two-year fellowship structure for entering students so incoming students won't have to TA in their second year. But traditionally if you're "TAing" or "RAing" it's hard to complete all of your courses in your second year. So a lot of people will postpone some field courses until their third year. This is especially the case for people who are switching around and don't know exactly what field they are interested in.

**How long do students normally take to complete their degree?**

*Kurt*   Five years, maybe six, tends to be about the median for people who are going academic.

**What do you mean by "going academic"?**

*Adam*   There's a tail of people who just sort of hang around and do other things, rather than follow the academic path. They might do applied work or work for consulting firms. For them the dissertation often doesn't matter.

**In terms of micro and macro would you say there is a particular slant that students get at Stanford that might be different at other schools?**

*Kurt*   I have no idea. I don't know how they do it at other schools.

*Greg*   I have no other macro experience. They didn't teach macro at my undergraduate school.

*Adam*   I think the macro guys here don't like Keynesians. I've heard some nasty talk about Keynesians.

*Greg*   There was a great line at the skit party that the students put on each year. It referred to the fact that all the macro economists at Stanford had left all at once. They did a skit about how they were going to teach macro. This one student said that he would teach macro in nine words: "Keynes is dead, dynamic programming, Keynes is still dead."

**How about rational expectations? How much does that show up?**

*Adam*   It's hard to compare; dynamic programming imposes rational implications, it's everywhere.

**Do you have much relationship with students at other graduate schools, and how would you see Stanford relative to them?**

152

*Greg*  I can't name another economics graduate student who is not at Stanford.

*Adam*  I can name a couple I met recently. I met one at Harvard and she seemed to me very different, but I can't quantify what that difference is. I think it is fair to say that we don't have a good sense of the other graduate schools.

**Where would you see Stanford ranking in relation to the other top graduate schools?**

*Kurt*  It really varies by field. IO here is pretty good; macro has gone up and down.

**On the questionnaire, it was quite interesting that there was lower interest in macro here than at any other school. At Stanford 15 percent thought macro was very important compared to an average of 33 percent.**

*Greg*  At some schools such as Cal Tech the percentage would be 0 percent.

**No, the schools in my study are Chicago, Princeton, Harvard, Yale, MIT, Columbia, and Stanford. Cal Tech is definitely off on its own. There was also very little interest in money and banking here at Stanford.**

*Adam*  Yeah, I don't think anybody does that. That term won't ever be used. What is money and banking? I would say that there's definitely a tracking. International students would probably do international development or something, and most U.S. students here do IO or micro theory.

**What's the percentage of international students compared to U.S. students?**

*Kurt*  It varies by year. It's probably about 50–50. It depends on who does admissions. If the person cares about things such as undergraduate senior thesis, they give more weight to dimensions where U.S. students are stronger.

**Would you say your views are representative of the Stanford student body, and if they are not representative, how might they differ?**

*Adam*  I'd say we are a little less disgruntled than the average student. There are a lot of students who aren't doing well in the program; they're more critical about any number of things.

153

**What would some of the disgruntlement be?**

*Kurt*   I think a lot of people just lose their way; here, once you lose your way, nobody goes and finds you.

*Adam*   I heard that at MIT they have a faculty meeting every year where they go around and read each student's name off and then somebody has to explain who that student is. Here I don't think there is any such procedure.

*Kurt*   You can just get TA jobs and hang around for ten years or so.

*Adam*   There is no cutoff for financial aid either, so you certainly hang around for a long time. There are examples of students who have completed their fifth year and have not completed their second-year paper yet.

*Kurt*   All the Stanford facilities are great; it's tough to leave; it's like a country club where they pay you.

**What would you say makes a successful economist?**

*(long silence)*

*Greg*   Define "success."

**If you were to say, "Here is an economist who is really doing great work." What would you describe that great work as being?**

*(long silence)*

**Let's try a slightly different question. Can you describe success in terms of how the person does, for example, whether they get published, or whether they get a job at a top school, or is there some other way to define success?**

*Greg*   It's trite, but, for me, a successful economist would be someone who solves a problem or who explains some interesting economic phenomenon. If someone could explain the equity premium puzzle, that would be a really cool economist. Someone who tells us something we didn't already know.

*Adam*   I don't have a good way of answering that question. You can come at the question from so many different ways. I was reading the *NYT* article on Steve Levitt recently. It seemed that his strategy for success is very different from other people's. But I can't say that he's a bad economist or a good economist. I think he does do good work and that people recognize that.

**Will good work be recognized or do you need to have the right contacts, and a willingness to operate within the existing mode of doing things? Is Levitt an outlier or a normal example?**

*Adam*   I think that you really have to sell your work. You can't sit in your office and talk to yourself, and expect people to read your work. I think that a lot of people get into a shyness trap; students will not approach a faculty member with their ideas. The same trap exists for faculty members; if you just don't go to conferences and interact so that people know who you are, who is going to care about your work?

**How unified do you see the economics profession?**

*Kurt*   I have no idea.

*Adam*   I think it's pretty unified, at least compared to other disciplines I've read about. I hear the anthropology department has split in two, with one group called anthropological scientists and another group called cultural anthropologists. I don't see any movement to do that in economics.

*Greg*   I have a slightly different view. When you look at physicists, you see much more unity of ideas. True, they argue about ideas, but you don't have the equivalent of a Keynesian physicist. You might see someone who does superstring theory; you don't, however, see someone identified by which particular superstring theory they work on. In economics, that's not the case; you have Keynesian macroeconomists and rational expectations macro economists, and many more strains.

*Kurt*   Are there still Keynesians?

*Greg*   Well there are Neo-Keynesians, how's that? Okay. But I mean occasionally you see these labels attached based on which theory people ascribe to, whereas I've never seen that in physics or chemistry.

155

**What would Keynesian economics be? How would you define "Keynesian" or would you? You don't think it exists?**

*Kurt*   Where I went for undergrad we never did the whole IMSL model, or whatever it is.

*Greg*   It's IS/LM.

*Kurt*   I remember reading the GRE economics book and seeing this once. (*laughter*) But that was three years ago and I haven't seen it since.

**So you never saw IS/LM?**

*Adam*   That's a really confusing model.

*Kurt*   We teach this to the undergraduates here.

*Adam*   You do?

*Kurt*   Yeah, I remember a friend of mine was complaining about having to learn it.

*Adam*   I think that Keynesians exist, or at least economists who would be called Keynesians; people like Brad Delong, exist. But I don't work in that field, so I don't recognize the fine points of what they're working on, and what the differences in views are on some fundamental level.

**So, none of you are macroeconomists?**

*All* (*in unison*) No.

**Now how about micro? Are there different styles or types of micro, or is there only one micro?**

*Greg*   There certainly are different types. There are people who study different facets, but not to the degree that exists in macro.

*Kurt*   Labor is somewhat fractured.

*Adam*  Yeah, maybe theory's not so bad, but there is certainly an internal feud going on in labor. We're associated with a particular style of labor economics here, which is different from the style practiced at, say, Princeton or Berkeley.

**How about behavioral micro versus full rationality micro? Do you consider behaviorial to be a whole different approach to micro, or is it just part of a much broader approach?**

*Greg*  I don't think we know yet, it's too young.

*Kurt*  I don't know; I spent a lot of time with the marketing guys, so I see it more as just another way of looking at it.

**If the students were coming here, what suggestions would you have for them?**

*Greg*  Have a car. (*laughter*)

*Adam*  Take it easy, don't stress out over stuff.

**Sometimes the economics profession is called "Neoclassical." How would you describe the economics you do?**

*Kurt*  I don't know what the labels for what we do are.

*Adam*  I don't know any other types of economics; I didn't do those as an undergrad.

*Kurt*  I remember our first year here. One of our professors here said, "I'm not here to teach you; I'm here to brainwash you." And that's been pretty much successful.

(*laughter*)

**Do you have any history of economic thought?**

*Kurt*  You mean like Heilbron [Heilbroner] or something like that? That's about it.

*Adam*  Did you read that in undergrad or grad?

157

*Kurt*   Undergrad.

**If you were asked about Alfred Marshall, would you have any sense of his economics, or is he just some old economist that existed?**

*Kurt*   Is he the guy in the econ murder mysteries? The Marshall Jevons mysteries? That's about all I know of Marshall.

*Adam*   He wrote a book, but I never read the book.

**Have any of you ever heard of the Cambridge Capital controversy?**

*Adam*   Was that a *JEP* article? If it was, I didn't read the article. There was a survey of it earlier in some other journal.

**In the survey, in answer to the question, "Was neoclassical economics relevant for today?" Stanford thought it was less relevant than some of the other schools. Would that be consistent with your view? Any explanation for it?**

*Greg*   It would probably just be that the people didn't know what neoclassical economics was.

*Adam*   Yeah, they felt I don't know what this is, so it can't be very relevant.


*(laughter)*

**Another question on the survey was, "What's the difference between normative and positive economics?"**

*Greg*   I always get the two terms confused. Normative is like trying to figure out the welfare implications; positive is trying to figure out what's going to happen. Right?

*Kurt*   One concerns the way the world is and the other concerns the way the world should be.

*Adam*   Yeah.

**The answers at Stanford indicated that very few students thought that you could draw a sharp line between the two. Would that be any information or just a reflection that the students haven't thought much about positive and normative economics?**

*Greg*  At least from my perception that sort of makes sense because if you are doing theory you write down a model, and the first thing you want to know is what happens and then you want to know how to tweak it so to make it better. It seems a very natural next question.

**So you're a micro theorist.**

*Greg*  Yes.

**How do you test your theory?**

*Greg*  I don't. That's someone else's job. (*laughter*) Was that an erasable answer?

**How about you?**

*Adam*  I'm empirical.

**Do you see your job as testing his theories or other theories that theorists develop? Or do you see your job as somewhat different?**

*Adam*  Testing theories might be too strong a term. What I'm certainly trying to do is present evidence that would inform theory. I don't see much of a difference between normative and positive either. Most of the work I'm doing is what one would consider policy relevant. Sometimes maybe positive and normative work should be distinguished, but it's not often done.

**So you're not testing theories in the sense of trying to refute a theory? Instead you're trying to shed light on theory and provide information about how the theory relates to the real world? Would that be a better description?**

*Adam*  Right.

*Kurt*  Right, and figure out what is going on.

In the survey, Stanford had the most students who said that math was very stressful. It also had the most students who said that math wasn't stressful at all. So there seems to be a fairly big division.

*Kurt*  I think that goes back to the admission.

*Greg*  In my class there are a number of math majors, and there's lots of people who did minors in math; they wouldn't find it stressful. Others probably would.

*Kurt*  Even within a year I think there's always a group of people who have no math skills. They get here for the math camp in the fall, and that is hardly enough to prepare them.

**And so that's probably an example of differing admissions committees bringing in two different types of students.**

*Greg*  Yeah, or even the same admission committee bringing in two different types of students. They may believe that some people are really good economists, and they believe that their math skills will come up to spec. Others, they believe have these great skills, and hopefully they can do something with them.

*Kurt*  Would you say that the chances of success are much higher for people with decent math skills coming in?

*Adam*  We should exclude the Asian cohort.

*Kurt*  Yeah, if you just look at the non-Asian population, then I think that the people who came in with better math skills tend to do better.

*Adam*  Yeah, I think that's definitely true.

*Kurt*  Many more of those who came in with weaker math skills either went away at the end of the first year or faded away.

**Compared to other schools Stanford had a very high percentage of respondents who said that being good at problem solving was very important. Any take on that?**

*Kurt*  Problem set solving?

No, this was just problem solving. Something that might be described as the Levitt-type approach. Here's a conundrum that I don't quite understand, can I come up with a reasonable explanation? Not a real theoretical one but a reasonable one that can empirically shed some light on the issue. Would you say that's the type economics they're trying to teach you here? Or are they trying to teach you lots of different approaches, so it depends on which professor you happen to get?


*(silence)*


**What are they trying to teach you here?**


*Greg*  Well, it's definitely professor-dependent.


**So there's no Stanford school?**


*Adam*  I don't know if we are qualified to judge, because we don't know the graduate students at Princeton, Stanford, MIT, and Harvard.


*Greg*  There is certainly nobody here who would speak against theory. There is certainly nobody here who would say theory's useless, or not say, "Let's write down a model on our paper." Even people who are not doing technical work seem to highly value at least simple theory. Maybe not the type of work that I'm doing.


*Adam*  But it is really simple theory.


**Any other observations on the questionnaire? It's been quite a while since you filled it out.**


*Adam*  There were some funny questions on there relating to stuff that was a bigger deal earlier.


*Kurt*  Like Marxian economics.


**Is there a Marxian economist here at Stanford, or was Marx ever mentioned in any of your courses?**


*Adam*  I remember that there was a guy at Stanford who wanted to study Marxian economics. This guy's like sixty-two now, but he studied econometrics. I guess there used to be a Marxian economist here.


161

There were big fights here about such issues in the 1960s and 1970s—one side was pushing for a slot in alternative economics.

*Kurt*   I think that side definitely lost

**How about Joan Robinson? Do you ever hear of her?**

*Greg*   Who?

*Adam*   I read her book, but I'm very rare. I remember reading her work on monopsony, but I think she had some other work that was more controversial.

**How about any dissident economists? Do you discuss any of them today in any of your courses? Have you ever heard of post-Keynesian work?**

*(silence)*

**Well, since you've never heard of Keynesian, it's not surprising that you haven't heard of post-Keynesian.**

*(laughter)*

*Adam*   I think it is fair to say that that dissident work is not a popular style of work here.

**When students come to Stanford, what do students normally get in terms of a financial aid package?**

*Adam*   For 2003–04 the standard package will be $28,000.00 plus tuition, from what I understand. Earlier, in the second year you had to TA, but that is no longer the case. This is a reflection of competition. Other schools have been offering this for a long period of time. I think it's a positive move; it's hard having to TA while you are taking all these second-year courses.

**Tell me about the acceptance process. Once you are accepted at Stanford, do they invite you for a visit?**

*Adam*  If you are accepted, you get an invitation to come in, say, early April, typically when it's cold everywhere else. You go to a Mexican restaurant or something, and then during the day you go meet with faculty members or attend a seminar. Then you go to a dinner. It's pretty much a social event where they give you some feel for what people do here.

*Kurt*  They try to keep you away from the first-year students.

*(laughter)*

*Greg*  Well, the problem is that it's right after they took their econometrics comps, and it's probably the low point of their entire career here.

**So there's a first year bitterness? When does that go away, or does it not go away?**

*Greg*  It's just the stress of taking the econometric comp; that's the only real issue.

**So by the summer, students feel good?**

*Greg*  Yeah, especially if they passed.

*(laughter)*

*Kurt*  If they passed; but if they don't they often eventually go away.

*Greg*  Or eventually pass.

**Is it a theoretical econometrics comp? Or is it more applied?**

*Adam*  It's pure theory.

*Greg*  Well, it's not all pure theory; there is usually one question that asks you to look at all these regressions and say what you can actually say from them.

*Adam*  But even then, the questions are theoretical.

163

*Greg*   Where do you draw the line between theory and empirics? I agree though; it's mostly theory.

**Would it cover much nonparametric econometrics, or is it all asymptotic theory?**

*Adam*   It's all asymptotic theory.

**Do you cover any Bayesian econometrics?**

*Adam*   No, we learn no Bayesian econometrics. There are some problem sets during the year that discuss small samples, but not much. You pretty much can't do anything with it using a pen and paper that you could teach a first-year grad student. Econometrics is clearly the hardest class.

*Greg*   Even with my math background I still found the econometric problem sets and exam a lot more annoying than micro or macro.

**How about the problem sets?**

*Kurt*   They don't count. The only thing that counts for your first-year grades is your score on the comprehensive exams.

*Greg*   In any case, your first-year grades don't really count when you're going on the job market.

*Kurt*   They do count for impressing faculty or whatever. The only thing that matters is your grade on the comps. I really took advantage of that by slacking off on problem sets. Most people, however, work pretty hard on them.

*Greg*   There's two reasons why. One is that problem sets are a fairly decent way of learning the material. The second is that you can sometimes impress a faculty member if that's the course he's teaching.

# MIT Interviews

## MIT Interview I

*Two MIT interviews are presented in this chapter. This interview is with one second-year and two third-year students. It was conducted in an economics office at MIT in October 2004.*

**At MIT what do most students study?**

*Ken*   Most do applied micro, but there is a second peak in macro theory. The students who take macro tend to be international students.

**Would you consider yourself a representative sample on various dimensions?**

*Ken*   We are probably representative in terms of fields. Politics doesn't really enter into many discussions. While people have views, it's not clear that their political views affect their views in economics.

*Bryce*   There doesn't seem to be much political sorting here.

**Is there sorting on other grounds?**

*Ken*   There is probably sorting of international vs. U.S. students. The department is split 50 percent-50 percent, while the groups tend to stay together.

*Larry*   Part of the reason for that is that they come with different histories; the Americans have often worked in policy. That's less the case with international students.

**Is there any distinction between men and women?**

*Bryce*  The men tend to be more inclined toward theory; the women more toward applied work.

*Larry*  Controlling for the international/U.S. distinction, that would probably not be that strong a pattern. The women in the graduate department at the moment happen to be U.S. citizens.

**How did you decide to come to graduate school at MIT?**

*Ken*  I did well in undergraduate work, and felt I wanted to go into academia, which allowed more independent thinking than the private sector. I chose economics because I was interested in policy, but I wanted a field that emphasized mathematics. I was originally planning to go to Berkeley or Stanford, but I chose MIT because they push students through faster. They also bombarded me with placement statistics, which in retrospect I'm not sure were all that relevant.

*Larry*  I came to MIT to do a math Ph.D. and my interests changed. I talked to the program here, and given that Peter Diamond had done the same thing, it was an accepted change.

*Bryce*  I studied physics in college, but decided that economic questions were more important to me than the questions they were asking in physics. I taught high school economics and decided that teaching was what I loved doing.

**In terms of math, were you prepared?**

*All*  (*in unison*) Yes.

**Did the math preparations make a big difference in the first-year courses, and what math did you use? For example, did you use much real analysis?**

*Ken*  I'm the only one who did not do a math-oriented undergraduate, so I will try to answer that question. It didn't seem that the math was all that difficult. In college everyone had said that it's really helpful to have taken real analysis, and maybe it is, but it didn't show up much. The math is more for the pattern of thinking, not the specific use of math.

*Bryce*  I think it's important to be familiar with the method of deductive proof that is used, but the actual theorems are not particularly relevant.

**How does the MIT program differ from other top programs?**

*Larry*   We're not all that familiar with the other programs. The department likes to think of itself as student-oriented, and I think that is true to some extent.

*Bryce*   Here, one gets the idea that the professors are here for the graduate students, whereas the sense I get is that that is less the case at other schools.

**There is a belief at other schools that they prepare students here to write a job market paper. Would that be correct?**

*Bryce*   I think the goal is to produce a substantial and important contribution to the field of economics.

*Ken*   That's my objective, so maybe we don't realize it.

**Would a paper that you do for research differ from a job market paper?**

*Bryce*   What you want is a paper with a great instrument that answers an interesting question.

**What do you mean by a "great instrument"?**

*Bryce*   That you can defend that the appropriate restrictions hold and that it is not correlated with the error term—that it is almost as good as randomly assigned.

**Can you tell me about the normal progression here?**

*Ken*   In the first year you take your core courses—micro, macro, and econometrics—and one field course.

*Larry*   That's something that they try to sell the program with—that you get to do a field course in the first year.

*Ken*   The sense I got is that the first-year courses are things you are supposed to get done with, so you can move on to field courses.

*Bryce*   I'd agree with that.

*Larry*   In the second year you take field courses, plus a few remaining core requirements. Then you take general exams, which have a high pass rate, although not 100 percent. People take these exams seriously, but it is not quite clear why they do rationally.

**Do the same teachers grade the generals who gave the course?**

*Ken*   The general exams are in your field. We don't have comprehensive exams.

**How about financially?**

*Ken*   Most students have fellowships in their early years, either university or external. In later years, many students have TAs. Some have RAs, but in general you can't support yourself with an RA.

**Can you summarize the micro you learned here?**

*Bryce*   I waived the intro micro courses by passing qualifying exams.

*Ken*   Our micro sequence is divided into four subcourses, each with a different professor. The first subcourse is consumer and producer theory, although we get some applied issues here since the professor who teaches it talks about cases he has worked on. The second subcourse is game theory; general equilibrium is the third subcourse, and the fourth covered contract and information theory.

**How about macro? What did you learn in macro, and was it representative of the state of the profession?**

*Larry*   Macro also has four subcourses. There are growth theory, business cycles in the traditional MIT style, consumption, and rigidities and imperfections.

**I didn't hear much about real business cycles.**

*Larry*   It shows up as a comparison, but there is not much on it.

**What do you think of the dynamic stochastic general equilibrium model?**

*Larry*  We certainly look at them, and the younger people on the faculty are very much into them, so there is an age-divide in the faculty about this approach. It depends on whom you work with. I do that stuff, but there is a divide depending on whom you work with.

*Ken*  The perspective of the micro people who take the macro sequence is, I suspect, somewhat different from the macro people. The general perspective of the micro students is that it is pretty worthless. We don't see why we have to do it, because we don't see what is taught as a plausible description of the economy. It's not that macroeconomic questions are inherently uninteresting; it just that the models presented in the courses are not up to the job of explaining what is happening. There's just a lot of math, and we can't see the purpose of it.

*Bryce*  It's not only micro people who believe that.

*Larry*  There is definitely a divide in the opinions. I think people here are quite open-minded about whether macro models are good descriptions of things. Maybe that's not the impression you get in a course where you have to learn about them, but the department is not didactic about which model is right.

**How about views on monetary and fiscal policy?**

*Bryce*  Monetary and fiscal policy are not abstract enough to be a question that would be answered in a macro course.

**On the questionnaire, MIT was the most likely to see fiscal policy as effective. Any comment?**

*Ken*  I think that in the macro course we never talked about monetary or fiscal policy, although it might have been slipped in as a variable in one particular model, but that wasn't the focus, so it didn't come from the courses.

*Bryce*  My guess as to why that would have come out is that there are a lot of people here interested in doing applied policy work, often in public finance where one considers incentive effects of policy. People who study that are inclined to believe that government policy is actually relevant to the world.

*Ken*  I can believe that the faculty here may believe that more than the faculty at other places, but they never really state it in the courses.

**MIT also came out least likely to say that inflation was a monetary phenomenon. Any explanation?**

*Larry*   I think it has to be a selection issue—that that view is correlated with other things. It certainly doesn't come from the courses.

*Bryce*   It might also be the lack of emphasis of that here. We don't actually get taught views on policy, whereas they might be taught that elsewhere.

**MIT came out least likely to say that rationality assumptions are important.**

*Larry*   I think that that result is much more integrated into the curriculum. There is a lot of behavioral work being done here.

*Ken*   I don't think the MIT view is that rationality is not important; it is simply that it is not valid.

**Would you see the views that you are learning here to be representative of the profession's views?**

*Bryce*   One of the reasons I decided to come to MIT is that I felt that there was less of an emphasis on a school aspect. I might be misguided, but I felt that if I came here I would be exposed to all the research that was on the cutting edge, and not be told what to think about it.

*Larry*   Although we do lots of theory here, there is less being wedded to a theory for its own sake, and more emphasis on the internal consistency of a theory and applicability. It is such nuances of differences where MIT may differ from most schools.

*Ken*   Within labor there is a MIT/Harvard/Berkeley approach, and a Stanford/Chicago approach. If you want to do something more like what is done in Stanford, they won't prevent you from doing it, but no one really does it here.

**Do economists test theories meaningfully?**

*Bryce*   I think so—yes.

*Larry*   At their best they do.

*Ken* I'd have to say no. I remember from my undergraduate days, when we used Peter Kennedy's book. It has a statement to the effect that no meaningful theory of economic behavior has ever been rejected on the basis of a formal statistical test, and I think to a large extent that is true. Maybe my different view is because I do more empirical work than the others.

Theorists come up with something, and say that the rational model underlies some behavior, and then the empiricists come along and say, well, it's failing these tests, and the theorists respond that there is something wrong with the tests. Frequently there is, and it is very hard to conduct a convincing test in the social science setting.

I'm not saying that they are dismissing evidence that they shouldn't be dismissing, but at the same time we have to recognize that we are not really testing if we are not willing to reject the theory on the basis of the empirical tests available.

*Bryce* I would regard that as indeed testing. Even if you do not come to the conclusion that it was convincing evidence, the act of going out there and unsuccessfully testing it is still the act of testing. If you are unwilling to change your mind, then you are not testing, but I would say that most economists are willing to change their mind; it's just that it would take a large amount of evidence to convince them.

*Larry* Obviously there are some things that are easier to test than others; the core assumptions are very hard to disprove.

**Do you read anything by Hayek, Robinson, Keynes, or Marx here?**

*Larry* No. Some are represented in secondary versions, but we read nothing in the original sources.

**How about literature?**

*Ken* No, we read almost no literature in the field.

*Larry* The point of the second-year exams is that you are meant to read your way through a lot of the literature. But the reality is that people know what is going to be in these exams, and there is a certain temptation to work toward them. It's such a big field that you can't survey everything, but I think there is an effort to do it.

*Bryce* I think the public finance sequence does a pretty good job of giving us a wide exposure to various topics. The first day of the course, we were introduced to Musgrave's topology of the field.

171

*Larry*   That said, you don't spend a lot of time reading things written before 1995.

*Bryce*   In public finance, we go back to the 1970s.

*Ken*   Let me restate my answer, because I wasn't quite sure what you meant by "literature." Certainly, there is, in our course, a very long list of articles that are on our syllabus. In theory you could read them, but in practice you don't have time to read most of them. I guess the reason I said "no" was that there was no sequence or progression in which we were connecting all these topics.

**Can you tell who the stars will be right at the beginning?**

*Bryce*   The answer might well be, yes—but we're wrong.

**Last time we labeled the MIT interviews "Ambivalence and Security." Would you say that is still a good title?**

*Larry*   Security?

**By "security" we meant that there was a sense conveyed in the interview that MIT is about the best. By ambivalence we meant ambivalence about what is right theoretically—that there was not the self-assuredness that they were right that, say, Chicago had.**

*Larry*   I think that's probably still true.

*Ken*   I wouldn't disagree with it.

*Bryce*   I don't like the word "ambivalence." I prefer "open-mindedness."

*Larry*   We're ambivalent about the word "ambivalence"—meta ambivalence.

*(laughter)*

**What would you describe as the economic method?**

*Larry*   I don't think that there is one economic method. The way theorists do economics is very different from the way an empirical economist would do economics. A theorist looks for stylized facts rather than the real details and then tries to write models that try to explain them.

*Ken*   An empirical economist looks for a question that is interesting, and then thinks of empirical tests that we can do to answer it.

**How would that differ from a sociologist's approach?**

*Ken*   Probably in the use of models. We wouldn't start off thinking here's a model, but at some point we will decide that there is a model with which we should frame the question. Sociologists don't do that. I also think that our empirical methods are somewhat more robust and sophisticated than are sociologists'.

*Bryce*   Economics is more focused on the importance of getting causality out of the tests.

*Larry*   Some of the most interesting debates I've had with people concern what are economic models and what they are for.

**What type of jobs are you looking forward to?**

*All*   Academic.

**If you said you wanted to go teach at a liberal arts school, would that be frowned upon?**

*All*   Yes.

*Bryce*   It already has been. When I came, I was told that, since I come from a high school teaching background, I might be thinking of teaching at a liberal arts college. He said to give that up at least for my time here. Here I should consider myself a researcher, not as a teacher.

**How about if you said you wanted to work in public policy?**

*Larry*   I think that would not be discouraged; the faculty moves in and out of Washington occasionally. It depends on the field; theorists don't go into public policy, and public policy wouldn't want them.

**Any regrets? Would you do it over?**

*All*  No regrets, and yes.


**Any suggestions for anyone applying for economics programs?**


*Larry*  I think that unless you are very sure about what you want to do, it is important to be in a very broad department that offers many styles. That's something that this department does very well.


**Any relationship with the business school here?**


*Ken*  Surprisingly little. There is some overlap, especially with the Ph.D. students in the business school, who take core courses with us, but overall we are in the humanities and social science department and that is where we belong.


## MIT Interview II

*This interview is with four fourth- and fifth-year MIT students. They are all U.S. students. It was conducted in an economics office at MIT in October 2004.*


**Would you consider yourselves a representative sample?**


*Judy*  Definitely not; there aren't any international students or theorists; also macroeconomists are not adequately represented.


*Nate*  And I'm not a typical macroeconomist. There are very few Americans who do macro.


**Any reason for that?**


*Barb*  Macro sucks.


*Judy*  A lot of Americans are interested in the U.S. economy.


**Isn't macro about the U.S. economy?**


*Adam*  There is a general feeling that the technical requirements of macro are greater, and that it is removed from actual policy.

*Barb*   Public finance and labor tend to be very focused on the U.S., so you have U.S. students there, and international students in macro. In development there's a good mix.

**What's the percentage of U.S./foreign students?**

*Barb*   50–50. It would appear to be a strict quota system, as that seems to be the case every year.

**The response rate in the questionnaire had a much higher percentage of U.S. students. Any reason why?**

*Barb*   I suspect that one reason is that many more Americans were probably familiar with your first book. I've also heard that Americans are remarkably likely to answer surveys; we are unsuspicious. My advisors told me to read your book and if, after reading it, I still wanted to go, that I would be a good candidate to go.

*Judy*   Reading the book made me just not want to go to Yale; everyone seemed so sarcastic there.

**MIT had more women than any other top school. Any explanation?**

*Judy*   I heard that they try to get a critical mass so that a woman in the program will not feel like she is the only one.

**Do they succeed?**

*Barb*   It can still be the case that often you're the only woman in the room.

*Judy*   Some of the younger women feel that they take too many women, and they wish they were the only woman in the program.

*Barb*   That was a joke. We have a women's lunch here, which the men complain about.

*Adam*   Do they really complain?

*Barb*   Some say, "I'm the only (fill in the blank); shouldn't I get a lunch?"

*Judy*  They seem pretty happy with the leftovers.

**Is there a split between women and men, or between international and U.S. students?**

*Nate*  I think there's definitely a split in fields. There is also a social split in the first year.

*Judy*  In my cohort, I was in a group of twelve women and one guy, and then I broke off and went with this married group, instead, because it was better for my schedule. That group was all men except me.

*Barb*  My first study group was three U.S. women and one guy.

*Nate*  My study group was all U.S. men.

*Adam*  We were three to four Americans, two foreigners, and both men and women.

**Can you discuss your decision to come to graduate school in economics and to MIT in particular?**

*Adam*  I had taken the first two years of graduate theory as an undergraduate, and I thought I wanted to do it. But then I got sick of it; I went to work. Then I decided that I wanted to do work in development, and it made sense to get a Ph.D. MIT seemed the best program for my desires. Some of my friends were coming here.

**Have you lost your disaffection with theory?**

*Adam*  I still don't have a lot of faith in the usefulness of equilibrium models; I see some role for theory, but I don't want to do it.

*Nate*  I did economics as an undergrad after trying out a lot of other majors, and I knew I wanted to teach at a college level, so graduate school seemed a reasonable thing to do. I chose economics because I like applied policy and math; I originally started out as a math major. I didn't know anything about MIT when I applied, but I saw it ranked at the top, so when I got in, I came.

*Barb*  I went to a policy school, and I wanted to do policy research. I decided to do a Ph.D., and the general consensus was that economists are the most influential, so I chose economics. I did think about whether it would be miserable, and I fully expected that it would be much more miserable than getting a sociologist degree or some similar degree, but since I had the math background—I was a math major in college—I figured it was the appropriate path for me. I chose MIT because they had a reputation for treating their graduate students well, which, now that I'm here, makes me concerned about how they are treated at other places.

*Judy*  I didn't know what to do with my life in my junior and senior year in college. I thought about what I liked, and I liked math and psychology and history, and I realized that I could do all those things with an economics degree.

My second major was economics; my first major was math. All my economics professors told me that I had to do all kinds of math, but the reality was that I think that I was over-prepared in math and under-prepared in economics.

**How about the others? What did you think about your preparation in math?**

*Adam*  I came over-prepared in real analysis, and under-prepared in dynamic programming.

*Judy*  All of my professors told me that you had to take real analysis, because they had graduated in the eighties. I haven't used it ever.

*Barb*  I'm really proficient at a lot of math that I have never used here. But I did not know how to do the math that they wanted us to do here. I faked my way through a lot of the math part of the courses in classes that I didn't care about anyway.

**How do you fake your way through the math?**

*Barb*  You do it, but not really understand it. In the core classes, if you have a good intuitive understanding, you can get by. I learned the math for the things that I cared about.

*Judy*  If you are missing any math, they teach it to you. I got so sick of statistics, because I had it so many times.

**One of the major differences between this survey and the last is that the anxiety about math is much less now than it was. What would your explanation of that finding be?**

*Judy* I think it is a combination. I think that the reason is that MIT will only take students from small liberal arts colleges if they have a math major or minor, or possibly physics, so the selection is better. But the other reason is that there isn't a whole lot of math here. You can be an empirical researcher here and not do any math.

*Barb* That's one negative view that some people have about MIT—that they can't do the math.

*Judy* In macro there is a lot of dynamic programming, but I see that as useless; no offense.

*Nate* No offense taken; I agree. I think a lot of what they do in macro is in the wrong direction—huge models with little or no intuition and forty or fifty pages of math. That's where a lot of the young macro people are going; you can see it happening here.

*Judy* It seems like philosophy.

**What do they teach you here in macro?**

*Nate* They're starting to teach that dynamic programming macro here.

*Barb* Yeah; I suspect you'd need more math in macro now than we needed.

**Can you tell me about the program here at MIT? How does it differ from other programs?**

*Judy* No orals.

*Adam* My view of MIT is that in the first year they cut as much of the bullshit as they can out of the program, and get you through. You don't have comprehensive exams; you don't have orals. You can start working with professors early.

*Judy* Different people have different experiences. I felt that no one paid any attention to me.

*Barb* Those are choices you made; you could have emailed a professor and asked to work with him, and he would have responded positively.

*Nate*   I had a really good experience with professors helping me.

*Judy*   My cohort was really large; it was in the mid-thirties—and they normally shoot for twenty-five, so that made it harder to interact personally with professors. There are a couple of professors here who really care about students; if they are on sabbatical, it's not as good for the students. We didn't get the "early research" talk until the second year.

**What's that?**

*Judy*   In that talk they tell you about the research minor, and they tell you to graduate in four years.

*Barb*   They also tell you not to worry too much about generals—that people spend way too much time studying for generals, when they should be thinking about what they want to do research on. They deemphasize course work and emphasize research.

**At other schools there is a sense that MIT has students focus on preparing their job paper.**

*Judy*   I think that's true; for a typical dissertation we have to have one really really good paper, which is our job market paper, one solid paper; and one throwaway paper.

**What would a throwaway paper be?**

*Judy*   Something that you do in the last six months so you can graduate. Or something that you've written with a professor.

**Could it be history of thought?**

*Judy*   No, although maybe, if you worked with a Harvard professor on it; I don't think anyone has done that. Almost no one does anything in history here.

*(Here a general discussion about other schools occurred, with Barb asking what else one would have done in the past five years, and others discussing alternatives and different programs.)*

**So a job market paper differs from a research paper?**

179

*Barb*   That's probably true; I've had plenty of people say to me that that's a great paper, but it's not right for the job market, because it doesn't sell the important aspects of you, or that it seems too much like an MIT paper.

**What's an MIT paper?**

*Barb*   In labor, an MIT paper is an instrument paper that is just differences and differences, with no economics. This is something I am just learning, because I am making sure that my paper has enough economics in it.

*Judy*   I have this paper that was a labor market experiment, and I was told by some professors that that is a great paper, but it is not a good job market paper because it doesn't show what I can do econometrically. They said that I either have to have a second paper that is a really solid econometric paper, or I need to have something else as my job market paper, depending on what schools I am aiming for.

*Barb*   The best paper is one that generates a buzz.

**How about macro?**

*Nate*   My advisor told me that the paper I'm working on now is not really a macro paper, so I may not be the person to ask that to. A macro paper today is a dynamic stochastic general equilibrium paper or growth model. My paper will be more marketable as a development paper.

**How would you summarize the economics you've learned here?**

*Nate*   The main areas that we learn here in macro are economic growth, dynamic general equilibrium work, consumption theory, and old school macro such as credit market imperfections and frictions.

**Any discussion of Keynes?**

*(laughter)*

*Nate*   A little bit, but not much.

*Barb*   Our macro class began with a statement "All that stuff you learned in undergraduate school—it's incorrect."

180

**What is your view of econometrics?**

*Adam*   I think that the econometric theory we learned is probably very similar to what is taught elsewhere. We go through all the standard models and the theory gets very advanced, even in the required classes. There is no Bayesian taught, and only a little nonparametric work. But these courses are not especially helpful to applied researchers. For the most part, the people who do applied research learn their econometrics on the job.

*Barb*   The econometrics courses don't teach us what to do if you are faced with the type of problems that come up. It is simply the theory. You get the practical econometrics in the field courses, lunches, and from meeting with professors.

**So, would you agree that Ed Leamer's distinction between the theoretical econometrics done on the top floor and the practice done in the basement?**

*Judy*   None of us has heard of Leamer, but it sounds like an apt description.

*Nate*   In private conversation, there will be some interaction between theory and practice, but it is definitely not in the classroom.

*Barb*   There are a number of professors who will give you a lot of suggestions of alternative techniques to use.

**How about your views on monetary and fiscal policy? I ask this because MIT's views were an outlier from the other schools in the survey.**

*Nate*   I'd agree that fiscal policy is effective, although with a delay, and that inflation is not a monetary phenomenon.

**What would you say about inflation? What's the theory of inflation that you have? What causes inflation?**

*Nate*   Not much; it's bad. As to what causes it, expectations can cause it; too much money being printed can cause it.

*Barb*   These are all opinions that we had coming in. We've never talked about either of these issues in our classes.

**Did you see any IS/LM in macro?**

*Judy*   When I did the undergraduate intermediate class.

*Barb*   But the intro macro section on business cycles teaches glorified IS/LM analysis.

*Judy*   Which is actually the first time I learned it.

**Would you say that economists test theories?**

*All*   Yes.

*Nate*   But theorists don't test theories; they leave it for someone else to do.

*Judy*   One of our professors complains that public finance doesn't do enough theoretical work; we do too much playing with an econometric model and grinding through until it works, whereas others think that we should have a background model. One professor who just came here from the University of Chicago is complaining about that.

*Barb*   That's what I meant about the earlier comment about having more economics in my job market paper. There is a sentiment here from people that I've talked to that if they want a model, we can give them a model. We sit down and make up a model, and we play with it until it gives us the empirical result that we find, even though you could have just as easily have written down a model that would have given a different result. We've even had seminar speakers say that. "Oh, I worked on a model that predicts it; of course I could have written down a model that predicts the opposite, but why would I do that?" In general you can write down a model that predicts just about anything.

*Judy*   You know which parameters you can change to get the outputs that you want. That's what the theorists in my office do a lot. They know these things.

**If you can do that, what role does theory play?**

*Judy*   I think the best models are the simplest ones.

*Adam*   I think there was a useful theory presented at a recent seminar on corruption. It wasn't obvious which effects you might expect, when you were varying the variables. Writing down the model and computing the outcomes helped structure what you should look for.

**Can you tell who the stars are right at the beginning?**

*Judy*   No, the people who you think are going to be stars sometimes are and sometimes not. One top student in the classes did great initially but didn't have any research ideas and dropped out. Others do well at every level.

**Have you read any older economists, such as Hayek, Robinson, or Keynes?**

*Judy*   No. One of my complaints about the history class is that we don't do any history of economic thought.

*Nate*   There is a political economy class that does some of it.

*Judy*   But the person who teaches it isn't really an economist; he's a sociologist; he's treated very marginally in the department.[1] Nobody takes that class.

**Isn't that self-fulfilling?**

*Nate*   It's a choice; the class is there.

*Barb*   It's self-fulfilling, but it's really self-fulfilling on the part of the professors, because the professors who are going to get you jobs say, "no" you can't take that class; you need to take X class instead. So it's not our choice that we are marginalizing him and therefore not getting the material.

*Nate*   It is our choice, because no one would stop you from taking the class.

*Adam*   If you said, "I want to do my research in that," they'd say, "Okay, I can't advise you and there are only three jobs in the area."

*Judy*   One professor told a male student not to take urban economics the first year, but he didn't tell any of the rest of us that. It was a good class; perfect for the first year.

**Last time we labeled the MIT interviews "Ambivalence and Security." Is that an appropriate title? "Security" meant "comfortable with what we**

are doing." "Ambivalence" referred to theory. There was a sense that it is there, but we don't take it too seriously.

*Judy*   I think we have a healthy dose of reality. There's a real world out there.

*Barb*   As I was saying about the theory lunch. I was told that the best approach is to think of my own reactions and to see if it fits. If I found that it didn't fit, I would ask what is wrong with the theory, not what is wrong with my perception of the world. That may not be the case at a lot of schools.

*Judy*   One former student told me that the best theory papers are the ones that you start out and make a statement that doesn't quite fit for people. Then you go through the theory and explanation, and people go, "Oh, of course, that's the way it has to be." I agree with that.

**What kind of jobs are you looking forward to?**

*Adam*   Academic at a research university.

*Nate*   Academic job; I like liberal arts.

*Barb*   My dream job would be a policy school job.

*Judy*   I don't care as long as I can keep living with my husband.

**Nate, have you told your professors you want to teach at a liberal arts school?**

*Nate*   No.

*Judy*   In labor and public finance, they are supportive of liberal arts.

*Barb*   I don't think they are as supportive of you if they know that that's where you are going.

*Nate*   There is definitely a perception among the graduate students that you're better off not advertising that you're not interested in a research university.

*Barb*   And definitely not advertising that you're not interested in an academic job.

*Judy*   I've heard rumors that if you don't graduate in six years, that they give you a thesis, but make sure that you don't get an academic job.

*Barb*   It is also not wise to advertise that you have a "two-body problem."[2]

**Any regrets?**

*Judy*   I would not do it over.

*Barb*   If you had asked me a year ago, I would probably have said no, but I like research a lot better than I did the courses.

*Judy*   I remember the pain of the first year. I wish I had known not to put so much time into classes. If I had just not gone to any of those econometric classes, I think I would have been a little happier.

*Barb*   I knew that we didn't have to put that much time into them. Everyone thought it was pointless. What made it so difficult to get through was that I did not care.

*Adam*   I'd do it again in a second.

*Nate*   I'd do it again too. I really enjoy it here.

**Any suggestions to anyone applying to economics programs?**

*Barb*   Be prepared for it.

*Judy*   If you went to a liberal arts school, it takes a while to adjust to getting your exams back with just numbers on them with no explanation of where that number comes from or what it means. You have to get used to the lack of feedback.

*Nate*   My suggestion would be to keep perspective on the economics and not the math. Keep the big picture in mind.

*(The men had to leave for a class. After the men left, the women stayed on and discussed the economics graduate school experience from the perspective of women.)*

**What is the difference between the experience of women and men?**

185

*Judy*   I think women are more hesitant to talk to a professor because you think you are wasting their time, and a lot of guys don't feel that. Then, you're not getting any feedback.

**Would that be a liberal arts issue or a women's issue?**

*Judy*   I think it's both. Women are more likely to need external validation, because you don't have a lot of internal validation. Then, there's also a problem that you've got the homework that is written by the TAs, who don't go to lecture; you've got your lecture; and then you've got your exam; and the three things don't relate. If you drew a Venn diagram, the three things would not fit at all. If you do badly on one of those you tend to internalize that, and think that you're stupid, and need therapy or something.

Another thing that I notice is a change when your adviser discovers that you are married. They don't seem to care if the men are married, but they do care if the women students are married. They ask what your husband does. I have the two-body problem, and I know it is a choice that I want to live with my husband, because I care about him more than I care about economics, which isn't necessarily true for a whole lot of people.

When you TA as a woman for a woman, the male students can be awful. When I TAed with a male professor, they gave me more respect. They do this horrible work, and they come up to you sobbing, and if that doesn't work they come up to you angry. The male TAs don't have that problem.

We have a woman's lunch here where we talk about things. The younger women don't seem to be having as many problems as the older cohort did. It may be because there are fewer of them, so they are selected better.

Also, we have this horrible problem. One of the reasons that I left the woman's study group was that we do this thing where someone will say, "Oh I can't get this; I'm so stupid." Instead of saying, "No, that's not true; you're smart," which would be the healthy thing to do, girl #2 says, "No, I'm stupider than you are." It just keeps spiraling downward; we all have these self-esteem problems. There is a certain breaking point, when one needs therapy.

One friend didn't want to go to MIT because she knew another woman with a liberal arts background who she considered very bright but who had dropped out. I failed an exam once because I hyperventilated. I went in and looked at the exam, and it was completely different than the practice exam that I had done. I could have passed it if I had just sat there and gone through it, but I couldn't breathe, so I left.

The guys who leave the program seem to leave because they have outside earning opportunities that they think are greater. Women tend to leave it because of the program.

**Is there something about economics that is anti-woman?**

*Barb*  I've heard that, but I don't think so. You're trained to think as an economist. I think making economics friendlier to women hurts the cause.

**What could be done?**

*Barb*  A lot of the problem with graduate school is that there is not enough information out there. They don't give you advisors. One really nice thing about MIT is that if you say there is a problem, and you give advice on how to fix it, they listen to you. They will even throw some money at you if you need it.

They've put up a web page. They send out emails periodically. For a little while they gave us money to have dinners at the beginning of the year, but they dropped that because of money problems. They also established informational sessions, such as, "How do you write your thesis," which really helps. As a first-year student, it is scary to talk to upperclassman, and to professors. I think information really helps. I think it would also really help if the program paid a bit more attention to people when they first come. With a smaller cohort, that's been happening.

187

# Chicago Interviews

## Chicago Interview I

*Three Chicago interviews are presented in this chapter. The first is with two first-year Chicago students. It was conducted in the Graduate Student Lounge in February 2004. This interview was unscheduled, and the students had not been part of the original study. When they heard, however, that I was coming to interview students, they expressed an interest to be included.*

**Would you consider yourself a representative sample of the first-year students?**

*Emma*   We're a pretty diverse crowd. I'm probably representative of the American students.

*Pria*   In terms of qualification, I'm not representative. I have far less preparation, but I'm also different in the way I think about economics and what I'd like to do with it. But these things have a way of changing and evolving, and so at the end I might think that I am more representative.

**You came in having done a major in both economics and math, and yet you don't feel you have the background. Can you explain that?**

*Pria*   I went to a liberal arts college where they focus a lot on broader issues, and not as much on the technical skills required to do well in economics. I've had math, but it isn't math geared toward economics, and a lot of my undergraduate courses were simply not rigorous enough. They did help me develop an intuition, which I think will pay off in the end, but not in the first year. I think that reflects most liberal arts programs in the United States.

*Emma*  My first major was engineering, so I had a lot of a certain kind of math. Then after doing various things I got a masters in economics in a department that wasn't super technical. That's when I realized that I needed to do a lot of other preparation. I worked for a while and took some other courses in math, such as real analysis, to try to prepare myself. And I still feel a bit under-prepared. I think grad school does that to you.

**At Chicago there was a much higher percentage of foreign student respondents than at other schools. Is that representative of Chicago?**

*Emma*  Yes, definitely.

*Pria*  We have three or four Americans in our class; there may be a few more who are not American citizens, but who do have American degrees. But by and large the majority of the class has South American and European degrees.

**How do the Americans compare to the foreign students?**

*Emma*  It's hard to say. The first year is overwhelmed by what you knew before you came in. I think Americans feel as if the international students all have masters degrees, often where the Chicago style of economics is taught. So initially, foreign students have an advantage. But I've been told from students in more advanced years that after the first year, there is less of a gap.

**What do you mean by "Chicago style of economics"?**

*Emma*  That's a difficult question, and what is meant probably changes over time. Before I came to Chicago I had a very naive view of a salt water/fresh water distinction.[1] In the fresh water schools, the view was that markets work well; the salt water view was that market failures are where all the action is. Since coming here, I don't see that as the distinction. Now the distinction seems more methodological, although in many areas, such as in macro, there has been a merging of the various views under the dynamic stochastic general equilibrium mantle, as opposed to that ad hoc macro that was done before. All schools of macro now accept that we need individual rational foundations. Still, in my masters program we talked about sticky price models and monopolistic competition. It is now second quarter, and I haven't heard either of those concepts mentioned here at Chicago. Even when we talk about permanent income, which we're doing in macro now, you don't get the critical papers that I thought might show up on the reading lists.

189

*Pria*  The one thing I thought about Chicago that has proved to be right that distinguishes it from some other programs is that Chicago economists believe that economics is all-powerful and important, and can be used to analyze almost anything. Part of what we've been seeing in micro is that; they are not focusing as much on the techniques as other programs might. They focus more on the applications of the techniques, especially in the first year. I think that's different than other schools.

**So you are getting applications of the techniques in the first year?**

*Pria*  For micro, yes. Our first-quarter micro is different than anything else, and it appeals to me, although I don't know what others feel about it.

*Emma*  I think it is a great privilege to have someone like Gary Becker teach us. But I think many students would have preferred to have the standard producer and consumer theory before launching into applications, because we don't really know what we are applying to the problems. I think it is a great characteristic of the Chicago program that we do get the perspective that Becker gives us.

*Pria*  I agree; I think the sequence should be changed; it would be better if that were taught in the third quarter. But I think that it is wonderful that it is there for the first year. But I also agree that I did not know enough classical demand theory, as I should.

**What other courses would you take in the first year?**

*Pria*  We have income theory, or macro; theory of price, or micro; and econometrics, which is called quantitative analysis.

**What did you do in macro?**

*Emma*  We did Hamiltonians. It was strictly methodological; the professors posed it that way. Apparently, we use it a lot later in all the other quarters.

**Do you get any context at all in any of the courses?**

*Emma*  I think we do get some context in micro. The nature of the course you take is greatly affected by the instructor. For example, some econometricians here teach Bayesian methods, which can be a problem for those doing classical econometrics.

190

**Chicago is a bit different than the other top schools because they accept a bigger class and fewer graduate. I think about a quarter or a third of the entering class will not make it through. Does that create a lot of tension? Is that a better or worse system than one in which once you're in, you're highly likely to graduate?**

*Pria*   It definitely creates tension. It probably affects the first year more than it should, but eventually it is all right. We are all here knowing that that's the way it works. There's no information asymmetry. Actually, when you get here you realize that it's a little better than people make it out to be. It does not create the brutal competition—the dog-eat-dog atmosphere—that it has sometimes been described as creating.

**Do you do problem sets together?**

*Pria*   Absolutely.

*Emma*   Rather than being divisive, I think it helps people to work together.

**Is it clear right from the beginning, who the stars will be?**

*Pria*   It's really hard to tell in the beginning, because there is such a discrepancy. The learning curve is so much steeper for a lot of people. It is encouraging to see that in the second or third year, there are people with not too much background doing well. It's not precisely based on how much math you have, or whether you have a masters degree coming in. It doesn't quite work like that, which is comforting.

*Emma*   I think that just about every department at Chicago has the same thing at the end of the first year. In the sociology department, though, the core exams cover a body of literature that they feel all students should know. In economics, it's not so much a body of knowledge that they feel you need to know but instead a set of techniques. I think that some students see learning these techniques as "jumping through hoops," which is a little unfortunate. I do think that one of the bad things about the high failure rate is that it fails out some students who in another environment at another school would likely have done very well.

**Would you say that the views you are learning here are representative of the profession?**

*Pria*   I just don't know other views well enough. That said, I think what we are learning at Chicago is representative of a significant portion of the profession, and that's enough for me at this point. I remember something that a professor said when we came here for the orientation. He said, "We don't care what you do in your second or third years here—become a Marxist economist if you want—as long as you learn the things that we are teaching you. You can question them; you can address contradictions; but what we teach you in the first year is what we think that an economist should know." I tend to agree with that. I think the things that they don't teach us are things that we can learn on our own; they are equipping us with the tools to do that. And yes, that's a very politically correct answer.

*(laughter by all)*

*Emma*  I have a more qualified response. I think methodologically we are being trained in work that is being done in the profession; that is certainly representative. When there are opposing models, the opposing models get short shrift here. If they are presented, they are presented derisively. For example, behavioral economics does not get what I would consider a fair presentation here. It's the same with some of the sticky price models. I think it seems a little anti-intellectual not to present views fairly, and not to have a debate. Of course, the presentation we got may be idiosyncratic to our professor.

**How important are rational expectations?**

*Emma*  It is an assumption that we make for analytic simplicity. I don't take it super seriously. I hope that one day we will have a better way of closing models.

*Pria*  I think that it is really important and that it is not important at all.

**You are totally politically correct; you can tell your liberal arts background.**

*Pria*  I think that rational expectations is important for the methodology and for the way you move on. But once you have made the assumption, it's not going to take you far without other solid theory or a model. It's not the end, but the beginning; you need it to move on.

**If you were estimating the politics of the students here, what percentage would you say are conservative, what percentage moderate, and what percentage liberal?**

*Pria*  I don't understand what you mean by "conservative" and "liberal."

192

**I don't understand what I mean either, but if faced with that question on a questionnaire, how do you think students here would respond?**

*Emma*   Chicago has a reputation for being conservative, but that may be more the case with some faculty and the undergraduates. The graduate students are less so.

*Pria*   I would assume that the majority of the students would have checked conservative. I also think that that's a reflection on economics, not necessarily this program.

**For your information, 50 percent at Chicago checked liberal, and 20 percent checked conservative.**

*Pria*   Wow; that's definitely not what I expected.

**Do you think Chicago is changing students in their views, or whether Chicago students self-select?**

*Emma*   I think that there is some degree of self-selection, which makes it more conservative than some of the other programs. Some of the people I've talked to have a libertarian ideology, which can be interpreted as either liberal or conservative. I think libertarians are attracted to Chicago. That's not what attracted me, however.

*Pria*   That is precisely what attracted me, and that's how I would identify myself. I think that if you pick this program for its approach to economics, that the program will reinforce those ideas.

**Have you read Hayek, Robinson, Keynes, or Marx?**

*Emma*   I read Keynes before; I also read Marx and Smith in my previous studies. I've read none of them in the economics department.

*Pria*   I've read Keynes and Marx before, not here. We read none of these here.

**At Harvard, the students said that the methodological difference between a sociologist and an economist is that a sociologist picks an interesting question and tries to answer it as best he or she can. Economists look at the same range of questions but pick one to study for which the tools provide some answer. Would you agree with that?**

193

*Emma*   Yes, but I would amplify that a bit. I would agree that in sociology people are driven by the substance of the question and that economics is more methodologically driven. The thing is, in sociology nobody can agree on methodology, and so the entire approach is a bit disorganized. I think sociology is useful for its ability to generate hypotheses, while economics is useful for its ability to clarify issues and be clear about what assumptions you are making.

**Would you say that economists test theories?**

*Pria*   I would say yes.

*Emma*   Some economists just theorize; other economists test theories.

**Take Steve Levitt. Would you say that he is testing theories or finding interesting relationships using statistical methods?**

*Emma*   He is pretty atheoretical in the sense of having a formal model in mind, but his approach is fundamentally economic in that he often relies on the principle that people respond to incentives.

*Pria*   I agree; it would be the latter.

*Emma*   I would also say that economists do test theories but that they do not acknowledge the joint assumptions that must be made in order to test theories.

**How would you describe the economic method?**

*Emma*   I would say the cost/benefit approach emphasizing the importance of incentives.

**What type of jobs are you looking forward to?**

*Emma*   Just an academic job.

*Pria*   Definitely a non-academic job. That's how I feel at the start of the program; I might change my mind. The job I go into might even have nothing to do with economics.

**Are most of the first-year students happy they are here?**

*Pria*   I'm happy I came. I got into it knowing what to expect. It turned out to be exactly what I expected, only a little more of everything—a little more stress, a little more work.

*Emma*   It's also been a bit more stressful than I thought it would be.

**Any suggestions for students applying to grad school in economics?**

*Pria*   It is obvious that they should take as much math as they possibly can, but students should recognize that just because you are good at math, or able to do math, does not mean that you are going to be happy in a Ph.D. program in economics. You also have to be happy doing the math. Sure I can do it, but is that how I want to do a problem all the time? I think it is hard to find that out before, but how one answers that question is the key factor to whether one will be happy in graduate school. The best way to determine if a graduate program is for you is to take graduate-level economics courses. It is one thing to say that there is a lot of math; it's another thing to know that everything you will be doing is colored by that. Recognize, however, that this view is from a liberal arts person.

*Emma*   The math is a minimum requirement. I would say that the one thing students should keep in mind is that students in the program feel that they have to lose a sense of themselves when they are in a graduate program, especially in the first year. This means that you have to find parts of what you are doing rewarding, or you will get totally demoralized.

**What would you change in the structure of the first-year program at Chicago?**

*Pria*   I think that there is a certain lack of structure in the first-year program at Chicago. What they taught us in the first quarter does not tie in with what they teach in the second quarter. For example, in micro we are learning applications before we are being taught a grounding in theory. That, however, may just be a first-year problem.

*Emma*   One thing that I think is idiosyncratic at Chicago is that what we are taught is very specific to the interests of the professor. It is up to us to get the foundations. In other programs it is probably better.

**From my interviews, I would say that the belief that what is taught is specific to the professor is pretty common among graduate students. Moving**

195

**on to a different topic, how connected are the students with the faculty here?**

*Pria*  While theoretically we are told that we can talk to any faculty member about any concerns we have, in practice, I really do think that I could break my leg, stay in my apartment for a week, and no one would know/ care/or even be aware that it had happened. They wouldn't even ask me why I didn't show up. There is no organized structure to check on students, even just to say "How are you doing?"

*Emma*  I would agree. I think it is a characteristic of this department. In other departments in the university you are given an advisor; here you are not. Some older students have said that they don't bother getting to know you in the first year because they are not sure that you are going to be around. Students do feel neglected here.

*Pria*  Before I applied, I didn't know how graduate programs go out to recruit students. The faculty were so caring after I was accepted but before I chose to come here. Three separate professors called me, really taking an interest in my coursework and my statement of purpose. This led me to believe that there would be some sort of interaction in the first year. There wasn't. It's just very ironic. Maybe it will change again if we survive to the second year, but I'm not betting on it.

It is important, however, to keep the broader picture in mind; we're pretty happy here. I think that as a class we are pretty satisfied. After we got over the initial shock, we were generally happy. The first half of the first quarter was brutal, but then you figure out your strategy for surviving. I don't think anyone has dropped out.

I think that Chicago loses some good potential economists because of its core exam structure. There are a number of people who would be great economists who freeze up on the exams, and that is a loss to economics. I think economics in general has a loss because the field doesn't attract really intelligent-thinking generalists. It attracts technical people, not generalists.

**What about the position of women in the program?**

*Pria*  When you look around economics, it is clear that there are not many women, and this is something that disturbs me. A disproportionate number of students who fail to make it to the second and third year are women, and it is not because women are less mathematically capable of passing the program.

**What percentage of the class is women?**

*Pria*  In our class I think there are five women out of twenty-five; that's probably typical. I think the number of women here is more than in other
programs. There is only one tenured faculty member who is a woman.

**Have you heard anything about feminist economics?**

*Pria*  I read some stuff in college, but nothing here. I don't take it very seriously.

*Emma*  It is not something that I would pursue. Many of us here would like to
think that we are not ideologically driven, but we kind of are.

**What do you mean ideologically driven?**

*(silence, as I wait for an answer)*

*Pria*  How would you define it, Emma?

*(laughter)*

*Emma*  I guess what I mean is that we are driven by social and political goals
that economics does not address directly, and that the methodology of
economics does not deal with. For example, libertarianism is an ideological justification for a certain type of economics.

**Any final comments?**

*Emma*  Just one. I think that the Chicago program has changed since the last
time you did your study. I think the program is more open now than it
was.

# Chicago Interview II

*The second Chicago interview is with a second-year foreign students and
two third-year students. The interview was conducted in the Graduate
Student Lounge at the University of Chicago in February 2004.*

**How would you describe the Chicago program?**

*Nino*  I think that this program has some really good features. It brings you to
the frontier. The professors are very interesting. Before coming here, I

197

never studied anything that was beyond the 1970s. Coming here was a huge change. There is an enormous amount of stress in the first year; they don't manage to get the best out of each student. It is an incentive system that works well with most of the students, because they get good results, but probably they lose some individual students. Still, it's a good program.

*John* I think it is a great program too. The University of Chicago is really special and has so many resources. The faculty is excellent; the classmates are great. All the resources and other departments are all strong. The way I see Chicago is as a buffet table—everything is there for you; it's up to you to use them; it depends on how hungry you are for knowledge.

*Shaikh* Previously when I studied in England, the emphasis was on learning a broad range of arguments and learning to synthesize those arguments, and see where they go. Here in Chicago, what we learn is a way of analyzing something, and digging deeper along analytical lines. It's more a case of giving me the fundamental machinery to study various economic problems in a relatively narrow mode. There is not as much emphasis on reading alternative views. In summary, it is narrower and more structured analytical tools that we learn here compared to broad synthesis elsewhere.

**Would you consider yourself a representative sample of the Chicago students, and if not how would you differ?**

*Nino* In the sense that I care a lot about economics, yes, I am representative. On other issues I'm not. Most of my fellow students want to become professors. I see that as one of my possible objectives, but what drove me into economics was the idea of doing policy. I see economics more as a type of medical science for society, and in this respect, my views are quite different. When I talk to my fellow students, they want to be professors.

*John* I'm not sure I'm typical. There is a lot of diversity here. I consider myself liberal, and there are other liberals, but there are also conservatives and libertarians. What makes me most different is that I'm American. There aren't that many Americans in the program.

*Shaikh* I don't think that there is a unique generic student. But I differ from many students in my background. Most students come into this program having a masters or some sort of postgraduate degrees in economics. I think the Americans and those studying in England are the only ones having only an undergraduate degree in economics. Most students from Latin America and Southeast Asia seemed to have racked up a few degrees before coming into the program.

*John*   The fact that it is so international diffuses a lot of the political issues that are usually associated with Chicago. "Conservative" and "liberal" are construed differently in different countries.

**One of the questions on the questionnaire was whether you would consider yourself liberal, conservative, or moderate? What do you think the answer to that question was?**

*Nino*   I think 60 percent liberals, 20 percent are conservative, and 20 percent are moderate.

*John*   I'd say moderate 50 percent and the rest split between liberal and conservative. You have to be careful, because "liberal" can mean different things to different people.

*Shaikh*   I'd consider many more conservative.

**Was the core a useful experience?**

*Nino*   You learn a lot, a lot—a lot. They put enormous pressure on you. You're pretty sure that many of your fellow graduate students won't be there the next year. So sometimes you get so stressed that you don't appreciate things that you do like. However, without the pressure I never would have been able to learn that much in only one year.

*John*   It is definitely a hurdle that you have to get past. It's hard; it's tough. In the end it seems that the faculty wants you to pass, and I felt that I was supported the whole way. I didn't feel like I was being attacked. Well, maybe in the fall quarter I did. It took me some time to get settled in.

*Shaikh*   In terms of stress, it wasn't significantly different than it was in my undergraduate degree. Degrees in England differ from degrees in the United States because the entire assessment comes at the end. The material was challenging, but the difficulty of the material was well within reach.

*John*   I think the tests during the year were much harder than the actual core. Maybe that means I was prepared for the core.

199

**Is what you learn at Chicago the same as what they learn at other schools?**

*Nino*  Chicago has its views, and they teach you their view, but I think it is like other places. Maybe here they have a more coherent view.

**What is that view?**

*Nino*  There are some facts that you cannot go against. When a professor here writes a paper, of course he has his view of the result he wants to get, and then he designs a model to get this result. For example, trade must make countries better off. So I do a model in which trade makes countries better off. The theory is really, really coherent in this aspect. But the theory seems to be an instrument; the beliefs are there before. They put their views into the models. It is not only Chicago; it is most places.

**Do you both agree?**

*John*  It is good to deconstruct models; you cannot take models at face value; you have to really think about them and recognize why people have come up with them. But that doesn't mean that models come from nowhere. People do look at the real world and come up with models, and have a preconceived notion of what they are going to get. That's typical of many subjects. As long as people understand that, that's fine.

*Shaikh*  I would strongly disagree with Nino; I don't think there is a Chicago school of thought or method. I don't think that they start with the result. The caliber of professors at Chicago is so high that they can't pull the wool over each other's eyes. They jump past that. They are interested in predictive power and policy analysis.

*Nino*  Predictive power is never an option.

*Shaikh*  I would say that the way Chicago differs from the other universities is in the way they teach. In the program here when they teach you things, they will focus more on economic content rather than mathematical content; they leave a lot of the mathematics for you to work out on your own. I certainly don't think that professors start from a result and work backward.

*John*  I agree with that.

*Nino*  I disagree. If you look, their models are calibrated so they get the results they want. This is not looking for predictions. Calibrated models don't do good forecasting.

*Shaikh*  To be frank, calibration is not a substitute for estimation; it is something else, and if you don't have anything better to offer, there's nothing wrong with it. The question is how to interpret calibrated results. Do you really think you could publish in top journals if people know you are doing some useless procedure? These are seriously clever people here.

*Nino*  I'm not saying that they are not clever. That's not the point.

*Shaikh*  Do you think that when someone publishes something, they would publish something that wasn't good?

*Nino*  This is how they do economics; it is not Chicago. Why do you think you write a paper? Because you have an idea about how the world works and you make a model to fit your idea. It is how you do models in every science. It is just how it works. It is not a view specific to Chicago, but an approach of economics. Where you cannot do experiments, getting information through data is really difficult.

*John*  Regardless of people's motives or the approach that they take, whether it be estimation or calibration, the workshops systems should ferret out problems. There is competition of ideas.

**Is there anyone at Chicago coming up with a model that markets aren't working?**

*Nino*  No.

*John*  Definitely.

*Shaikh*  Bob Townsen looks at credit markets in Thailand, and is considering how to improve them. I don't see anything contrived in that.

*Nino*  If you talk to various professors, and you come to a seminar with a paper about incomplete contracts or one with complete contracts, they would tell you to do one with complete contracts. There are people in the department who think that there are enough prices in the world to cover all the shocks. Hence complete markets are a good approximation to reality. I agree that not everyone thinks that way, but the underlying view of this department is that whenever you can, you should go with complete markets.

Shaikh   I think the reason for that is not a fundamental belief that the markets are working. The reason they do that is to avoid being ad hoc. Departures from complete markets in the literature are ad hoc. It's not a reflection of a preconceived notion that markets work. If you can do it with the benchmark model, fine and dandy. It is for elegance, conciseness, and uniformity of analysis. Take something like the equity premium puzzle; you have all these bounded rationality explanations; that's fine, but the best paper I've read on it is one that shows that if you look at individual data, three-quarters of the problem goes away. I don't see it as an ideological preference for markets.

Nino   I agree a bit with what he says, but I think it is not totally that.

**What are your plans when you graduate?**

Nino   My ideal job will be at a central bank, even though I know that most economists think that these are useless institutions. I would like them to get useful.

John   I want to work at a research university.

Shaikh   Me too.

**Is there a push toward research universities?**

John   It seems like they want Chicago people to be everywhere. If the students come from different countries, they want them to be in the government, to participate in policy; they want them to be at the IMF, at the World Bank; they want them to be in important positions.

**If someone said he or she wanted to teach at a liberal arts school, how would the faculty respond?**

Nino   I think they would be neutral. If they think you are a brilliant economist, they might complain, but otherwise they wouldn't be against it. They do, however, push for research. That's what we're here for.

**One of the questions on the survey I distributed concerned the importance of various factors to succeeding as an economist. Various skills were listed. What skills do you think are most important for an economist?**

*Nino*   I believe that to become a good economist you have to have a good idea of how the economy actually works. You need a good feel for the economy to supplement the other skills.

*John*   I think it depends on which field you're going into, but I'd say the most important aspects of success are creativity and hard work. Mathematical ability is great, but creativity is much more important.

*Shaikh*   I'd agree with John, but I put a strong weight on knowing the literature. Being able to synthesize what has already been said is critical in the idea-developing process. It's nice to have a stylized view that an idea just pops into your head, but 99 percent of all research is incremental. What you do is defined by what's been done in the past.

*John*   You also have to keep your eyes open—read the paper, know current issues, talk to people about stuff that isn't related to economics. Of course here in Chicago they teach us that everything is related to economics.

**In the first year can you tell who the stars are?**

*Nino*   Since backgrounds differ so much, the first-year success is not that good a predictor. The mathematicians do well initially, but that doesn't necessarily translate to success in economics.

*John*   I don't see much of a correlation between how you do in your courses and your success as an economist.

*Shaikh*   I think class grades are a Mickey Mouse indicator of how good you will be. A fifteen-minute chat with an individual will give you a better indication.

**In France there has been a post-autistic movement. Are you aware of it, and do you have any views of it?**

*Shaikh*   When I was in England, I heard of it. To be frank, I never really explored it.

**What is your overall view of the economics profession?**

*John*   Positive, moving ahead.

*Nino*   I think economics is, for sure, a useful thing. The models are great; they catch a lot of intuition, but economists still do not forecast well. Forecasting in economics is like forecasting the weather. Economics should become more like weather forecasting.

*John*   I don't look at economics like weather forecasting. I don't know much about macro, so maybe in macro it is like weather forecasting, but for me economics is just a tool to explain behavior.

*Shaikh*   There's a lot of good stuff in economics, and there's a lot of junk too. I don't know other disciplines, so it is hard to compare the good-to-junk ratios. Junk may be inevitable in any academic literature. What I don't like is when you see some economist on TV saying something incoherent, inane, or obvious. That's the image most people have of economists, and that is very different from what a professional academic economist is.

**Could you compare economists to other scientists?**

*Shaikh*   Compared to lab scientists, the cutoff point for being useless is much higher for an economist than it would be for a lab scientist. Even a bad lab scientist will contribute much more to society that a half-decent academic economist.

**Why is that?**

*Shaikh*   It is because of the nature of economics. The structure of what gets published and listened to means that what is considered good economics doesn't always constitute good economics. In my view, good economics has to have some sort of policy implication. That is incredibly difficult, and good applications require top-quality economists. In the physical sciences, good applications do not necessarily require top-quality scientists.

**What percentage of the work is useless?**

*Shaikh*   In a top journal like the *Quarterly Journal of Economics*, I'd say at least half are useless. Probably 20 percent are useful and the rest are unclear.

**Would you both agree?**

*John*   Ideas that don't have any ready policy implications could have policy implications later.

*Shaikh*   I take that into account. I am including all future policy implications when I say that 50 percent are useless. Fifty percent will never be cited or read again.

**Do you agree?**

*Nino*   Yes.

*John*   I don't know enough to say, except for maybe in my area.

**Well, how about in your area?**

*John*   I haven't read enough yet in my area to be sure about my answer. If pushed, I would say less than 50 percent is junk, but that the junk is still a sizable amount.

*Shaikh*   My 50 percent is complete junk.

# Chicago Interview III

*The third Chicago interview is with a second-, a fourth-, and a sixth-year Chicago student. It was conducted in the Graduate Student Lounge at the University of Chicago in February 2004.*

**Do students' perspective of the program change as they progress through the program?**

*Ken*   I guess I'm more aware of the current research interests of the faculty as opposed to their published work.

*David*   I have to agree. When I thought about Chicago in my first or second year, I thought about the coursework, which is annoying in some ways, but there are useful aspects. Now when I think about Chicago, I think about the workshops and the general ideas floating around.

*Paul*   I think in the second year there is already a change occurring. In the first year you think about problem set after problem set, with exams for breaks. You get to the second year and suddenly you are supposed to write papers and come up with novel ideas. Even the courses you take have papers for requirements, so that is a big transition.

**Would you say that Chicago differs from other programs?**

*David*   I think it is a lot less humane than other programs. Everything I've heard about other programs is that in other programs there is more faculty caring about students; the professors want to help students progress. Here, especially in the first year, the goal of many faculty members is to create roadblocks.

*Ken*   I don't agree with that. I don't know about other programs, but my experience has been on the one hand faculty are not especially forthcoming with suggestions and with handing out topics. But on the other hand I have found them almost frighteningly susceptible to all kinds of crazy ideas that I paraded into their offices with. They were willing to entertain those ideas and play them through their minds. I felt no constraint at all in the topic I chose.

*Paul*   I think there is much less structure in the courses here. There are big-name faculty teaching the first- and second-year courses. They are not looking at textbooks very often. They are suggesting papers, talking about rough ideas, and structuring it the way that they want. I think that this approach is really helpful in fostering creative thought and helping students to think like economists. My feeling is that the way of thinking about ideas differs among schools. Chicago has its own perspective, and there are a lot of concepts that come to workshop participants who work here that are not familiar at other places. I'm sure there are concepts coming to people at MIT and Harvard that are unfamiliar to people here.

**How is the split between foreign and U.S. students?**

*David*   There were about five Americans in our entering classes of about forty.

*Ken*   In our class, two Americans left after the first quarter, and another two left later. We just got a job notification that is for U.S. citizens only, and there were three people on the email list out of the thirty on the job market coming out of Chicago.

206

**Why is that?**

*David*   I don't know why it is, but the Americans are just vastly under-prepared.

*Paul*   At least on average, the kind of training that we get as undergraduates is just not comparable. Mathematically, in terms of the depth, American students simply don't have the appropriate training. For example, in microeconomics, my experience is that most of the foreign students had read Mas Collel's book already and knew pretty much everything that was in there. There weren't a whole lot of models that were a surprise to them. For me, everything in there was a surprise. Similarly, the math tools that I have were not comparable. When you don't have that background you're just constantly catching up. That, I believe, is the curricular difference with other countries. In the United States there is an emphasis on liberal arts, which means that in general in any field you come out with less depth than you would in another education system.

*Ken*   The other aspect may be the selection of the candidates who could get into any of the top five programs. I wouldn't be too surprised to learn that the top American students chose MIT or Harvard over Chicago, whereas that may be less the case for foreign students.

**How would you summarize the state of microeconomics?**

*Paul*   I think that there are some really good empirical approaches today, and that empirical micro is getting closer to being a science like physics, with the emphasis on experimental evidence, and trying to simulate experiments with natural sources of variation—natural experiments, instruments. There are a few people in the profession who are really good at recognizing what important questions are, and I really appreciate that. My opinion is that the big advances in micro in the future will be from people who have a good understanding of basic price theory, which they then apply econometrically. There are huge branches of the profession who are working on esoteric theoretical questions that don't have much to do with basic price theory. I don't think this work explains a large fraction of the economy.

**Where would behavioral economics fit in?**

*Paul*   There are some behavioral economic questions that are useful. There is a lot of money in them, and they are explaining a large fraction of the economy, say in terms of advertising or people's savings behavior, but

I'm not really excited about the esoteric psychological questions; I lump those together with principle/agent work under esoteric theory.

*David*   I would agree. I think there is a core body of microeconomics that people are taking and using as a vantage point to do empirical work. I think empirical work is becoming the dominant strand of microeconomics. We have the computing power, we have the datasets, we understand identification issues, and the combination of the three makes the analysis much more credible than in the past, and therefore more readily consumed by policymakers.

*Paul*   One of the big challenges is to connect where microeconomics and empirical microeconomics have gone in the past several decades with where macro has gone. The dominant macro models have representative agents and minimal-to-no heterogeneity, while the dominant realization in micro has been that people are very heterogeneous and that we need to account for that in everything that we do. It seems that there is a lot of ground to be gained by trying to understand how heterogeneity affects the macro economy and in trying to use micro datasets to try to understand macro problems. People are starting to do that.

*David*   I totally agree on that. Macroeconomic theory is going to go out the window. In the future we are going to look at the models they do now in the way we look at the pre-Copernican episode.

**What did you learn in macro; did you do the dynamic stochastic general equilibrium model?**

*Paul*   We learned a lot of junk like that.

*David*   Probably the best description of the curriculum right now is Sargent's latest book. For quite a while now, whatever that book is has been the latest macro.

*Ken*   I mostly remember the growth theory, but this is classic established work that has been around since Solow. It's been refined a bit, but it is not new.

*David*   I had some really good courses. One was by Lucas on monetary theory. I wasn't too crazy about all the Bellman equations, but he raised interesting questions and concepts. I audited a second-year course on growth from him that was similar. It raised important questions and basic empirical issues. I also likes Mulligan's course on lifecycle models, labor supply, and consumption smoothing. He focused on Friedman's book *The Theory of Consumption*. I thought that was a really well-designed course.

*Paul*   Mulligan is much more applied than the other macro economists here. The other macro economists present almost endless math—Bellman equations, Hamiltonians. It may as well have been physics problems. That was fine for me because I was a physics major, but I never saw what this had to do with real human behavior.

*David*   Yes, I think I really lucked out in macro in my year.

**What are your views on monetary and fiscal policy? Have they changed in the program?**

*Ken*   I think that they have become more explicit. I think one of the big things that I am taking away from my graduate studies is going to be a normative framework that I can apply to policy questions. I wasn't aware of the criterion of efficiency as a criterion to evaluate policies. I wasn't aware of that before I came here. But, again, I'm not really a macro economist. I guess I am reluctant about big deficits, but it is not well thought out.

*David*   I'd say that I moved farther to the right, which in my case means closer to the center politically, since I've been here. I feel I'm pretty moderate now. I am willing to trust prices a lot more as indicators of value, and in terms of looking at whether a policy is important or not by looking at how many dollars are involved. I'm willing to accept that as a good rough measure now. That's not something I was willing to do before.

*Paul*   I don't know that my political views have changed that much, in part because the way economics is done right now does not speak to policy issues that I am interested in. For example, if you are interested in distributional questions, macro economists will say that we don't do that, or they desperately try to create models where there are distributional questions, but they turn out not to matter. So if you are interested in redistribution, economics has nothing to say on that right now, and in a way refuses to have anything to say on it.

**Is that an ideological bias in economics?**

*Ken*   I think that with some economists it is an ideological bias, but with other people, it is simply an acknowledgment that we just don't have the models to deal with it. You can do a lot of empirical studies of inequality, but ultimately it is very hard to analyze.

*David*   I'd say definitely that Becker, Murphy, Mulligan, and Lucas have an ideological bias toward the right, and do not like the distributional question. They are more interested in the question of convex returns, especially to things like ability, wanting to encourage innovation. That leads them to focus on efficiency.

*Ken*   I don't know. I think you can analyze distributional questions from the positive side. Economics can illuminate how to measure inequality properly, and how to interpret the figures, but ultimately the question of inequality reflects a value judgment.

**Couldn't economics provide a discussion of the most efficient method of reducing inequality?**

*David*   Murphy's response to that is to question why you are talking about inequality. That's not a good in itself. Why not, if you are interested in the well-being of poor people, focus on their well-being? Who cares whether the rich people are really rich, or only moderately rich?

**Isn't that a normative question? Who cares where the taste for equality comes from? Who are economists to question people's tastes?**

*David*   I don't like framing poverty in terms of inequality. It's like you get penalized every time someone is really really happy or really really rich. I prefer to frame it in terms of the income level of a certain group of people. Forget about the rest of the people; that's not really relevant to the question of poverty.

**Are you saying that economists should be worried about the normative goals—that if an economist is not comfortable in framing a question in the way a lot of people would, that he or she shouldn't look at his or her frame? Doesn't that involve integrating the economist's normative goals in the approach that he or she is taking?**

*David*   Definitely. Economists should be aware of what goals they are pursuing. You have to have some sort of normative view of the world to arrive at research questions, and argue that they are important in your introductory paragraphs. You want to supplement that with positive science. Hopefully, you make contributions in positive science that help achieve these normative goals.

*Ken*   I think that Chicago economists are more keenly aware of the unintended consequences of some policies that they would find naive. It is important to point that out. Some policies may be counterproductive, and Chicago economists will not hesitate to suggest policies that to others might seem outrageous. Economists have a number of creative ideas to solve social ills by methods other than legislation and regulation. I think those views are pretty prominent here.

*Paul*   It disturbs me that there is this normative undercurrent to a lot of directions that economics is taking, especially here at Chicago, and yet we get no education in philosophy or ethics or any of the thousands of years of thought on these issues on how such normative judgments can be made. If we think that economists should be making these normative judgments, maybe our graduate training should include some training in how to make good normative judgments.

*Ken*   I think such issues have come up a lot when I have talked one-on-one with professors. You ask them questions, and I have felt that my advisors have had intelligent responses to how they arrived at their normative judgments.

**If there were any change you could make to the Chicago program, what would it be?**

*Paul*   First, I think they should get rid of time series econometrics, and cut back on the theory a lot. They should cut down on the mathematics a lot. They should add some people who know something about macro policy. You mentioned macro policy and we have almost no discussion on any such issues. Lucas's class was an exception, but he does not teach in the core anymore. If we had someone like John Taylor or Alan Blinder, who really know macro policy, that would be great.

**Why get rid of time-series econometrics?**

*Paul*   Panel data is very useful, but when you are working with panel data, you use almost nothing that they teach in the typical time-series econometrics course.

*David*   I would disagree about time series; I had a very different time-series course. My course gave me a good sense of what econometrics is and what you are trained to do. One of the things I got from my course is that the panel data models that we use are very limited in the way they describe the time-series process, and that there are ways to make the

211

analysis a lot more credible by applying the insights we have about individual time series to panel data. We may need to apply the time series tools to different types of data, but I don't think we should be dropping it. Also, there are certain types of data, such as stock market data, which are inherently time series, and if we are going to study them, it is going to have to be with those methods.

I can think of two big changes that I would suggest. The first is that we need a smaller first-year class. There are a number of professors here who are very interesting people, but they are not good at lecturing to large classes. . . . [A] better job [should be done] in the admissions process . . . so that we get the the courses down to a size that suits some of our professors.

*Ken*   I don't know that it is the size; some professors are just much more interested in teaching what they are doing, which is fine, but it sometimes leaves serious gaps in the curriculum that we are not exposed to. This means that we have a real problem reading the literature, or identifying the references from people outside this school. So I would force everyone who wants to teach in the core to cover the basics. They can point out what they think is interesting, but they should present the established body of techniques, and the issues that these techniques are used to analyze. In the first year you teach what the questions are and what are the tools, and in the second year, they can take you to the frontier. I sometimes had the feeling that they were jumping way ahead. I would prefer to get a more solid grounding.

**What would you think of the idea of having the core exams graded by outside examiners, or at least by the department separate from the people who taught it?**

*David*   It's not only that the professors teaching the core grade as a group; they often grade their own questions.

**Would you support such a change?**

*Paul*   I would.

*David*   I think it depends on the field. In micro I really like the perspective that they have here; there are a lot of schools where they just go through Mas Collel chapter by chapter. I'd much prefer a course where you don't go through a single chapter of that book.

*(laughter)*

*David*  In terms of econometrics, they cover a lot of irrelevant material; it is way too teched up. If they could just teach people how to work with data and how to answer simple questions, it would be great.

*Ken*  This brings up my huge complaint with the Chicago program. David got to take a second-year econometrics course. I didn't, because they didn't hire someone to teach it. I fail to understand how a top-five school cannot have a second-year econometrics field.

**Any final comments?**

*Ken*  Regarding outside examiners: I agree that there should be incentives for the faculty to teach a more coherent set of material, but I think that doing it to the extent of reducing the certainty of students about how it would be graded is not the way to do it. The course is terrifying enough when you know the three people who will grade it. The more uncertainty you have about the exam, the worse it is going to be. I think the solution is to get the faculty to teach what they should teach.

**How might the answers have differed if foreign students were in this interview?**

*Paul*  It depends on which foreign students.

*Ken*  I know a couple of foreign students who want to practice a certain type of macroeconomics; they specifically came to Chicago to practice this. I don't think they would be unhappy with macro, as most of us were. They are getting what they came in for. They will go back with reputation and skills that will put them at the forefront of their country's economics. The Latin Americans are more likely to be coming here primarily for the macro.

*Paul*  If you take the average number of equations in a foreign-born student's dissertation versus the average in an American student's dissertation, you will find a significant difference.

*Ken*  Foreign and U.S. students are prepared very differently. A lot of them have really strong technical skills. The Americans seem more interested in the end result of economic science, which Becker would describe as ex-

213

plaining social phenomena and human behavior. It's not just solving differential equations.

*Paul*   I'd agree with that on average, but there are significant outliers.

*David*   There is a feedback effect with particular countries. I have one classmate who said that 90 percent of her undergraduate professors have their pictures on the wall.[2] Such undergraduate programs are a subset of Chicago macro.

# Columbia Interview

*The interview was conducted at the graduate student lounge at Columbia University in February 2004. It is with four students: two second year, one third year, and one who has just completed his dissertation.*

**Are you a representative sample, and if not, how do you differ?**

*Ichiro*   I am perhaps representative of the later students—in the final stage, but definitely not of younger students.

*Fidi*   I am older than most students, and am much more critical than most students.

*Wolf*   I don't see myself as representative, but I can't capture why.

*Joan*   As a U.S. student, I also probably am not representative.

**How did you decide to come to Columbia?**

*Ichiro*   This was where I was admitted.

*Fidi*   That's also the same for me; it was the highest-ranked school that I got into at a location that I found acceptable. There is so little information if you apply from another country.

**In terms of math, did you feel prepared when you came in?**

*Ichiro*   I felt prepared; I think East Asian students are in general well prepared.

*Fidi*   I, too, felt prepared. Our first-year math course was taught at a very high level, so it was a challenge; but in terms of all the other courses, my background was fine.

*Joan*  I did not feel prepared. I had never taken calculus when I came in. I was able to do the work, but it wasn't pretty. Now I feel confident about my math facility. I was carried a lot by some in my study group who had a strong background.

**Did you know what you were getting into before you came?**

*Joan*  No, not really. I think I had an idea and was scared, but I had no idea about how hard it would be because I had no concept of what it is.

**What is the percentage of foreign and U.S. students?**

*Joan*  My class has a high percentage of U.S. students; we've got thirteen in the class and three U.S. students. All the other classes average one U.S. student a year.

*Fidi*  That sounds right to me.

**How do you think Columbia differs from some of the other schools?**

*Joan*  I have no idea; I know people at Yale, and they sound a lot friendlier with the faculty. But once you finish the courses, it doesn't matter. I have a great relationship with the professors I deal with, and that's all that is necessary.

**Columbia and Chicago seem to be the two schools that have the least guidance. You come in and you learn it or not. Is that a fair description of Columbia?**

*Joan*  That's definitely true for Columbia, but at this stage in your career, is that really the worst thing? I look at it as a job; nothing is really handed to you. But you can get a lot out of it if you put a lot into it.

**Tell me about the program here.**

*Joan*  It is pretty standard; the first year is coursework, then you start your dissertation work your third year, and you keep up with that until you finish.

*Fidi*  We had fourteen students starting, but one voluntarily dropped out after two months. After the second year, two more dropped out. I think they shoot for about twenty students starting each year.

*Ichiro*   I was in the older tradition at Columbia. We had about forty students entering when I started. Five or six students dropped out during the first year; at the end of first year another ten left, either voluntarily or involuntarily. So about twenty people left. Then over time another five left, so about fifteen of the original forty will likely finish.

*Fidi*   In terms of core courses, there are four professors teaching (two each semester) each specialty (micro, macro, and econometrics) over the year. At the end of the spring term, you have the final for that course, and also have a certification exam for the entire year. These are in addition to the finals for the courses. The way it works is that the fall-term professors essentially add some questions to the spring-term final. So how well one does in one's courses is a good indicator of how one will do on the certification exam. In math we only have a fall course, so the math final counts as the certification.

*Joan*   Some of the courses are very small. Sometimes they combine it with CEEPA (Center for Environmental Economics and Policy in Africa) students, which creates a problem since they are learning it at a lower level. The attrition rate has varied with the size of the class. Now they are guaranteeing funding, which cuts down attrition a lot.

**With such small classes is there a lot of interaction with other departments?**

*Wolf*   In some cases yes; there are ties with political science and with the business schools.

**Are the certification exams prepared by the department or by the professors of the course?**

*Fidi*   They are prepared by the professors of the course, so they are very similar to the finals.

**Do the first-year courses provide an overview of the field, or do the courses focus on the professor's research?**

*Fidi*   The micro course is centered around Mas Collel in the first term, and in the second term we learn information theory. In econometrics we learn measure theory in the first semester and the second semester we learn about estimators. In macro it is probably the most difficult to get an overview. For the most part, the macro course is highly focused on advanced research, rather than providing an overview.

217

*Ichiro*   Our macro course was highly advanced, but because different professors taught it, there was a good mix of ideologies when we took it, but it depends on who is assigned in a particular year. Each year can be quite different.

**How would you describe the macro they teach here?**

*Joan*   Eclectic. I think that is the way macro is now taught. I don't really know where macro is today. My supervisor is in the business school. I certainly haven't gotten a uniform feeling from my experience.

**What are your views on monetary and fiscal policy?**

*Fidi*   Both monetary and fiscal policy are effective.

*Ichiro*   My quick answer is that it depends. Specifically, it depends on whether or not the country is an open economy. It also depends on what length of time you are referring to. In Japan, for instance, they keep trying to use fiscal policy, but it didn't work. It also depends on what instruments in monetary policy are used.

*Joan*   I guess I've decided that monetary policy is weakly neutral. But I'm still not sure about fiscal policy. Generally the way I feel about both is that bad fiscal and monetary policy are really bad, and good fiscal and monetary policy is at best neutral.

**Did you learn that from macro theory or from following events?**

*Joan*   More from economic history. I also found the empirical evidence on monetary policy persuasive.

**Are the views you are being taught representative of the profession?**

*Fidi*   I think that the profession is a bit to the right of the department. Actually our department is quite polarized. I remember once that I had a discussion with the dean of the graduate school; he noted that the department is very polarized.

*Nike*   I'd say that macro is nonstandard. The others are standard.

**Is that good or bad?**

*Ichiro*   I think it is good, although sometimes it is difficult in finding compatible advisors for your committee, and the students can be caught in between the various views. In micro, the policy views are less noticeable since we have a standardized course centered around Mas Collel.

**Is there much psychology in economics taught here?**

*Joan*   None; I really wish there was. Actually, I'm being unfair. The psych department actually offers an interdisciplinary seminar, which I've not attended. It is not advertised in the department. But it's there.

**What do you learn in econometrics?**

*Wolf*   The first semester of econometrics is about probability foundations; the second semester is about estimators and asymptotic properties of estimators.

**Do you do nonparametric and Bayesian econometrics?**

*Wolf*   In the first year we don't, but in the second year there is a class on nonparametric econometrics, but it is not required. We don't cover Bayesian econometrics.

**Is the econometrics course mainly theoretical or applied?**

*Wolf*   It depends on the professor, but it probably focuses more on theoretical, especially in the first year.

*Fidi*   My course was definitely theoretical. There were very few problem sets on applied issues.

*Ichiro*   My course was also theoretical, which I liked. Many of my classmates complained that we didn't cover time series issues or panel data issues—issues that would be relevant for our applied papers. We actually now have a third required course in econometrics that is more applied, but that came after me. I think it was started because the department was responding to complaints by the students about the lack of applied training in econometrics.

**Would you say that economists test theories?**

219

*Ichiro*  I agree with Professor Helpman, who says that they would like to see more simple correlations being done, rather than the really strange and asymptotic estimators and the fancy things. What econometrics should be about is finding what relates to what and why. Data analysis can be a starting point about causal issues. That isn't the way we are taught econometrics, but it is, I think, the way econometrics is used.

**Have you done much outside reading—say Hayek, Robinson, Keynes, or Marx?**

*Fidi*  Unfortunately not. I think that it's a loss. I still hope that sometime in the future to be able to catch up on my reading.

*Ichiro*  I've read Plato, Aristotle, Cicero, and Machiavelli, but I have not read any classical economics.

*Wolf*  I've heard about them but I have never read them.

**Is there much distinction between foreign and U.S. students?**

*Ichiro*  My impression of the difference between U.S. students and foreign students is that foreign students have much better math preparation. U.S. graduate students may be a bit more pragmatic.

*Fidi*  The U.S. students often have difficulty keeping up mathematically initially. That could be because the really mathematically well-trained Americans get into, and go to, the higher-ranked schools.

**How would you rank an academic career versus another type of career?**

*Ichiro*  I'm a strict academic person; my only interest is in academic institutions.

*Joan*  I'm more open. I plan to apply for everything and take the best offer I get in a reasonable location. If I get a good academic job that would be my first choice, but I'm not going to live in a place I don't want to live in.

**How do the faculty look at academic versus nonacademic jobs?**

*Joan*  Students definitely have to have a lot of enthusiasm for academia if they want the faculty to spend time with them. And I do.

**How much help do students get in their job search?**

*Joan*   I don't get the sense that they get a lot; I think a lot of people leave Columbia bitter because of the lack of help that they have gotten. I have found here that if you are really aggressive, you will do better.

*Ichiro*   I got a lot of help; my advisor sent out lots of personal letters; those turned out to be the most helpful.

**Can you tell who will be the stars at the beginning?**

*Fidi*   There is some correlation, but it is far from one.

*Ichiro*   One of the top stars in my class was a bit naive, so even though he was really good in the coursework, he didn't find a good advisor, and he floundered. In Asia, the professors assist the students in choosing topics and guide them. That doesn't happen here. Students here are left alone. We have to approach the professor, and fight for an advisor. Students who can't do that don't do well here.

**How would you describe the economic method?**

*Ichiro*   The approach we follow is deductive, focused on theory; I think the approach we should follow should focus on empirical regularities, and on economic and social problems. Then it should try to come up with solutions to those problems. In that sense it is a very inductive approach that we should follow.

*Fidi*   In my view there is not one economic method, because I think that economics is inherently schizophrenic. There are theoretical and empirical, and positive and normative, branches. One is a natural science, the other is a social science, and their methods differ completely. That's what I like about economics.

*Ichiro*   Among the social sciences, economics has a major advantage of using mathematics as a language to maintain the logic of ideas. In any discipline, logic is the most important thing. For that reason economics can take out many ambiguities in explaining things using logic. Having said that, if I include all the new developments in behavioral economics and bounded rationality, then I really like economics because not only do they use mathematics as a language, they also try to explain real-world issues. I might have a different feeling if I went to another school like

Chicago. But as long as they allow us to pursue different ways of looking at things, I'm happy with economics.

I'm not happy with the status of empirical economics, partly because it is often not really testing the theory. In a paper I did, I came up with a result that did not conform to my theory, and the question was what to do? I decided that the result was inconsistent with the theory, and I gave four reasons why. My professor told me that the paper was only an A- because it is not complete as an econometrics paper. You have to be able to correct for this standard error and whatever. The implication was that you cannot turn in an econometrics paper unless you have the appropriate results; I think that is ridiculous. To test you have to have two different theories, which you test one against the other. But much of the econometrics work by applied economists is not that at all; it is simply manipulation of the data to say what they want to say—to achieve the level of significance they need. I don't like that aspect of economics. We can't really have an experimental environment with that attitude.

**In the survey, Columbia students said that there is less agreement of fundamental issues here than at other schools. Any reason why?**

*Wolf*   I suspect that is accounted for by the different teachers. We have a couple of strong personalities teaching here who disagree significantly on most issues.

**There was also less interest in the rational expectations hypothesis at Columbia than elsewhere.**

*Ichiro*   This probably also reflects the people who teach macro here.

**In the survey, Columbia had the lowest use of optimization among students. Any comments?**

*Ichiro*   This could be partly because of the way theory is taught here. In theory, we simply don't see optimization; for example in trade, maximization may be behind the models, but the models are not taught in reference to maximization.

*Joan*   I use it; but everyone I know at Columbia does general equilibrium micro theory, so why would they use it.

**There was greater agreement that markets tend to discriminate against women at Columbia than at most other schools.**

222

*Ichiro*    Is there any disagreement that markets discriminate against women?

*Wolf*    Maybe it is because we have a lot of women here. In my class we have more women than men.

**At Columbia the relationship with faculty was the most stressful of any the schools.**

*Ichiro*    Yes, but there is an improvement going on these days. It was really hard for me to find an advisor; it took over a year.

*Wolf*    Here I think we can best define the relationship with faculty by an absence of a relationship.

*Fidi*    You have to work at it, but it is possible to establish a relationship. To me it wasn't very stressful.

**There was more interest in macro at Columbia than in the other schools. Any comments?**

*Ichiro*    One possibility is finance macro concentrations. There is a feeling that the finance professors in the business school place people well, which may be being reflected in the survey. Several friends of mine took that path.

**Any suggestions for anyone applying to an economics program?**

*Ichiro*    To get in, or whether they should do it?

**Either.**

*Ichiro*    Be prepared to spend a year on math. Be prepared to work a lot. Have enormous motivation. You have to be convinced of your own stamina.

*Joan*    Learn a lot of math. Perseverance. People who get a Ph.D. aren't always the smartest; they are the most persistent. You will find some professor who likes you and supports you.

*Fidi*    If you are sure you want to do it, then do it. If you are unsure, then a Ph.D. is not the right thing for you.

*Ichiro*  No, I wouldn't agree with that. You can try out the first year, and then decide.

*Wolf*  In terms of getting admitted, I think that a lot of focus should be put on letters of recommendation.

*Fidi*  There are many people who are going into economics because they want to work in a policy program like the IMF or CEEPA as a job. For those people, I can only say—study math. Take a Ph.D.-level course in math; see if you are comfortable with it. If you are not, then really question whether you want to go into economics. If you are a person like me, who has no problem in math, and wants to be in academia, I would offer different advice. To them, I suggest that you study as much economics as possible—different fields like IO or public finance. There are many interesting intuitions you can learn on the undergraduate level. You don't have time to acquire that once you get into the Ph.D. program. You get specialized very quickly, and you never have any time to learn economics.

**Last time we labeled the Columbia interviews "Eclecticism and Concern." Would that be a good label again?**

*Fidi*  I don't know; I guess I would agree. I think there is concern, and that there are many different views here.

*Ichiro*  I agree.

*Joan*  Because it is such a hands-off program, your experience is very personal to you. There are some people who get some help, there are others who are left behind, and there are others who make their own way.

# PART III
## Reflections on the Survey and Interviews

I BELIEVE THAT THE RESULTS of this survey presented in Part I, and the conversations presented in Part II, give the reader a good picture of graduate economic education at elite schools in the early 2000s. But I also believe that research is never neutral, and cannot be. The questions one asks, the way one interprets results, and the way in which one organizes the material reflects the researcher's interests and biases. You are seeing graduate economics through my eyes.

As a partial counterbalance to that author bias, I have asked two top economists whose views on graduate economics education differ from mine to comment on the surveys and the conversations. Chapter 11 is written by Arjo Klamer. I see Arjo Klamer as representing the more heterodox critique of graduate economics education. Heterodox economists are far less satisfied with the direction that the profession has taken than are the majority of economists at these top schools, and I wanted someone who could articulate their views. Klamer is perfect for that role both because he is such an insightful observer, and because he did the earlier study with me.

Chapter 12 is written by Robert Solow. I see him as representing the concerned mainstream view of graduate economics education. In my view, Robert Solow is everything an economics professor should be— brilliant, insightful, caring about his students, and about economics. He has cared most about pedagogy over the past forty years than any of other top mainstream economist I know. His former students still rave about his teaching—how he would come into class and ask them what they wanted to learn, and then teach them that. Moreover, he can always be counted on for an honest, straightforward answer to a question. We haven't always agreed about graduate education—in fact, we have had serious disagreements about how ideally graduate school education would be structured—but I, and the entire economics profession, have always had the highest respect for his views. His comments add a necessary perspective to the study.

They were both free to write what they wanted; I simply sent them the manuscript and asked them to comment on the study, and on graduate economics education generally. I think you will find that their views add insight and depth to the book.

In the last chapter of the book, I give my concluding reflections on the study, this time being a bit more direct in where I think there are problems in graduate economics education, and what I think should be done about them.

# Does This Have to Be Our Future?

*Arjo Klamer*

IN HINDSIGHT, the paper that Dave Colander and I wrote on graduate students back in the 1980s was polemical. We were looking for confirmation of our dissatisfaction with the state of economics. Could we be right in fearing that the practice of economics was becoming more and more abstract, and less empirical? Might the elite schools indeed be training idiots savants, knowing a great deal of technique but little about the actual economy or, for that matter, the history of their own discipline? And was the training of economics making Ph.D. students more conservative? We had spent many hours speculating and swapping anecdotes— as economists are wont to do when discussing their own discipline—and then decided to gather some evidence to wake up the profession and bring about a change. At least that was our intention as I recall it.

Our findings were good for a wake up call all right. As Colander tells in the introduction to this book, the media picked up on our finding that students found problem solving very important and a thorough knowledge of the economy unimportant for success in the field. How could economists train their people ignoring the economy? It did not make sense to journalists; these findings confirmed the reputation of economists as being out of touch. Within the profession the leadership took notice of the frustrations that these very best students showed with their education and ordered a more thorough investigation and evaluation of graduate training. The American Economic Association appointed the so-called COGEE committee that went to work with significant financial support. Colander reports here what happened in the wake of its final report. Nothing much, so it seemed, at least if you trust the usual anecdotal evidence. The report disappeared in the drawers of directors of graduate studies and it was business as usual. But was it?

It is good that Colander redid the survey and went back to speak with the new cohorts of graduate students to find out what actually changed.[1] Of course, his research cannot determine what the impact has been from our book and the subsequent investigation by the American Economic Association. It does convey, however, a sense of how the current cohort of graduate students compares with the cohort in the mid-eighties.

The findings do not appear to be remarkable. Most of our earlier findings stand. For many questions, the answers deviate by only a few percentage points. Given the limited and nonrandom nature of the sample, these differences do not allow the drawing of firm conclusions. In interviews, the teaching of core courses continues to be a cause of concern. Colander does not see an improvement here. Despite the recommendations of the COGEE committee that the content of the core courses should be the concern of the entire department, no change was made, and the structure of the core remains unchanged; it is technical, mathematical, and untied to reality. He also does not see greater attention to writing and communication skills, nor a smoother transition from coursework to the dissertation. Noteworthy, however, is the reappreciation of empirical research. This does accord with the recommendations of the COGEE committee (as well as those made by Colander and myself).

Instead of a further differentiation of departments, as recommended by the COGEE committee (and applauded by Colander), we see actually a fading of the differences between the various schools. In the earlier study, Harvard students expressed an outspoken bias against neoclassical economics, but after the outspoken neo-classical Bob Barro joined the Harvard faculty, Harvard students have moved into the direction of the Chicago position (with 41 percent finding rational expectations very important versus a mere 14 percent fifteen years ago.) These findings suggest that the divide between fresh and saltwater departments has all but disappeared. The ideological battle is over. These graduate students are more or less in step with each other. The question is whether this is a good development or not.

The same question concerns the level of frustration of the students. Colander and I were surprised to find such strong frustrations with graduate training and the state of the discipline among our interviews at the time. We saw in those frustrations a sign that graduate training was going in the wrong direction, that graduate students were molded in a way they did not care for. Maybe they would change things for the better, so we hoped. Maybe they would help open the profession up for alternative approaches, diminish the emphasis upon mathematical dexterity and problem solving. Maybe. In this new round of interviews Colander encountered more contentment and hence fewer frustrations. Students were experiencing fewer difficulties with the math and appeared better prepared and equipped for graduate training. Colander contributes this current contentment to a change in the screening of potential candidates. Graduate directors apparently have gotten better in finding students who are willing to go along with the training. (How Steve Levitt passed the selection at MIT is a riddle, given that he had no background in mathematics whatsoever, as he mentioned during the session on Colander's findings at the meetings in Boston. He said that he might have reconsidered his choice for a Ph.D. in economics if he had read our book before coming to MIT. Then again, he did not find the math overwhelming. So maybe something has changed in this regard.)

So what to make of these findings? Is all well in the profession? Or are the results reasons for concern about the future of the profession? Surely, the reading depends on what you want to read in the numbers.

## Colander Has Mellowed Somewhat

Let us begin with Colander's reading. He appears to have changed somewhat along with the graduate students. He has grown more positive about the state of economics in general and graduate training in particular. He appreciates new developments such as behavioral approaches and the study of complex systems. He also approves of the increased emphasis on empirical research. All the changes that he registers in this study are positive, according to his reading. He appears to have mellowed: this book is not meant to be polemical. The profession can rest assured.

229

# The Tea Leaves Could Just as Well Be
# Read the Other Way

There is another, more critical reading. Granted, the survey remains flawed and the selection of the interviewees is even more arbitrary than it was the first time. Even so, the results may be considered more damning than they were before. If anything, the discipline has become more homogeneous, more single-minded, more hard-nosed about the science of economics and hence less heterogeneous and arguably less intellectually exciting. Problem solving continues to be the key to success, and so is mathematical dexterity. Intellectuals with a wide range of interest will not survive in the conversations that economists are trained to conduct. They do not even make the cut for graduate school. The fields of history of economic thought and economic history have all but vanished from the programs. Macro is on the way out. It's all micro now (to the chagrin of Robert Solow). Controversies are gone and with them the liveliness of the discussion. Nothing much seems to be at stake, except prestige, one's ranking, and the number of citations that an article generates.

Particularly worrisome is the perception of this cohort of graduate students concerning the science of economics. They have become more hard-nosed about their discipline compared to their counterparts in the eighties (see Klamer 2006 for more on the hard-nosed position). They have become more arrogant about their discipline vis-à-vis the other social sciences. To these hard-nosed graduate students, economics is the superior scientific discipline. In contrast to their counterparts in the eighties, they do not question the scientific approach that they are learning and do not wonder about alternatives. Modeling continues to be the way to go.

They have even less consideration for alternative approaches than their counterparts fifteen years ago. Austrian, feminist, Marxist, post-Keynesian, social and cultural economists, to name a few "heterodox" economists, do not exist as far as these students are concerned. Their silence could be symptomatic of a further marginalization of alternative approaches during the preceding decade. Colander finds comfort with the new interest in behavioral economics and the increasing appreciation for sociology and psychology, but I doubt that the so-called hetero-

dox economists share his comfort. I am actually certain they do not—
as further marginalization translates in fewer jobs and fewer slots for
heterodox sessions at the annual meetings of the American Economic
Association.

These students furthermore do not show a great deal of ability to
reflect on their discipline. They are satisfied with the commonplace,
the things that economists conventionally say about their discipline.
This cohort appears to be mindless, or at least resourceless, when it
comes to reflections on the nature of their science. They have no literature to fall back on. Even the text of Milton Friedman appears to have
dropped from their reading lists. (Needless to say, economic methodology has no place in the curriculum.) Apparently they are taught to do
what they are doing without giving much thought to the "how so" and
"why" questions.

To anyone who cares about the intellectual quality of the discipline,
about the ability of economists to reflect on what they do, or who is
working on alternative economic perspectives and approaches, the
findings of this study are rather depressing. If these very best students
are really so unaware about the meta levels of their discipline and are
so unconscious of what is going on in the academy at large, what does
that mean for the future of our discipline?

## No Matter How Interesting or Depressing Their Findings Are, Studies like These Will Have Little to No Effect on the Practice of Economics

When the students and their faculty show such little interest in serious
reflection on their discipline, studies like this one stand no chance in
influencing the practice of economics. Those who work in the margins
of the profession may take notice and may find confirmation of their
worst nightmares, but those who work in the core of the discipline
have no reason to take these findings seriously. Nothing is at stake.
The discipline is doing fine, thank you. More undergraduate students
register for a major in economics than departments can handle. Even if
American students do not apply for graduate school, more than enough
foreign students are eager to fill the open slots. There is no crisis and

therefore no need to start rethinking current practices. There is no need to read in the history of thought or the methodology and philosophy of their science. There is no need for self-reflexivity.

## Shouldn't Intellectuals Want to Be Knowledgeable about What They Do?

A student of the methodology and philosophy of science myself, I am somewhat taken aback by the lack of philosophical sophistication of graduate students and their teachers nowadays. Maybe Duke University during my graduate training there was an exception in this regard, but my fellow students and I made a point of reading Kuhn, Lakatos, Popper, and other philosophers who could help make sense of the science of our discipline. Encouraged by faculty members like Craufurd Goodwin, Martin Bronfenbrenner, E. Roy Weintraub, and Neil de Marchi, we read in the history of thought to gain some understanding of how the discipline had changed over time. All this knowledge made us certainly less sure of the science and more open to the possibility that methods and insights once beyond dispute are likely to be reevaluated and possibly discarded. We believed that true scholarship asks for self-consciousness on the part of the researcher and of a keen awareness of what one is doing.

Current graduate training stresses the techniques and takes the students through the compulsory notions without asking the important questions: "why?" and "what for?" As a consequence, these students are quite unscientific when it comes to answering questions about their discipline. We are left wondering whether they are prepared for crises in the discipline that are inevitable from time to time. How will these students fare when they are in the company of other scholars who are so much more aware of new developments in thinking about science? One thing is sure, this cohort is even further removed from the ideal that Deirdre McCloskey displays when she pleads that economists rejoin the human conversation (McCloskey 1983; see also her contribution to Klamer, McCloskey, and Solow 1988).

# The Relevance of Economics

A lack of reflexivity does not serve these students well when they have to elaborate on their claim that the science of economics is relevant for society. Although they appear to be firm on that claim, they have no evidence. They have even no theoretical framework that would allow them to investigate such a claim. Apart from the usual anecdotes they have no well-supported arguments to show that the science of economics has an impact on policymaking, the running of business, or the behavior of individuals. It remains interesting to note that even though economists are willing to study any phenomenon that strikes their fancy (and fanciful the phenomena that Levitt studies surely are), their own behavior and the impact of their science are not among them (with a few not widely noted exceptions).

Surely, with the rational expectations hypothesis economists implied to say that their knowledge was too important to be left out in the model. A claim, however, is no evidence. Even when politicians appear to apply insights of the science of economics, as in the case of NAFTA, they actually follow other, political, interests and keep economists at bay (for the evidence see Klamer 2006). Even though the relevance of economics is beyond doubt—why else would economics continue to be a popular study and why else would economic concepts pop up left and right in everyday conversations?—these students do not seem to have a clue why that is. It is even doubtful that their faculty has a clue.

By continuing to pursue the discipline of economics mindlessly, without capacity for serious reflection on the nature and history of the discipline, the economic profession is at risk. Apart from that, the lack of reflexivity renders the current practice in the discipline so much less intellectually open-minded and challenging than it could be. Colander is well advised to do another round of interviews in ten years to see whether the discipline has learned to take itself more seriously.

# Reflections on the Survey
### *Robert M. Solow*

THE SURVEY AND INTERVIEW responses have to be full of interest for anyone who cares about the teaching of economics or, for that matter, anyone who cares about economics. It is nevertheless hard to know how to treat the detailed survey results and the interviews. The samples are small and haphazard. Over and above the biases that David Colander mentions—underrepresentation of foreigners, for instance—I suspect there may be a tendency for happy campers not to fill out survey questionnaires or volunteer for interviews. The meaning of a question and the answer may be understood slightly differently by respondents from different backgrounds: a Chicago student may not mean quite the same thing as a Stanford student in responding to a question about the "importance" of rational expectations. Common understandings may change even more during a fifteen-year interval.

Here is another example. Colander asks students how they rate the importance of certain characteristics as contributions to success as an economist. It's a good question. One of the characteristics is problem-solving ability. So I asked myself what I thought, and discovered an ambiguity. If problem-solving ability means the ability to solve analytical puzzles (if Sam is twice as old as Dolores was when Sam was 13, etc.), then I think that sort of talent has some use, but not much. If problem-solving ability means, however, the ability to start with an apparent anomaly or counterintuitive pattern observed in the economy, and then find a coherent and plausible explanation of it according to basic economic principles, then I think that this talent is very important, and a student should be willing to kill to acquire it. What did the respondents have in mind when they answered? Probably not all the same thing.

Nevertheless, these responses clearly contain a lot of information about the perceptions of graduate students and the teaching of economics in these elite departments. That information has to be interpreted (self-servingly, no doubt, but that's life), but it should not be ignored. I am inclined to avoid fussing over the response fractions and their variation from time to time and department to department. I would rather think of them as hints about professional beliefs and practices and as a stimulus to reflection. That is, in fact, the way Colander uses them.

What struck me most, and horrified me most, was the widespread feeling among these elite students that the macroeconomics they were taught was the least "relevant," least applicable, least enjoyable part of their curriculum. That would not have been true thirty years ago. In fact the truth—and the perception—would have been just the other way round. Macro texts and macro teaching were full of data and data analysis, model-based data analysis aimed directly at current policy issues; micro teaching and micro texts were full of invented curves and arbitrary functions. It is major progress that microeconomics has changed, with the availability of large datasets and the analytical and statistical methods to deal with them. The problem is with macro and— here I apparently disagree with Colander—the problem is with the substance, not with the teaching.

This is not the place for me to mount my private soap box, so I will just say that the macro community has perpetrated a rhetorical swindle on itself, and on its students. (Evidently some of the students realize this, but not their teachers!) If you pick up any "modern macro" paper, it tells you it will exhibit a "micro-founded" model that will then be used to study this or that problem. When the model turns up, it is, of course, the representative-agent, infinite-horizon, intertemporal-optimization-with-conventional-constraints story with its various etceteras. This model has no valid claim, except by reiteration, to be "micro-founded." Basic microtheory tells you no such thing. The analogy I use is that it is as if my diet consisted entirely of carrots, and, when asked why, I reply grandly that I am a vegetarian. Being a vegetarian is no excuse for choosing and, worse, promoting a ridiculously restricted menu among the thousands that are available. Believe me, I could go on, and the temptation is great, but I should stick to the topic.

It is a puzzle how this happened to macroeconomics; and a good explanation might apply to similar developments elsewhere in economics as reflected in the interviews. I do not have a pat answer. No doubt there were flaws in the "hydraulic Keynesianism" that preceded "modem macro." That would provide an initial impetus to any "new" approach that could claim to correct old errors. But that would not explain why the macro community bought so incontinently into an alternative model that seems to lack all credibility as applied to quarter-to-quarter or year-to-year events. Maybe there is in human nature a deep-seated perverse pleasure in adopting and defending a wholly counterintuitive doctrine that leaves the uninitiated peasant wondering what planet he or she is on. I guess there is something like that, but I am not wholly convinced.

The common story is that it is technique-happy aficionados who grab the initiative and defend it behind walls of mathematics. This view gets some support from the students who say their macro courses are all abstract mathematics, and it puts them off. The mathematics, however, is not that hard, nor is it beautiful. The students master it, just to pass their examinations; and then they go off to work at a more interesting branch of economics. Maybe that's the point: it drives away all but a high-morale ingroup that is enough to keep the sacred flame burning.

Another possibility is that occasionally a pied piper turns up who can create a school and fire up a coterie. I suspect that the heyday of pure monetarism owed a lot to the sharp mind and powerful personality of Milton Friedman. I don't quite see that in modem macro, though obviously it has its heroes.

If all this had to do only with macro, it would be a fairly parochial matter. Something similar, if not so intense, however, seems to characterize many of the survey responses and Colander's reaction to them. He wants the core courses to focus less on model-building and more on "economic reasoning." There I cannot go along with him. I think that, for better or worse, economics is irremediably a model-building project. I am unclear what "economic reasoning" can be, other than pointing to models without actually teaching and learning them.

For instance, you can talk about the importance of incentives in class, and you can give neat examples of this principle at work, even some that are far from obvious. Probably you should do that, for a week or two. But then—these are graduate students, after all—you have to get down to the nitty-gritty. Exactly how does this work? Why does it work? Under what circumstances might it cease to work? How could you figure out what happens if there are incentives that work at cross-purposes? And then, I confess, I see no alternative to continuing: Well, how could we make a simplified model of a market with imperfect information? How could we make a simplified model of a work place in which the employer cannot accurately observe whether workers are shirking? Or even, how could we make a simplified model of an economy in which employers and trade unions can bargain over employment as well as wages? How is it possible to allow for strategic interaction in such cases?

The key to engaging students' interest may not lie in postponing or minimizing the model building. Maybe it is more in choosing assumptions about motivations, constraints, and beliefs that smell more like life than the standard ones. In his introductory remarks, Colander notes correctly that you become an "economist" by going to graduate school, not by working in a business, real or financial, and seeing "how markets work." That is not accidental or arbitrary. Economics is an *analytical* subject. It is not about the experience of participating in the economy, but about analyzing the economy. Experience in a business or in the labor market or in anything is almost certainly a useful reality check, but it does not teach economics. You do not become a chemist by working in a petrochemical or pharmaceutical company; you study chemistry. You do not become a sociologist by living in a community; you study sociology. The same is true of economics. The point I am making is that our job is to teach our students how to analyze the economy or some of its parts. That certainly entails teaching them "tools," though it may include more. I do not see how the core courses can entirely evade this responsibility.

My last thought is about an aspect of graduate education that may be underplayed in the survey and in its interpretation. I am not sure. We can take it for granted that graduate students and professors differ in the things they are good at. To coin a phrase, they have different comparative advantages within the set of activities that economists undertake. The question is whether the typical Ph.D. program tends too much to the cookie-cutter approach. And, if that is so, whether there is any efficient way to play more to the comparative advantages of our students.

Presumably the required "core" courses should cover the material that "every economist should know." Is there a tendency to try to crowd too much "advanced" material into the core courses, partly to woo good students into a specialty, partly because professors enjoy it, partly out of sheer athleticism, and partly to compete with rival departments? If four courses a year is the average load, and if two years is the average time to general exams, and if the core consists of a year of micro, a year of macro, and a year of econometrics, is it a good idea for the core to eat up three-eighths of our teaching time? I don't honestly know. Like any well-trained economist, I believe that the answer depends on the alternative.

In our discussion at the AEA session considering Colander's findings, we seemed to agree that it is important to teach Ph.D. students how to recognize a good research problem when they see one. I share that view; but I wish I were confident I knew how to do that. Chemistry and biology students have the advantage of early experience in someone's functioning research laboratory. Maybe we could invent a near equivalent. Just keep in mind that recognizing a good research problem is not remotely a theory-free activity. What strikes an alchemist as a good research problem will strike a chemist as a foolish dead end.

# The Academic Research Game
# and Graduate Economics Education

ECONOMICS HAS CHANGED over the past twenty years, in my view, for the better. It is more empirical and more concerned with applied problems than it was, and it focuses more on applied mathematics and less on pure mathematics than it did. All of these changes have made economics more relevant. The changes are evidenced in the survey by a decrease in student's perceptions of the importance of mathematical skills, and an increase in student's perceptions of the importance of empirical skills as determinants of success. It is these changes that, in my view, have led to the better feeling among the students about what they are doing, and the disappearance of the extreme cynicism that Arjo Klamer and I found in the previous study. In short, today's students are happier with their studies and have a better feeling about economists' role in society than yesterday's students. That said, there are still issues of concern, and in this concluding chapter I discuss some of those concerns.

## Hazing, Selection, and Relating Theory and Practice

One of those issues of concern is that changes in the core (the set of required courses in micro, macro, and econometrics) have not kept pace with the changes in the profession.[1] While economics gives less prominence to pure mathematics unrelated to applied policy problems than it did, the core has been much slower to make that adjustment, which means that there is a mathematical hazing that goes on in graduate schools in economics; students unwilling to put up with that hazing do not go into economics, which decreases diversity of thought processes and approaches in the pool of economists. In the interviews a number of students made this point.

At these top schools, which my study focused on, the hazing is manageable, both because of the high mathematical prowess of the students and because the students are not pushed truly to be able to use the math in novel settings—just to be able to reproduce it.[2] Students recognize that the core is not economics, and they also recognize that how they do in the core courses is not closely tied to how they do as economists. So when the pass requirements of the core are set low relative to the technological nature of the material taught, as they are at almost all these top schools, the core does not present an insurmountable barrier—if the student can maintain the willpower to stick with it.[3]

To say that the core is a surmountable barrier is not to say that it is serving the purpose it should be serving. In my view, there are serious questions about what function the core is serving. It is definitely not serving the purpose that I believe a core should serve—providing a core of knowledge that all economists should share and will build their research on. Instead, the core is primarily a selection and hazing device that insures that only highly analytical individuals become economists.[4] Only after getting through the core do students learn how to be an economist—how to structure a workable model, and how actually to do empirical work.

The problem with the core goes beyond its not serving the role a core should be serving. It also causes two additional problems for the profession. The first was alluded to earlier; it biases who becomes an economist, limiting diversity of approaches and thought patterns within the economics profession. There's no one left in economics to argue that the emperor has no clothes. The interchange of people with diverse views and methods is lost, and the result is intellectual inbreeding, with all the problems that inbreeding brings about.

The current structure of the core also biases how those who do become economists approach problems and how they integrate theory and applied work. Because students currently learn theory in the core courses, and not as a natural part of their applied work, they do not learn how theory and applied policy are connected. In fact, the current structure of the core tends to separate theory from applied policy in students' minds. Students come away from the core with the belief that theory and applied work are separable, not mutually reinforcing, activities. They see economists becoming either applied economists or theoretical economists, rather than simply economists. That does a disservice to both theory and applied work. As one of the Harvard students said in the interview, "So the math hurdle is bad because it keeps some people who would have been good at economics out of economics, but it is also bad because it keeps some who might have been good theorists out of theory."

In applied micro, the heavy concentration on mathematical theory in the core has, ironically, decreased the importance of standard micro theory in applied work. With the development of behavioral economics, and the decrease in the importance given to formal specifications of rationality, there are many different theories that empirical results can fit. This has led to a tendency for one branch of applied empirical work to become primarily statistical analysis. Shared knowledge of what used to be known as price theory—Marshallian or Walrasian micro theory, such as presented by George Stigler or Paul Samuelson—is no longer the glue that holds the economics profession together. Instead, it is more likely to be a shared knowledge of statistical techniques that holds the profession together.[5] The problem that this deemphasis of the once-standard price theory presents can be seen in the students' comments. One MIT student stated,

> There is a sentiment here from people that I have talked to that if they want a model we can give them a model. We sit down and make up a model, and we play with it until it gives us the empirical result that we find, even though you could have just as easily have written down a model that would have given a different result. We have even had seminar speakers say, "Oh, I worked on a model that predicts it; of course I could have written down a model that predicts the opposite, but why would I do that?" In general, you can write down a model that predicts just about anything.

A Chicago student put it this way:

> When a professor here writes a paper, of course he has his view of the result he wants to get, and then he designs a model to get this result. For example, trade must make countries better off. So I do a model in which trade makes countries better off. The theory is really, really coherent in this aspect. But the theory seems to be an instrument; the beliefs are there before. They put their views into the models. It is not only Chicago; it is most places.

These two statements capture the difficulty with the separation of theory and applied work, which the current structure of the core instills in students. If a formal model can be developed to explain any empirical result, then what purpose is that formal model serving? A useful model is one that guides the researcher in what he or she is looking for; it precedes empirical work. Because most applied micro graduate students see their theory classes as mathematical hurdles, they do not learn how to use economic models as engines of discovery (the role that Alfred Marshall saw for them). Rather, they see formal models as a caboose, which journal editors require them to add to their applied statistics papers in order to publish them.

In macro, the separation of theory and applied policy created by the core has led to a different situation. Applied macro theory of thirty years ago—when students learned about monetary and fiscal policy, macro institutions, and sectoral econometric models—is no longer taught in the core. It has been replaced by a strong theoretical core theory—dynamic stochastic general equilibrium theory—supported by loose abstract statistical analysis, such as calibration, which relates the two. The problem is that much of modern macro theory is quite removed from real-world applied policy macro problems.[6] This has led to the situation in macro that Bob Solow (chapter 12) describes in his comments.

The heavy concentration on theory and technique in the econometrics portion of the core is also problematic. Because core econometrics focuses on abstract theory and proofs, rather than on how statistical theory relates to actual problems, students generally come away from the econometrics core with little grounding in actually applying statistics to problems or in making judgments about whether their statistical findings are relevant. The results are very bright, technically competent economists who tend to rely too heavily on pure statistical tests, not their judgment, in determining the relevance of their empirical research, and who too often in their work fail to distinguish statistical precision, statistical significance, and economic significance. Unfortunately, because of the nature of economics data (and the difficulty of finding on-point natural experiments), statistical precision and even statistical significance are often of less importance than a variety of other issues that are not captured by statistical tests, but which can be discerned only by judgment.

The core econometrics courses do not even teach the importance of judgment in interpreting one's statistical results.

## Applied Empirical Micro: A Bit Too Much Cleverness?

The focus on statistical techniques separated from theory and judgment has led to an increase in the value of what might be called cleverness in applied micro empirical research. Cleverness is an important skill, and if that cleverness is embedded in a broad theoretical vision tempered by judgment and knowledge of the limitations of statistical tests, it can be the foundation for wisdom. This is a big "if," however, and the current structure of graduate economics education, and the current incentives in the profession, do not guide students toward combining cleverness, judgment, and knowledge. Instead, the incentives tend to direct students toward cleverness for cleverness's sake. By that, I mean that students strive to find a natural experiment, or an instrumental variable, that provides a statistically significant (precise) result, without pushing as hard as they might to determine whether their results are economically significant and thus provide wisdom. That is not surprising, because it is such cleverness, supported by good statistical tests, that will get them published in the "right" economic journal, and that leads to their advancement as academic economists. The article, not the knowledge, is the goal upon which their advancement depends.

Having judgment and wisdom can actually be a detriment in generating articles, because judgment causes one to be wary of statistical relationships regardless of statistical significance level. Significance of results can be determined only by having a deep understanding of all aspects of the issue. One must have knowledge of all the relevant theory relating to the subject, knowledge of the broader literature on that subject, and knowledge of institutions that are central to the issue being looked at. Acquiring such information takes enormous time and effort, and it generally will not lead to a journal article publication within the narrow set of economic journals that graduate academic departments tend to focus on. Since the students' core training does not drill the limitations of statistical study into them, when they are faced with publishing incentives pushing them away from in-depth consideration of issues, they are likely to ignore these limitations and concentrate on their short-run goals. With theory separated from applied empirical work by the structure of the core, and with the importance of literature and institutions downplayed as insignificant in graduate economic training, an emphasis on empirical cleverness, rather than on knowledge, is the natural result.

In the previous study Arjo and I did in the 1980s, when students had a stronger grounding in, and higher regard for, standard price theory (a grounding often acquired in their undergraduate education), the problem I identified was that students were told to empirically test theories that could not be empirically tested in a formal sense. This led to the cynicism I described in the earlier study. Today, many applied micro students no longer see themselves testing a carefully delineated economic theory; there are many theories. Instead, they see themselves as discovering interesting empirical relationships and then relating those relationships to a wide range of models developed by theorists, even if they have to modify the models to fit the empirical findings.[7]

Moving toward a more inductive approach in which empirical evidence rather than theory guides research is, on balance, a positive development, but it increases the need for the students to have wisdom guiding their interpretation of the empirical results. Where does such wisdom come from? Most fields see wisdom as being embedded in the past literature and in the practical knowledge of actual people in the institutions being studied. That is why the graduate cores of fields such as political science and sociology have students study the past literature and the current debates in the field. The graduate core in economics does not do this; it focuses almost entirely on techniques and the particular cutting-edge work that the professor is doing. When the professor changes, the core changes. There is very little attempt to teach students about the problems with the techniques their professors are using, nor about the current debates within economics. One Chicago student nicely summarized the problems with this approach:

> Some professors are just much more interested in teaching what they are doing, which is fine, but it sometimes leaves serious gaps in the curriculum that we are not exposed to. This means that we have a real problem reading the literature, or identifying the references from people outside this school. So I would force everyone who wants to teach in the core to cover the basics. They can point out what they think is interesting, but they should present the established body of techniques, and the

issues that these techniques are used to analyze. In the first year you teach what the questions are and what are the tools, and in the second year, they can take you to the frontier. I sometimes had the feeling that they were jumping way ahead. I would prefer to get a more solid grounding.

The approach that he suggests seems very reasonable, and the fact that it is not followed is a serious problem with the core at almost all the schools I surveyed. The lack of training in a core of literature allows simplistic methodological views to prevail, and reduces the value of the student's technical expertise. It makes it unlikely that economists will graduate with even the beginnings of the acquired wisdom of the past.

## Did Macro Lose Its Way, and If So, Why Did It?

While the focus on pure theory in the micro core has led to a tendency for applied empirical micro economists to emphasize statistical work, the focus on pure theory in the macro core has led many potential applied empirical macro economists never to become macro economists, leaving macro to the pure theorists. In my view, this happened because economists followed Robert Solow's methodological advice always to develop clear, formal models. Students in the 1970s, following Solow's methodological prescriptions, were taught that one needed a formal macro model if one was going to provide insight into an issue. So they developed a formal model, making whatever assumptions they had to in order to make the model tractable. In my view, new classical economics is the "Solow methodological approach" applied to macro, and thus what happened to macro is precisely what happened to micro when it went through its general equilibrium phase—thirty years later.[8]

In his comments Solow criticizes my desire to have the core courses "focus less on model building and more on 'economic reasoning,' " stating that he cannot go along with me because "economics is irremediably a model-building project." He further states that he is unclear about "what 'economic reasoning' can be, other than pointing to models without actually teaching and learning them." Perhaps, by referring to the developments in macro, I can be clearer about what I mean by economic reasoning. Teaching economic reasoning involves teaching students methods of judging the relevance of the models that they are learning; in macro it would involve a consideration of Solow's views that "the macro community has perpetrated a rhetorical swindle on itself, and on its students" and that "what passes as micro foundations in macro" has no "valid claim to be micro foundations." Students are not taught such debates in the core; such debates are part of the economic literature that has been jettisoned to make room for more technical models.

I agree; economic reasoning cannot be taught directly, but it can be taught; it is embodied in a knowledge of the nuances of past debates, and in the practical knowledge gained by real-world experience with the institutions being studied. If more students had studied those past debates, and the experience of earlier macro practitioners, I suspect the majority of students would never have followed the approach to macro that Solow dislikes. But they didn't, and they did because they didn't. My point is that economic reasoning does indeed involve learning formal models, but it also involves learning about the degree of precision that the models are capable of achieving, the value of the model, and what claims can be made for such models. These are more matters of judgment than of technical expertise, and unless you teach these skills, or at least the importance of these skills, by a study of the literature and institutions, the result is precisely what happened in macro, which Solow nicely described as "technique-happy aficionados who grab the initiative and defend it behind walls of mathematics" that are not all that hard or beautiful but are sufficient to "drive away all but a high-morale ingroup that is enough to keep the sacred flame burning."

Ironically, my reaction to the developments in theoretical macro are nowhere near as strong as Solow's, in large part because I am far less satisfied with the macro that it replaced than he is. The problem I had with macro in the 1970s was the pretension of theoretical science that underlay it. Results were claimed for macro econometric models that didn't pass my reasonableness test; theoretical micro foundations were selectively used when convenient and placed into formal models that had no strong analytic foundation, all the time calling the work "scientific." The result was a macro in which theory and empirical results reflected the policy view of the researcher. Somehow, it seemed that "Yale" economists were always going to find "Keynesian" results and Chicago economists were always going to find "monetarist" results.

Had the earlier macro been presented as a type of imprecise engineering, and applied macro as something similar to weather forecasting, with no deep micro foundation theoretical core, I would not have had a problem with it—but that's not how I remember macro being presented. I recall it being cast as a set of formal models that were theoretically grounded in individual optimization; I further remember macro econometrics being presented as empirical tests of these formal theoretical models. Thus, in my view, the classical revolution succeeded so quickly because of the problems in the Keynesian/classical synthesis. It was necessary to purge what came before.

If I am so much more positive on developments in macro than is Solow, what accounts for my suggestion that macro, as it is currently being taught, should be eliminated from the core? It is because the macroeconomics being taught sees itself as advanced micro theory—dynamic stochastic general equilibrium theory—which suggests that it should not be taught until students are firmly grounded in micro analysis. Whereas the game theory and the mathematical tools that students learn in micro theory will likely show up in other courses, that is far less likely to be the case with the tools they learn in macro. As one student stated, "It is beyond me what the relevance of what we learned was." If macro is only advanced micro theory, then it does not belong in the core.

I, along with Solow, and I suspect many other macro economists, do not believe that macro is advanced micro. It is for that reason that I could see all students benefiting from an applied policy macro course, which would give them some sense of macro institutions and macro policy and theoretical debates in macro. In fact, I would see such a course as a wonderful addition to the core—a course that would be useful background for any economist. It would be a quite different course, however, than what is currently taught. It would be a policy- and problems-oriented course that would teach students how to appreciate the macro models and the difficulties of empirically dealing with macro data; it would not teach them how to produce the theoretical models.

## Matching Training and Careers

Hal Varian (2001) once argued that the best way to structure content in a course is through backward induction—start with the goals one wants students to have at the end of the course and then teach so that students can answer questions that reflect those goals. As is the case with most of the things that Varian says, there's much in that insight, and it is useful to think about the training that graduate economics students get in reference to the goals we have for students. Currently, the goal of graduate economics training seems to be success in the academic research game. In that game, success is measured by journal articles (weighted by journal quality), and advancement is in large part determined by the quality-weighted sum of one's peer reviewed publications. Students' graduate training is devoted to creating efficient journal article writers.[9] Making an important contribution to a public policy debate through other means than journal articles, or even making a contribution to a broader debate in a field where economics plays a role, is given much less value and can even hurt you.[10] Doing a good job teaching is given even less importance. I am told that at one school the "Best Teaching Award" is known by the students as the "Kiss of Death Award," since it demonstrates that the student who wins it is not sufficiently dedicated to academic research.

When the goal is publishing journal articles, not advancing knowledge, you get all kinds of perverse incentives. For example, a student working on nutrition would be poorly advised to delve deeply into the nutrition literature, even though such research might make his or her research more relevant. Doing so would take time away from his or her academic economic journal publishing. Similarly, students would be ill advised to study the relevant institutions or to gain a deep knowledge of the history of a policy debate, or even the current literature on that debate, because again, it will not lead to an appropriate publication. For the approximately 50 percent of students who end up in a graduate economics position at a research institution, this is probably relevant advice for their short-run advantage. At research universities teaching is not highly valued, and the first six years of work (or until tenure) will be almost totally focused on getting appropriately quality weighted journal publications.

For other students who are not going into such positions, these academic research skills are less important. Students going on into policy work, teaching undergraduates, government, or consulting will find that their training has not prepared them well. In these other positions, communication skills, the ability to answer real questions, and the ability to come to a reasoned policy conclusion are much more highly valued.

Many of the theoretical economists who currently teach in the core, and thus control the content of the core (because that content is determined by those who teach it, not by the department), will respond to this argument by saying that training applied policy economists is not their goal; they are training individuals to become theoretical economists like themselves. But that is not the large majority of the students whom they are teaching, even at these top schools. Most will become applied economists. I suspect that the broader group of the economists at these schools—those teaching in the field courses, and those leading the way in applied policy work—feel differently; they would favor a broader core training, with advanced theoretical work being an elective. That's the way the profession has moved over the past twenty years; it has reduced its focus on theory and increased its focus on empirical work. But even as the profession has changed and has elevated its view of applied policy work, the graduate core has lagged behind. It is time that the applied economists were given control of the core.

When I have asked people at top graduate schools why abstract theorists tend to be the ones who teach in the core, I have been given a number of different answers. The most common is that it isn't worth the political fight it would involve to change the situation. Others have told me that if the departments didn't assign the theorists to the core, there would be almost no students who took their theory courses, so what would theorists do? Still others have told me that if they did push the issue, they would have to teach the core, which would mean they would no longer teach their field courses, which they love. I can understand all these reasons, but I can only lament the consequences.

My argument for change is that even at these top schools, the large majority of students are not going to become pure theorists. If the core exam were determined by the entire department to reflect what they see as the core of economics, or better yet, were determined by representatives of the institutions that hire their graduates, the core exams would be quite different. The core exam could be just as challenging, but it would likely involve a better knowledge of institutions and literature and give more emphasis to creativity of approach, and not be simply "problem sets lite."

The current structure of the core does not do irredeemable damage to the majority of the students at these top schools.[11] These students are very bright and highly motivated. They will adjust and learn what they need to learn on the job or on their own. To say that they can do it on their own, however, does not offset the fact that graduate programs are not serving the students' needs.

One can see the disconnect between the training in skills that students get and the training in skills that are most appropriate for them in the survey of practicing economists by Stock and Hansen (2004). In that survey they found that "at least half of the respondents to their survey report too little emphasis on *applying economic theory to real-world problems*, on *understanding economic institutions and history*, and on *understanding the history of economic ideas*" (their emphasis).

I found similar results in the survey that I did of economists who had participated in the original survey back in the 1980s. Comparing these economists' assessment of what makes a successful economist in their current position with the assessment they made when they were students, one sees a marked change (see chapter 4). Now, 28 percent report that it was very important to have a thorough knowledge of the economy, compared to 0 percent of those same students in the earlier study; 24 percent saw having a broad knowledge of the economics literature, compared to 9 percent earlier; 22 percent saw excellence in mathematics as important, compared to 53 percent then; and 46 percent saw empirical skills as very important, compared to 11 percent then.[12]

Graduate economics training has moved closer to the needs of students in decreasing the importance given to pure math and increasing the importance given to empirical research. But it has still not moved any closer to giving students a sense of economic literature or of economic institutions. The difference between the skills that economists need as economists and the skills that economists are taught in the core goes to the heart of what I see as the problem with graduate school training in economics today. Ideally, one would want a reasonable match between the training provided and the skills that students will need in their jobs. Currently, that match is not very good. In my view, the match could, and should, be made much closer.

# NOTES

*Chapter One: Introduction*

1. At liberal arts colleges, however, economics majors are a much higher percentage of total college enrollments, often making up 25 to 30 percent of all seniors. The reason is that most liberal arts economics majors are actually business majors in disguise.

2. Actually, the American Economic Association (membership: 18,000) has a requirement that you be recommended by a current member. Yet if you pay your $90 membership fee (less if your income is below a certain level), you will find that you can become a member; the secretary treasurer of the association is a friendly person: each year he recommends 18,000 people to be members.

3. One can also get a masters degree in economics, and there are a few programs devoted specifically to producing masters degrees. But most Ph.D. economists do not look upon these favorably as creators of complete economists. Most students who get masters degrees get them as a stepping-stone to a doctorate either at the school where they get the masters or at a separate school. For example, it is typical of Latin American students to complete a masters in Latin America and then come to the United States for a Ph.D. Approximately half the students entering Ph.D. programs already have masters degrees (Siegfried and Stock 2004). Some students who start the Ph.D. program never finish it, so they end up with a terminal masters. The bottom line: when economists talk about economists, what they have in mind is someone with a Ph.D. in economics.

4. After a ranking is published, someone at a school recognizes that that ranking measure did not cast his school in the best light, and therefore does an alternative ranking that casts his school in a better light. For the most part, the rankings at the top are fairly consistent, but the rankings at lower-level schools shift around greatly as different metrics are used. Jerry Thursby (2000), looking at the multiple rankings, notes, "There's not a hill of beans difference across large groups of departments" (383). He further finds that out of 104 departments, only 24 departments are distinguishable from fewer than 10 others, and 47 departments are not significantly different from 20 or more departments.

5. This period is shorter than the seven-year median time to completion found in the Siegfried and Stock profile. That difference is explained by the fact that this measure includes time completing other degrees such as law degrees, MBAs, or terminal masters again, and not just time in the Ph.D. pro-

gram. When adjusted for these, Siegfried and Stock (2004) estimate that it takes 5.4 years to complete a Ph.D.

6. We later expanded the study into a book (Klamer and Colander 1990) with the same title.

7. The members of the commission were Anne Krueger, Kenneth Arrow, Olivier Blanchard, Alan Blinder, Claudia Goldin, Edward Leamer, Robert Lucas, Jan Panzar, Rudolph Penner, Paul Schultz, Joseph Stiglitz, and Lawrence Summers.

8. This discussion is based on a survey of COGEE Commission members and informal discussions with friends in the profession. It is not based on hard evidence, but it is, I believe, correct in its essentials.

9. As we will see in the interviews, as of 2004, Chicago's micro is an exception.

### Chapter 2: The Making of an Economist, Redux

1. I did this study alone because Arjo has since moved to the University of Rotterdam in the Netherlands and is no longer involved in U.S. graduate economics education.

2. I checked the number of foreign students responding with the total of those in the programs in 2004, which is not an exact comparison since two or three years had passed, but it gives a good basis of comparison. Foreign students made up 62 percent of the survey, whereas, in 2004, they made up 70 percent of the student body at these schools. When I asked students about this difference, they said that foreign students were less likely to fill out questionnaires.

The percentage of foreign students in these top graduate programs is higher than the 52 percent found by Aslanbeigui and Montecinos (1998) in a more extensive survey of foreign graduate students for the period 1995–96. The difference could reflect a greater percentage of foreign students in these top schools, an increase in the percentage of foreign students over the past decade, or a combination of the two. In my survey results, schools reporting especially high U.S. percentages had especially low foreign student response rates, specifically MIT and Stanford. Whereas foreign students made up only 22 percent of these schools' respondents to my questionnaire, both had student populations with slightly more than 50 percent foreign students in 2004. Foreign students were in the majority at all schools in 2004.

3. Some tables on student stress can be found in appendix C.

4. Judged in terms of major U.S. universities, this may seem wishful thinking, but since 62 percent of the respondents are foreign, and, as Aslanbeigui and Montecinos (1998) report, foreign students are very likely to return to

their home country, where they will likely be hired at a major university, these expectations do not necessarily exhibit irrational exuberance.

5. Women also found coursework and relationships with faculty more stressful than did men; they experienced no more stress than men in finding a dissertation topic, in conflict between course content and interests, and in relationships with other students. They exhibited less stress in regard to their financial situation; 11 percent of the men found this stressful; 2 percent of the women found it stressful. Appendix C has tables on stress by gender and school.

6. Appendix C includes tables of these responses by gender, year, and school.

7. This finding is subject to different interpretations. In the 1980s, when we did the first study, the term "neoclassical economics" stood for mainstream economics and was contrasted with a substantial undercurrent of heterodox thought that existed at the time. Today, the term "neoclassical" is far less used, and mainstream economics has incorporated many elements that previously were considered heterodox in developments in fields such as behavioral economics and evolutionary game theory. When I asked a Stanford student why Stanford students' views on neoclassical economics differed from those at other schools, he stated, "It would probably just be that the people didn't know what neoclassical economics was."

8. The percentages reported in this paragraph are the percentages finding a skill as very important.

9. These percentages are the ones ranking empirical research as "very important." While Harvard students ranked empirical research lowest on this measurement; they were the highest in finding it moderately important. Only 6 percent of the Harvard students found doing empirical research unimportant, compared to 12 percent in the survey as a whole.

10. The percentages reported in this paragraph are the percentages finding math very stressful.

11. Stress by school tables are reported in appendix C.

12. The percentages reported in this paragraph are the percentages finding a topic of great interest.

13. When I did the first study, a well-known economist asked me whether I had given up economics because I was handing out a survey. Since that time, a number of economists have begun using survey techniques (Blinder et al. 1998; Bewley 1999), although survey data are still questioned more than are other data (Easterlin 2004).

14. A former chair of a major department once told me that I (because of the initial study) had discouraged more students from going on in economics than any other person has; I took that as a compliment because it meant that the students going on are more likely to be those who really want to go on.

15. One of the interesting discussions that I had with students concerned the greater anxiety of women students about the core exams. The male students in the interview could not understand the women's anxiety, since the rational expectation was that everyone was going to pass. The women agreed, but said that they still felt uncomfortable because they did not really understand what was going on; the male students didn't understand either, but since they were confident they could pass the exam, they were not concerned about it. I have explored the data about female students more carefully in Colander and Holmes (forthcoming).

16. At one school that had a department-written exam, I heard that a policy-oriented economist who was not teaching in the core wrote a question for the core macro exam about the likely effect on the economy of a change in interest rates. Almost all students taking the exam had no idea how to answer it. The question was discarded, and the department moved away from department-written exams.

17. Many other possibilities exist. Suggestions I have received from readers of drafts of this chapter include adding an additional price theory course focused on economic reasoning, a policy-based macro course, or an economic history course, to the core. Alternatively, some have suggested reducing the number of courses in the core.

18. I outlined my alternative proposals for structuring and grading the core in Colander and Brenner (1992). They involve outside examiners for the core exams and an additional general departmental exam on recent economic debates and policy issues based on a reading list, but without specific lectures, which students would have to pass as part of their core training.

The breadth issue is of special interest to me because liberal arts schools, such as mine, need macroeconomists who have some knowledge of macro institutions, macro policy, and some sense of the history of macro. Job candidates who have studied macro in top schools often have almost no training in such issues. In a related spirit, Stock and Hansen (2004) argue strongly that graduate training does not fit the nature of the policy jobs that many economists take.

## Chapter 3: Further Results from the Survey

1. Creating these rankings was fun, but they should not be taken too seriously. There was no context set for these, and many students did not put any response down. A different structure of the question would likely have brought about a quite different result.

*Chapter 4: How the Views of the Original Survey Respondents Have Changed*

1. Of the original survey of 212 students, there were approximately 97 students who listed their name and address. Most had moved, and so I had to use a variety of sources to find the latest address. These included the AEA directory, university alumni offices, and search directories on the Internet. This reduced the number to seventy-one. Of those seventy-one, forty-five responded, some to the initial mailing and others to one of two followup requests. Eight surveys were returned marked "addressee unknown," meaning that the response rate of those who received it was forty-five out of sixty-three. While the response rate is high, the sample size is small, and one should be hesitant to use the results as anything other than a quantitative glimpse of the modern economics profession.

2. A number of potential biases exist in the survey results if one is using them to interpret what economists believe today. First, the survey is of graduates from top economics departments, and it does not necessarily reflect the broader economics profession. It is likely that graduates from top programs are more satisfied with economics than graduates from other programs. Second, since it was easier to find addresses of students who had remained in the economics profession, it is more likely to include "satisfied customers," since the address selection bias is toward those who remained in the profession. This bias also existed in the first survey; there, respondents suggested that if we had contacted students who dropped out, we would have gotten a somewhat more negative reaction. This bias may be partially offset by the fact that participation in the survey was voluntary, as was the first survey; those who are less happy with the profession, and more concerned with the state of the profession, are more likely to have filled out both the original survey and this survey.

3. Because of the low number of responses from Columbia and Yale, I do not include them in any discussion; so the schools being compared are Harvard, Stanford, Chicago, and MIT.

4. We did not notice this distinction in the first study, but it was there. In the original study subsample, MIT students saw success in economics as dependent on being knowledgeable about one particular field much more than students at other schools did. It seems that MIT emphasized specialization more than other schools did.

5. This has not necessarily been the case elsewhere. In France, students have recently revolted over many of the same issues that underlay the concern in the United States in the 1970s and 80s—the lack of relevance and the overconcentration on math in the first years of graduate school.

6. See Colander (1998) for a further discussion of this point.

*Chapter 5: Harvard Interview*

1. As I mentioned earlier, one of the reviewers of this book was at Harvard during the previous study. He said that radical students had made a concerted effort to increase responses to the survey to influence the results, and that this may have influenced the previous results.

2. The Ec 10 controversy concerned the undergraduate introductory course. Seven hundred and twenty undergraduate students signed a petition asking that undergraduate students have the option of taking a more broad-ranging course as an alternative to the current Ec 10 undergraduate principles course.

3. Michael Woodford, a well-known macro economist, has since moved to Columbia.

4. The Cambridge controversy was a debate about the theoretical problems of measuring capital in the production function. It was a topic that was significantly discussed in our earlier interviews with Harvard students.

*Chapter 6: Princeton Interviews*

1. Ben Bernanke has since moved to the Federal Reserve Bank, where he serves as Chairman of the Board of Governors.

*Chapter 8: MIT Interviews*

1. The professor in question is trained as an economist.
2. A two-body problem is a husband and wife both looking for a job in academia.

*Chapter 9: Chicago Interviews*

1. This distinction was popular in the early 1990s. "Salt water" referred to schools on either coast—MIT, Harvard, Stanford, and Berkley, for instance. "Fresh water" referred to schools around the Great Lakes.

2. At Chicago, the graduates' pictures are in the economics hallway.

*Chapter 11: Does This Have to Be Our Future? (Arjo Klamer)*

1. I myself did a similar survey among Dutch graduate students to find out that even though the legacy of Jan Tinbergen remains clearly discernible,

Dutch graduate students are being Americanized, stressing less the empirical and policy relevance of their economics and more the importance of pursuing academic economics (Klamer and van Dalen 1997).

*Chapter 13: The Academic Research Game and Graduate Economics Education*

1. The core is changing, and in micro, at some schools, there is more presentation of behavioral economic theory and experimental economics, and their relation both to game theory and to empirical evidence in the core. These changes in the core are, in my view, highly positive and are not the focus of my discussion here. To discuss those aspects of economics would require a much longer essay.

2. The same teachers who teach the course almost always grade the "core exams," which usually are simply course exams, or duplicates of the course exams. The students sometimes describe the core exams as "problem sets lite," by which they mean that the core exams are simply easier versions of the problem sets.

3. At intermediate-level graduate schools, which have ambitions of being seen as top departments, the core exams are often more brutal on students, both because the students' math background is not as good and because the professors teaching there want to show their rigorousness by maintaining a "high standard." I am told that in one such school only two out of twenty-seven passed the initial prelim core exam in micro. Because of this hazing in some of these intermediate-level schools, a half or more of the students drop out. For a discussion of such issues, see the blog at *http://www.chrissilvey.com*. It has postings from graduate students from a variety of schools, and it recounts the life of a student who decided to drop out.

4. As with any hazing process, once through, the survivors gain a feeling of being special and of having analytic superiority for having made it through.

5. One interesting phenomenon I have noticed is that young applied micro economists seem to prefer to teach statistics rather than micro. In previous decades, they strongly preferred to teach micro theory.

6. Most applied micro policy students (the majority of students at most schools) have little sense of why they are learning what they are learning in macro, or what its relevance might be. Whereas twenty years ago it was possible to expect that a newly hired Ph.D. would be comfortable teaching undergraduate micro or macro, today many non-macro specialists would feel uncomfortable teaching undergraduate macro, and it is even unclear whether most macro specialists would be comfortable teaching undergraduate macro, based on what they learned in their graduate courses. They simply have not had any

appropriate training unless they got it on their own or in their undergraduate courses. Students from top schools are often hired by undergraduate colleges because the graduate schools have selected bright students, rather than because the students have gotten the training they need to teach undergraduates.

7. This is, of course, an overstatement, and there is important work going on in relating empirical results to theory. Such work is most prevalent in behavioral microeconomics, and to the degree that such work is presented in the core and in the research that applied micro economists do, my comments do not apply.

8. The optimistic part of seeing the history in this way is that it suggests that what happened in micro—it became more empirical—will also happen to macro, and, with the development of cointegration and vector auto regression techniques, that now seems to be happening. In my view macro has now gone through its hyper-formal modeling period—making whatever assumptions are necessary—and is moving toward a macro that is more pragmatic and that makes far fewer claims for having a solid foundation for its theory than what we currently have, and that instead will be about work-a-day predictions and discussions. (See Colander [ed.] 2006.)

9. As can be seen in the interviews, that training has now reached a higher degree of specialization in which students differentiate a good job market paper from a good journal article paper.

10. One story that I have heard is that an assistant professor was asked by Paul Volker whether he wanted to work on a book with him; the assistant professor asked his chair whether that was a good idea, and the chair stated, "One book probably won't hurt you too much, but I definitely wouldn't do two."

11. The situation is far worse at lower-ranked schools that, in order to be like the top schools, structure their core similarly. It drives enormous numbers of potentially wonderful applied economists out of economics.

12. The respondents to the later questions were from various fields—about half were in universities, 13 percent in liberal arts schools, 25 percent in government, and 13 percent in business, which reflected where they thought they would be.

# BIBLIOGRAPHY

Aslanbeigui, Nahid, and Veronica Montecinos. 1998. "Foreign Students in U.S. Doctoral Programs." *Journal of Economic Perspectives* 12, no. 3 (summer): 171–182.

Bewley, Truman. 1999. *Why Wages Don't Fall During a Recession.* Cambridge: Harvard University Press.

Blau, Francine. 2004. "Report on the Committee on the Status of Women in the Economics Profession 2003." *Committee on the Status of Women in the Economics Profession Newsletter* (winter).

Blinder, Alan, et al. 1998. *Asking about Prices.* New York: Russell Sage Foundation.

Card, David, and Alan Krueger. 1997. *Myth and Measurement: The New Economics of the Minimum Wage.* Princeton: Princeton University Press.

Colander, David. 1994. "Vision, Judgment, and Disagreement among Economists." *Journal of Economic Methodology* 1, no. 1:1 43–56.

Colander, David. 1998. "The Sounds of Silence: The Profession's Response to the COGEE Report." *American Journal of Agricultural Economics* 80, no. 3 (August): 600–607.

Colander, David. 2003. "The Aging of an Economist." *Journal of the History of Economic Thought* 25, no. 2: 157–176.

Colander, David. 2005. "The Making of an Economist Redux." *Journal of Economic Perspectives* 19, no. 1 (winter): 175–198.

Colander, David. 2006. *Post Walrasian Macro: Beyond the Dynamic Stochastic General Equilibrium Model.* Cambridge: Cambridge University Press.

Colander, David, and Reuven Brenner. 1992. *Educating Economists.* Ann Arbor: University of Michigan Press.

Colander, David, Ric Holt, and Barkley Rosser. 2004. *The Changing Face of Economics.* Ann Arbor: University of Michigan Press.

Colander, David, and Arjo Klamer. 1987. "The Making of an Economist." *Journal of Economic Perspectives* 1, no. 2, (fall): 95–111.

Colander, David, and Jessica Holmes. Forthcoming. "Gender and Graduate Economics Education in the U.S." *Feminist Economies.*

Easterlin, Richard. 2004. "Economists and the Use of Subjective Testimony" in *The Reluctant Economist.* Cambridge: Cambridge University Press.

Frey, Buno, et al. 1984. "Consensus and Dissention Among Economists: An Empirical Inquiry." *American Economic Review* 74 (March): 986–994.

Fullerton, Edward, ed. 2003. *Revolution or Evolution: Reflections on the Post-Autistic Movement.* London: Routledge.

Hansen, W. Lee. 1991. "The Education and Training of Economics Doctorates: Major Findings of the Executive Secretary of the American Economic Association's Commission on Graduate Education in Economics." *Journal of Economic Literature* 29, no. 3 (September): 1054–1087.

Klamer, Arjo. 2006. *Speaking of Economics: How to Be in the Conversation.* London: Routledge.

Klamer, Arjo, and David Colander. 1990. *The Making of an Economist.* Boulder and London: Westview.

Klamer, Arjo, and Harry van Dalen. 1997. "Blood Is Thicker than Water: Economists and the Tinbergen Legacy," pp. 60–91, in *Economic Science and Practice: The Roles of Academic Economists and Policymakers*, edited by Peter A. G. van Bergeijk, A. Lans Bovenberg, Eric E. C. van Damme, and Jarig van Sinderen. Cheltenham: Edgar Elgar.

Klamer, Arjo, Deirdre (Donald) N. McCloskey, and Robert M. Solow, eds. 1988. The Consequences of Economic Rhetoric. New York: Cambridge University Press.

Krueger, Anne, Kenneth Arrow, Olivier Blanchard, Alan Blinder, Claudia Goldin, Edward Leamer, Robert Lucas, John Panzar, Rudolph Penner, Paul Schultz, Joseph Stiglitz, and Lawrence Summers. 1991. "Report of the Commission on Graduate Education in Economics." *Journal of Economic Literature* 29, no. 3 (September): 1035–1053.

McCloskey, Donald. 1983. "The Rhetoric of Economics." *Journal of Economic Literature* 21: 481–517.

Siegfried, John, and Wendy Stock. 2004. "The Labor Market for New Ph.D. Economists in 2002." *American Economic Review* 94, no. 2 (May): 272–285.

Solow, Robert. 1964. *Capital Theory and the Rate of Return.* Amsterdam: North Holland.

Stigler, George. [1975] 1982. *The Economist as Preacher.* Chicago: University of Chicago Press.

Stock, Wendy, and W. Lee Hansen. 2004. "Ph.D. Program Learning and Job Demands: How Close the Match?" *American Economic Review* 94, no. 2 (May): 266–271.

Thursby, Jerry. 2000. "What Do We Say about Ourselves and What Does It Mean? Yet Another Look at Economics Department Research." *Journal of Economic Literature* 38, no. 2:383–404.

Varian, Hal. 2001. "What I've Learned about Writing Economics." *Journal of Economic Methodology* 8, no. 1:129–132.

# INDEX

academic advancement, and journal publication, 243

academic economics, prospects of, 103–4

academic jobs, activities of, 8

academic path, and Stanford interview, 152, 154

academic research, and success, 248

admission: and Columbia interview, 215, 216; to graduate school, 103; and Stanford interview, 162–63

advisors, and Princeton interviews, 144

AEA (American Economic Association): board of, 6; and COGEE, 10; and *Journal of Economic Perspectives*, 9

age, of graduate students, 20

agent-based modeling, and Harvard interview, 110

American Economics Association. *See* AEA

applied policy macro course, advantages of, 247

applied policy work, and current trends, 249

applied versus theoretical, and Princeton interviews, 141

Aristotle, and Columbia interview, 220

Arrow, Ken, ranking, 62, 63, 87

Arrow/Debreu, general equilibrium theory, 9

Austrian approach, and Princeton interviews, 142

Barro, Robert: and graduate education, 228; and political orientation, 110

Bayesian econometrics: at Columbia, 219; and Stanford interview, 164

Bayesian methods, and Chicago interviews, 190

Becker, Gary: and Chicago interviews, 190, 210, 213–14; and political orientation, 210; ranking, 62–64

behavioral approach, and change, 229, 230–31

behavioral economics: advance of, 15; and Chicago interviews, 207–8; and Columbia interview, 221; and Harvard interview, 110–11; and MIT interview, 170; and

shared knowledge, 241; and Stanford interview, 157

behavioral work, and MIT interviews, 170

Bellman equations, and Chicago interviews, 208

Bernanke, Ben: and Chicago interviews, 211; and Princeton interviews, 131, 144, 256n1(ch. 6)

Blinder, Alan: and economic policy, 131; and economics workshops, 14; and policy/theory, 127; and Princeton interviews, 144; and remedial math courses, 12; and testing, 130

bounded rationality, and Chicago interviews, 202; and Columbia interview, 221

Brookings Papers, 97

Buchanan, James, creative economist, 43

Cal Tech, and graduate education, 153

Cambridge controversy: and Harvard interview, 122; and Stanford interview, 158

Card, David: and Harvard interview, 115; and minimum wage, 98

career choices: and Harvard interview, 121–22; and Princeton interviews, 126–27

Center for Environmental Economics and Policy in Africa, and Columbia interview, 217

change: and the economics profession, 15–16; and graduate education, 42–43, 48, 227, 228–29

character of school, and Princeton interviews, 136–38

Chicago, as top-ranked school, 6

Chicago economists, and monetarist results, 246

Chicago style economics, and Chicago interviews, 189–90

choice, and MIT interviews, 174–75, 176

choosing graduate school: and MIT interviews, 166; and Stanford interview, 148

Cicero, and Columbia interview, 220

classical economics, and Robert Solow, 245

classical revolution, 247

class size, and Chicago interviews, 212